STUDIES IN HISTORY, ECONOMICS AND
PUBLIC LAW

Edited by the
FACULTY OF POLITICAL SCIENCE
OF COLUMBIA UNIVERSITY

NUMBER 462

A PIONEER MERCHANT OF ST. LOUIS
1810–1820

THE BUSINESS CAREER OF CHRISTIAN WILT

BY

SISTER MARIETTA JENNINGS, C.S.J.

A PIONEER MERCHANT OF ST. LOUIS 1810-1820

The Business Career of Christian Wilt

BY

SISTER MARIETTA JENNINGS

AMS PRESS
NEW YORK

COLUMBIA UNIVERSITY
STUDIES IN THE
SOCIAL SCIENCES

462

The Series was formerly known as *Studies in History, Economics and Public Law.*

Reprinted with the permission of Columbia University Press
From the edition of 1939, New York
First AMS EDITION published 1968
Manufactured in the United States of America

Library of Congress Catalogue Card Number: 68-58594

AMS PRESS, INC.
New York, N.Y. 10003

PREFACE

THIS study presents an account of Christian Wilt, a pioneer merchant of Saint Louis during the decade from 1810 to 1820, years that mark a well defined period in the development of the western community. In 1810 the Louisiana Territory had been in the possession of the United States for only six years and Saint Louis had for one year been a chartered village in that territory; in 1820 the Territory of Missouri, carved out of the Louisiana Purchase, was being rapidly settled, and Saint Louis, emerging from the pioneer stage, was ready to assume the duties and responsibilities of a city. This she did in 1822, just one year after Missouri had been admitted into the Union as a state.

In this study an attempt has been made to show the rôle played by the business man in the growth and development of pioneer life. The merchant was an outstanding member of his frontier community. As a distributor of merchandise, as a pioneer in building industry, as a banker, as an advocate and patron of social institutions, as a patriot, he was a citizen of importance. An appreciation of his work is necessary to an understanding of the general development of western trade, manufactures, and the social life of that day.

Out of the numberless courageous men who, undaunted by hardships and dangers, pressed on to distant points to open marts of trade in the western wilderness, Christian Wilt has been chosen as a type. In his story, told in detail, one may get in outline at least, a picture of the pioneer merchant and an estimate of the power he wielded in the building of the Middle West. In the early nineteenth century it required a man of courage to establish a business enterprise in the midst of the comparative wilderness that surrounded Saint Louis. At the time of which we write there was great difficulty in maintaining communication between the region west of the Mississippi and the older communities of the eastern states. In the Western districts, separated by a wilderness of hundreds of miles, by areas sparsely inhabited save for roving savages, by stretches of land uninviting in their untilled expanse and undeveloped resources, the people were badly handicapped by the lack of means of transportation. The courage and heroism, implicit in the record of the way in which the pioneer settlers faced their hardships and overcame innumerable difficulties, constitute a fascinating and inspiring chapter in the history of our country.

The most important sources for the story of Wilt's entrepreneurial career are his own letterbooks (1812–1815) and those of Joseph Hertzog (1811–1815). The first letter found in Hertzog's letterbook is dated March 20, 1811, while Wilt's first letter was dated almost a year later, January 18, 1812. The letters in both books are arranged chronologically, just as they were copied by the authors when the originals were ready for the post. The books, which are to be found in manuscript in the archives of the Missouri Historical Society in Saint Louis, have recently for the first time been given publicity. Because of limited space it has been impossible to include in this monograph a detailed account of all the projects described in this correspondence, or even to give a complete list of them. However, in the hope of encouraging further study of the early efforts to establish trade centers on the western frontier, an attempt has been made to select such portions as give a clear picture of this young merchant, his ambitions, his character, his successes, and his failures.

The present work had its source in a paper prepared under the guidance of Dr. Dixon Ryan Fox at Columbia University in a seminar in American History. The original material was found in the archives of the Missouri Historical Society of Saint Louis, to whose librarian, Miss Stella Drumm, I am deeply indebted for assistance in the use of the Society's remarkable collections. For their generous and willing aid in facilitating the research for this work, I wish especially to thank the staffs of the Saint Louis Historical Society, the Columbia University Library, the New York Public Library, the New York Historical Society, the Library of the Historical Society of Pennsylvania at Philadelphia, the Historical Society of Western

Pennsylvania at Pittsburgh, the Saint Louis Mercantile Library, and the Fontbonne College Library of Saint Louis. It gives me pleasure to acknowledge my indebtedness also to Mother Agnes Rossiter, former Superior General of the Sisters of St. Joseph of Carondelet, to Mother Rose Columba, present Superior General, and to Mother Angela, Superior Provincial, for their constant encouragement; to Mr. J. Felix Vallé, who made available for my use manuscripts in his private collections; to Mr. Alphonse H. Clemens, Fontbonne College, Saint Louis, to Mrs. Louis Houck, Cape Girardeau, Missouri, and to Miss Ellen Masterson, Quincy, Massachusetts, for their generous and valuable assistance in procuring original source material; and to Monsignor Charles Van Tourenhaut, Ste. Genevieve, Missouri, who put at my disposal his valuable collection of rare books on the history of early Louisiana.

To Professor John A. Krout of Columbia University, I owe a special debt of gratitude for his criticism, advice, and encouragement in the preparation of this monograph. I wish to express my thanks to Professor Allan Nevins for his reading of the manuscript, and also my appreciation for his helpful suggestions. To these and to all others who have in the slightest degree helped in the preparation and rounding out of the work here presented, I am truly grateful.

SISTER MARIETTA JENNINGS, C.S.J.

SAINT LOUIS, MISSOURI
DECEMBER 15, 1938.

CONTENTS

9

CHAPTER I

A WESTERN MERCANTILE ADVENTURE

ONE of the youngest and most enterprising of the pioneer merchants of Missouri was Christian Wilt, who settled in Saint Louis in 1810 as the representative of his uncle, Joseph Hertzog, prominent in the mercantile circles of Philadelphia.

The Hertzogs came to Philadelphia from Niederlustadt, Palatinate, Germany, where Andrew, father of Joseph, was born on October 20, 1730.[1] They arrived in Pennsylvania shortly before 1750, during the period of the greatest emigration from the Palatinate, when ships crossing the Atlantic "plied between Rotterdam and Philadelphia with almost the regularity of a ferry".[2] Fleeing from their homes in the beautiful valleys of the Rhine and the Neckar, they found refuge in America from the fierce religious and political persecutions then raging in South Germany.

Joseph Hertzog, Andrew's son, was born in Philadelphia on February 7, 1764. It was the year that Laclede mapped out the little town of Saint Louis to the development of which Joseph Hertzog, in later years, was to contribute so largely of his fortune and his talents. According to the records of the First Reformed Church of Philadelphia the little boy was baptized on February 23, 1764, with his parents Andrew and Barbara Hertzog standing sponsors.[3] It is not known where Joseph received his early training, but that he acquired more than the rudiments is evident from the fact that his letters are often written in French, sometimes in German. In his English letters his vocabulary is well chosen, his sentences, though long and involved, and for the most part innocent of punctuation, are perfectly clear. This young German was fond of music and

1 Collins, William H., *Geneological Records of the Descendants of John Collins, Sr., from 1640 to 1760* (Quincy, Illinois, 1897), p. 160.

2 Beidelman, William, *The Story of the Pennsylvania Germans* (Easton, Penn., 1898), p. 54.

3 Records of First Reformed Church, Philadelphia, in The Historical Society of Pennsylvania, Philadelphia.

played the flute well. One can easily imagine the family grouped on a winter's evening about the glowing fireplace singing old hymns or the folk songs of Germany to the accompaniment of his flute. He copied his own music scores, and devised a five pronged copper pen, which he found useful in drawing the lines of the music staff easily and quickly.[4] On January 30, 1789, Hertzog married Catherine Wilt, half sister of Christian and Andrew Wilt, whose ancestors probably came from the Palatinate at the same time that his own family emigrated. For his bride he built a comfortable home in Green Lane, Philadelphia, a section of the city where the members of both families lived. Later he made extensive improvements which contributed much to the comfort of his growing household.

The family consisted of Joseph Jr., who died in infancy, and four daughters—Mary, Rachael, Anne, and Elizabeth—who grew to womanhood and accompanied their father in 1819 when he went to Saint Louis. Elizabeth loved to recall going with him to the neighborhood of Germantown, where he had suburban property and where, under his guidance, she learned to work in a garden. In religious matters he was a freethinker, but his leading personal and moral characteristics were kindliness, gentleness, and charity; and he taught his daughters to be active and earnest Christian women.[5] He spoke of himself as "plain, friendly and honest."[6] Catharine Wilt Hertzog, his wife, was a woman of great vitality although in appearance slight and delicate. As a small child she spoke only German, but as she grew older her association with English-speaking children made her forget her native tongue; it was only as she approached "second childhood" that the German language, which she had used in her youth, came back to her. She was a member of the Presbyterian Church and carried out her religious convictions in everyday life, especially in her love and care for the poor.[7]

4 Collins, *op. cit.*, p. 161.
5 *Ibid.*, p. 166.
6 Hertzog to Zachary Mussina, Oct. 12, 1811, Hertzog Letterbook.
7 Collins, *op. cit.*, p. 167.

Hertzog carried on a thriving trade in groceries in a shop located on Crown Street; did an extensive wholesale business in supplying merchants in Philadelphia, Pittsburgh, and surrounding towns not only with groceries, but also with dry goods, crockery, queensware, and other articles needed in their frontier settlements; and he owned large properties in what is now the heart of the business section of his city.[8] For one of these properties, which extended from Second Street to Delaware Street, between Sassafras and Mulberry, he paid the sum of $8333.33.[9] He purchased various tracts of land outside the city of Philadelphia. From William Peltz's[10] heirs[11] he bought about 6000 acres in Beaver, Mercer, Crawford, Erie, and Venango Counties;[12] and he speculated in town lots in Milheim[13] and New Berlin,[14] as well as in land in Potter township, Penns Valley.[15] The extent to which he was interested in real estate is shown by the option offered him on 40,000 acres along the Susquehanna River in upper Lucerne County, part of the estate of the deceased Judge Samuel

8 Among the purchases recorded was one on March 15, 1803, when he bought of William Sansom, for $570, a piece of property, 20 × 175 feet, on the west side of Crown Street, between Callow Hill and Willow Street, and extending to Fifth Street. Edmund Physick acted as attorney in the transaction. Original Deed Book, I. C. No. 23, p. 337. Office of the Recorder of Deeds, City Hall, Philadelphia.

9 Original Deed Book, E. F., No. 26, p. 549. Recorder of Deeds Office, City Hall, Philadelphia.

10 William Peltz, Philadelphia grocer. *Pennsylvania Archives,* 3rd Series, XV, 211.

11 Hertzog to Zachary Mussina, Aug. 3, 1811.

12 Hertzog to Zachary Mussina, July 25, 1811.

13 Hertzog to Lyons Mussina, Feb. 14, 1812.

14 Hertzog to Lyons Mussina, Feb. 15, 1812.

15 Hertzog to Mussina and Patterson, Mar. 10, 1812.
"The following is the description (of the above tract) in Potter's township Penns Valley, bought 3rd April, 1798: running north by other land of Mr. Gunkle 2d (degrees), west 159 p (perches) to a stone thence by land of A. Kremer north 88 degrees, east 61 p to a stone thence by land of Charles Hag and Daniel Kremer north 66 degrees, west 61 p to place of beginning— 60 acres 152 per, part of a tract called David's addition. Recorded in deed book L. Pages 718–719, 16 Oct., 1802 (bond dated Oct. 10, 1798 and entered up)."

Wallis, one of the chief landowners in Pennsylvania at the end of the eighteenth century.[16] The price was 50 cents an acre, to be paid part in cash and part in groceries.[17] This appeared to be an enticing offer, but evidently Hertzog decided not to purchase the tract when he learned that the marshal of the district had sold the property four months before and that the owners held it only under warrants.[18] His speculative interests carried him far afield. It was probably between 1807 and 1809 that he financed the Philipson brothers, Philadelphia merchants, in their lead and mercantile venture in the Missouri Territory.

Hertzog was willing to consider any new enterprise that offered sure and profitable returns on an investment. To his countinghouse came reports of the steadily growing traffic between East and West. There were attractive profits to be made in furs, peltries, and lead from the Louisiana Territory, and in the commodities which were sent West in return. The back country was being rapidly settled. Every day settlers laden with household goods for their new homes,[19] adventurers seeking wealth in the mineral deposits of Missouri, and merchants carrying wares for the new stores in some village along the Ohio, Mississippi, and Missouri rivers, left the Eastern states for the Indian country. All of this indicated that the territory beyond the Mississippi offered encouraging possibilities of trade and investment for the enterprising business man with vision and confidence. Such a man was Hertzog. When Zachary Mussina, whom he had known for some years through his business association with Simon Philipson, returned to Philadelphia with glowing accounts of the growing importance of Saint Louis, Hertzog, after considering the reports together with the stories told by the Philipson brothers, decided to invest in a mercantile establishment in this the largest city of Upper Louisiana.

16 *Pennsylvania Archives*, 3rd series, XXV, 342, 353, 354, 655.

17 Hertzog to Jacob M. Kinney, Aug. 5, 1811.

18 Hertzog to J. M. Kinney, Aug. 13, 1811.

19 Birkbeck, Morris, *Notes on a Journey from Virginia to Illinois* (London, 1818), p. 25.

Zachary Mussina, who talked convincingly of the future of the West, was of Italian stock. He was industrious, a good salesman, and experienced in both the western lead and mercantile business, but he had a quick temper, was revengeful and at times sullen.[20] He had been in the employ of the Philadelphia merchants, Simon and Jacob Philipson, the former of whom was his brother-in-law. These brothers were interested in the lead traffic of the Missouri mines. Mussina had acted as their agent in the West and in this capacity had probably bought lead from the Vallé brothers, Francois and Jean Baptiste, who with J. B. Pratte and St. James Beauvais of Ste. Genevieve, owned Mine La Motte; or from J. Smith T,[21] a bold and daring speculator, who claimed Mine Shibboleth and Bellefontaine together with 10,000 arpents which embraced Mine à Liberty;[22] or from Moses Austin who since 1798 had been at Mine à Breton.

One may get an idea of Austin's extensive mining interests from the fact that between May 29 and June 9, 1810, there were 18,199 pounds of lead mined and melted at the Mine à Breton.[23] It is not improbable that with this output Austin could offer Mussina larger quantities of raw and manufactured materials at lower prices than could his competitors. But Mussina had become dissatisfied with his subordinate position as agent, a post that offered no opportunities for advancement, and he had determined to embark upon some adventure that would become more profitable as time went on. In the summer of 1809 he returned to Philadelphia and prevailed upon Hertzog to enter a partnership to carry on trade in the flourishing village of St. Louis. This project was only the first step in the realization of his great ambition, for Mussina's ultimate aim was to be associated with Hertzog in the dry goods business in Philadelphia, where he

20 Hertzog to Wilt, April 18–22, 1812.

21 "T" for Tennessee, his native state, and used for the purpose of distinguishing him from other Smiths.

22 Houck, Louis, *History of Missouri* (Chicago, 1908), II, 229.

23 Barker, Eugene C., ed., *Austin Papers* (Washington, 1924), II, 173.

fancied he could "make money like I. Moss[24] and some other favorites of fortune."[25]

The articles of partnership were formally signed February 24, 1810. The purpose of the enterprise was to "open and establish a store in Louisiana" with Joseph Hertzog and Zachary Mussina as partners. Christian Wilt, Hertzog's nephew, was to go with Mussina and share the adventures of this new experiment in the West.

The third party to the transaction, Christian Wilt, was born in Philadelphia on January 18, 1790,[26] the son of Abraham and Rachael Wilt, whose ancestors came to America on September 9, 1751, in the good ship PATIENCE. They settled in Philadelphia among their own people, and there as a merchant Abraham prospered. That Christian was well educated is evidenced by his correspondence. He was honest, adventuresome, and enterprising, but he had had little experience in business, and none in the manner of life and living encountered in a frontier settlement in 1810. The customs, habits, and codes that prevailed along the Mississippi were alien to the tastes of the young man of twenty accustomed to the culture and refinement of Penn's city of Brotherly Love. He was not yet of age at the time the partnership was formed but he was assigned to the western country with Mussina. If the western life appealed to him, and if he proved successful in operating the store, he was on gaining his majority, to assume responsibility for the Saint Louis investments and become co-partner in the business.

Of the total investment amounting to $15,000, Hertzog was to furnish $10,000. Mussina, whose contribution to the capital investment was a sum of $5,000[27] due him from the Philipson brothers, his former employers, agreed to act in the capacity of agent for this new firm in the cities along the Ohio, particularly in Louisville, Cincinnati, and Pittsburgh. In these localities he

24 Isaac Moss, wholesale dry goods merchant, Philadelphia.

25 Hertzog to Wilt, April 22, 1812.

26 Collins, *op. cit.*, p. 173.

27 Hertzog to Wilt, April 22, 1812.

was well-known, because he had been for several years the representative of the Philipson interests in that area.

The Philipsons—Simon, Jacob, and Joseph—were brothers, Polish Jews, highly educated and accomplished musicians. They came from Germany early in the century. In 1803[28] Simon and Jacob were partners in a business enterprise in Philadelphia, but in 1808 Jacob located in Saint Louis. Joseph, the youngest and best beloved of his brother Simon, had also sought his fortune in the West. He left Philadelphia early in September, 1807, by way of Baltimore, where he purchased supplies from the following firms, some of which are still in existence: Thomas Faulk, John Harvey, Galt and Thomas, George Price and Co., C. and John Comegy, Henry Schroeder and Company, Frederick Hammer, Jonathan Munro, Samuel Lyons and Co., John Kelly, Woods, Taylor, and Graighead, and others, on long term notes (twelve months' credit) to the amount of $10,000. He was able to pay only $552.90[29] in cash on his account, so that his indebtedness was very heavy when he began his business in the frontier settlement of Saint Louis. Joseph Philipson was, perhaps, the first Jewish merchant to establish himself in this new and thriving mart on the Mississippi. He arrived at his destination with his cargo in the winter of 1807 and opened his first account on December 13 of that year. He remained in Saint Louis for many years and carried on his business successfully.

In the spring of 1810, Wilt and Mussina started from Philadelphia with their first invoice of goods valued at $13,841. The cargo consisted of a large consignment of groceries taken from Hertzog's store on Crown Street; dry goods, some bought at auction for cash and some secured on short credit; and articles from the Pittsburgh stores which were charged to Hertzog's account and for which he was obliged to settle on sight drafts.[30]

28 Billon, Frederick L., *Annals of St. Louis in its Territorial Days 1804-1821* (St. Louis, 1888), p. 228.

29 Philipson, Joseph, Original Account Book, 1807-1809. Mercantile Library, St. Louis.

30 Hertzog to Wilt, June 6, 1812.

At Pittsburgh the young men procured a keel, loaded the boat and went down the Ohio and up the Mississippi to Saint Louis. In this little town Mussina was expected, according to the terms of the agreement, to establish a permanent place of business and build up a brisk and thriving trade. But on reaching Saint Louis, he immediately sold out the major portion of his supply for $20,000 at the small profit, according to Hertzog, of $4000. The buyers were the Philipson brothers, who manipulated the sale in such wise as to delay payments for months and tie up the little income that should have accrued from this transaction. For three-fourths of the amount of sale, Mussina accepted three term notes of $5,000 each, dated as follows: November 1, 1810, February 1, 1811, May 1, 1811; for one-fourth of the debt he took a quantity of lead and beaver which the Philipsons had ready at hand. The lead Mussina shipped by way of the Mississippi and the Ohio, but the furs he took with him to the East through the port of New Orleans. When disposed of in Philadelphia, the cargo netted a profit of $1,400 which amount was not received until September, 1811.[31]

Displeasure over this first transaction forced Hertzog to write:

Nor was I without great uneasiness for the greater part of that time lest an accident happen to the buyers, or the lead be lost in the Mississippi, or the sea swallow our beaver. For Mussina had taken the beaver to New Orleans to bring it by way of the Atlantic to Philadelphia. He came to Philadelphia more dead than alive, conscious that he had played a silly game and trembling lest my indignation might light on him, or at least, that I should no more place confidence in him.

The whole transaction was indeed a keen disappointment to Hertzog. He had hoped that his profit, considering the capital invested and the risks involved, would approach or reach $10,000,[32] but it amounted to only $5,400, and this sum was

31 Hertzog to Wilt, April 22, 1812.
32 *Ibid.*

not available for many months. As a result he was left without ready money for the necessary fall purchases. Last, but not least, the store in Saint Louis had not been opened. But Christian Wilt had remained in Saint Louis; and Hertzog, after deliberation and some misgivings, decided to send another invoice which reached Saint Louis late in the summer of 1810.[33]

33 *Ibid.*

CHAPTER II
SAINT LOUIS AND ITS EARLY MERCHANTS

THE Saint Louis in which Christian Wilt now found himself contained, according to the Census of 1810, fourteen hundred inhabitants; "one-fifth were Americans and about four hundred persons of color."[1] In no other town of the West was there such a mixed population; it was composed of the descendants of the early French colonists, Canadian voyageurs, Spaniards, Indians, shrewd Yankee traders, and lawyers, Scotch-Irish from Kentucky and Pennsylvania. People from "every nation, kindred and tribe under the heavens," from the islands and principalities of Europe, from the vine-clad hills of Italy, from the banks of the Rhine and from every state of the American Union were gathered here,[2] and in this motley crowd were many of that singular class of beings, the *Engages*, fellows who talked of a trip to the Rocky Mountains as one might speak of a holiday excursion, and who thought of an Indian encounter as one might of a bout with a midnight prowler. Voyageurs and coureurs-des-bois, dressed in buckskins and coonskin caps, with hunting knives and Indian tomahawks stuck in their belts, had been familiar figures in Saint Louis from the time of its foundation.

Little is known of its founder, Laclede, whose full name was Pierre Laclede Liguest. He came to Louisiana in 1755. Pierre Margry of the French Naval Bureau fixes his birth about 1724, in the Parish of Bedons in the valley of the Aspre, diocese of Olerm, in Bearn, about fifteen leagues from Pau, capital of ancient Navarre.[3] In stature Laclede was a little above medium size. He was very dark complexioned, with a large nose, high forehead, and dark, piercing and expressive eyes.[4] He was a

1 Brackenridge, H. M. *Views of Louisiana* (Baltimore, 1817), p. 222.

2 Washington Irving, *Astoria* (New York), p. 126.

3 Billon, Frederick, *Annals of St. Louis in its Early Days under the French and Spanish Dominations* (St. Louis, 1886), p. 411.

4 Edwards, Richard, *The Great West* (St. Louis, 1860), p. 263.

forceful and dominating character and his attention to detail in business transactions was recognized by everyone who had dealings with him. Captain Gordon, of the British forces under General Gage, who met Laclede in Saint Louis in 1766, described him as, "clever, sensible, active, and very well-educated." But Gordon was evidently disturbed by the aggressiveness of the Indian trader, for he added that Laclede

takes good measures that the whole trade of the Missouri, and that of the Mississippi northwards, and that of the nations near La Baye, Lake Michigan and St. Joseph's by the Illinois River, is entirely brought to him. . . . He will give us some trouble before we get the parts of the trade that belong to us out of his hands.[5]

Laclede was a member of the firm of Maxent, Laclede and Co., of New Orleans, which in 1762 obtained a license from Governor Kerlerec, the last French governor of Louisiana.[6] This license to "trade with the savages of the Missouri and all nations residing west of the Mississippi for eight years,"[7] was confirmed by D'Abadie, at that time Director General and Commandant of Louisiana. Houck says that

it is likely that Maxent, then one of the principal merchants of New Orleans, to secure this Upper Louisiana trade, furnished the goods and capital and that Laclede agreed to give his personal attention to the business, and for this received a share in the profits of the new establishment, and that thus the firm of Maxent, Laclede and Co. originated.[8]

However that may be, immediately after the terms and conditions were signed with the French Government, the firm undertook to import from Europe all the merchandise necessary to

5 Alvord and Carter, *The New Regime.* Illinois Historical Society *Collections,* XI, 300.

6 Houck, *op. cit.,* II, 1.

7 Chouteau's Journal of the founding of St. Louis. Missouri Historical Society *Collections* (St. Louis, 1911), III, 336. (The original French manuscript is in possession of the St. Louis Mercantile Library Association).

8 Houck, *op. cit.,* II, 3.

carry on extensive commerce with the Indian tribes of the trans-Mississippi region. While awaiting the arrival of the goods that had been ordered, the firm organized an expedition which it placed under the capable direction of Laclede.

With a cargo of merchandise likely to appeal to the Indian taste, Laclede left New Orleans the third of August, 1763.[9] Instead of the mouth of the Missouri, his original objective, he chose as the site of his trading post a "bluff on the western bank of the Mississippi at a sweeping curve of the river," eighteen miles below the mouth of the Missouri, where at all times much of the area would be out of the reach of inundations. Saint Louis was chosen as the name of the little settlement and these plans, made in 1763,[10] were put into effect after the opening of navigation in the spring of 1764,[11] when Laclede sent a boat in charge of his stepson, Auguste Chouteau, with directions to begin the work of laying out the village.

After the settlement was well begun, Laclede, relying on his partner Antoine Maxent, the leading merchant of New Orleans,[12] to attend to their interests in that city, spent his time exploring the interior of the country. He crossed the Missouri, Osage, and Platte rivers. He established trading posts up the Arkansas, the Red, and the Francis rivers. These travels through the forests, filled with danger, privation, and hardship, may have undermined a strong and rugged constitution, for on June 20, 1778, Laclede, just fifty-four years old, died suddenly on his way from New Orleans to the city he had founded. He was buried near the mouth of the Arkansas River in a lonely and unmarked grave.[13]

So rapid was the growth of Laclede's village that within three years after its foundation Saint Louis was the largest settlement

9 Chouteau's Journal, p. 350.

10 *Ibid.*, p. 351.

11 *Ibid.*, p. 352.

12 Gayarre, Charles, *The History of Louisiana, The French Domination* (New York, 1867), p. 86.

13 Edward, *op. cit.*, p. 263.

in the valley north of New Orleans.[14] This was undoubtedly owing to its position near the mouth of the Missouri, which was the highway of the fur trade, and to a continual emigration of French settlers from the towns east of the Mississippi. After the cession of Louisiana to the United States, Saint Louis became the seat of government of the territory. It was the place of residence of the supreme and lower courts, and became the political and commercial center of Upper Louisiana.[15] In 1808 on petition of the people the judges of the court of common pleas incorporated the town, the first so incorporated west of the Mississippi, in what is now the state of Missouri.

The boundaries of the town as defined in 1809 by William Clark, Clemens B. Penrose, and Bernard Pratte, trustees in and for the corporation of the town of Saint Louis, were as follows:

Commencing at the River Mississippi at low water mark, at or near the windmill of Antonio Roy, through a due west course, until the line intersects the eastern boundary of the forty arpent lots on the hill back of Saint Louis, thence along the line of said lots to Mill Creek, thence down said Creek to its mouth, thence up the River Mississippi along the low water mark to the place of beginning.[16]

The territory of the village was thus limited to the lower bluff between the river and the hill back of the town, from the "foot of what is now Poplar Street, northward over two miles to Rocky Branch."[17]

Parallel to the river were three long, narrow streets called, in the old French days, Rue La Grande, Rue L'Eglise, and Rue des Granges, names which, on the coming of the Americans were changed to the more prosaic Main, Second, and Third Streets. These thoroughfares were cut at right angles by five others, one of which, now called Walnut, found its way up a gentle slope on which the fort and soldiers' quarters were built.

14 Williams, Walter, *The State of Missouri* (Columbia, Mo., 1904), p. 10.

15 Houck, *op. cit.*, III, 161–62.

16 *Louisiana Gazette,* March 21, 1811.

17 Billon, *op. cit.*, I, 22.

The others lost themselves in country roads that wound through valleys and over the broad prairies back of the town. Only two streets, Vine and Market, were cut down to the river.[18] These had been quarried out by the first settlers to enable them to get to the river for water or to bring goods from the boats to the stores on Main Street. This street, in spite of the name MAIN, was only thirty-six feet wide (French measure) with, here and there, cellar doors protruding like skylights upon the foot-pathed way, making the space between the houses on either side only thirty feet. Second and Third Streets were equally narrow. The blocks fronting on Main Street were generally two hundred and forty feet, running back three hundred feet to the street north. Probably the reason for the narrow streets was need of protection; in case of Indian raids it would be easier to defend the village, since compactness meant a shorter line of palisades.

The principal cross streets were variously designated by to-pographers, but they generally agreed on the following notation: Rue de la Tour, now known as Walnut Street; Rue Bonhomme, familiar to Saint Louisans of today as Market Street; Rue Missouri, now called Chestnut. These were simply narrow lanes, ranging from twenty-five to thirty feet in width, and were still in their "natural state of hills, hollows and sink holes." Walnut Street, or Rue de la Tour, between Second and Third Streets, was used but seldom because it was low, and on wet days almost impassable along the slippery rock bed which in the course of years had been stripped of its protecting soil.

Along the dark streets at night the belated traveler made his way cautiously and fearfully, as best he could, with no light, except that furnished by the moon on moonlight nights, or per-haps a faint candlebeam from some friendly window of the near-by houses to guide his steps. These unpaved streets were "knee deep in mud" in wet weather, while they were very dusty during the hot and dry season of the year. As late as February 11, 1816, the *Gazette* complained that the "town presents to the

18 James Cartwright Essex, "An Autobiography," in *Glimpses of the Past,* Missouri Historical Society *Publications,* 1934.

stranger a despicable portrait of police management. Several streets are rendered impassable by the want of a common footway or a drain to carry off the rain water." In spite of complaints and numerous protests, no attempt was made to improve the roads or to lay sidewalks until 1818, when there was enacted a city ordinance requiring "that Front or Water Street be paved with stone."[19] Brackenridge tells us that in 1810 Saint Louis despite these physical drawbacks, was a place of refinement and fashion and the residence of many genteel families, both French and American.[20]

The houses of the town were built chiefly of logs or stone. There were a few frame structures, but up to the year 1810 there was not a brick building in the village. The log houses, built in the old French style of slabs or logs set upright in the ground and filled in with stones and mud, were usually only one story with porches extending around three sides.[21] The floors were of puncheon and the windows of glass. The homes of the more prosperous settlers were enclosed in yards which were fenced with pickets seven feet high and eight or ten inches in diameter. The pickets were driven into the ground and sharpened on the top, a device which helped to keep out intruders. Within these enclosures were gardens with the choicest varieties of flowering plants and bushes. Back of all this were orchards in which were to be found fruit trees bearing the numerous varieties of the best developed apples, plums, pears, etc.[22] Beyond, but still within the enclosure, were the stables, and yet farther on, the quarters in which were housed the slaves, for from the time of Renault, who brought the first Negroes into Upper Louisiana,[23] every family of means had its menial tasks performed by slaves, one of whom in the capacity of "Mammy," cared for the children.

19 *Missouri Gazette,* February 11, 1818.

20 Brackenridge, *op. cit.,* p. 223.

21 *Ibid.,* p. 217–218.

22 Ashe, Thomas, *Travels in America,* p. 291.

23 Houck, *op. cit.,* I, 282.

The most pretentious dwelling noted by Wilt, as he passed down the street, was that owned by Colonel Auguste Chouteau. On Main Street, extending from Walnut to Market and back to Second, there was laid out what was termed the town square. Chouteau's residence occupied the center of this square, which was entirely enclosed, not with pickets, as in the case of the other houses, but with a massive stone wall. The house was a large two-story French building with verandas around the entire edifice. The furnishings, which were in keeping with the imposing exterior, included every variety of drape, furniture, fixture, and wall-trapping. The floors were of black walnut, so highly polished that they reflected as do mirrors.[24] It was here that the young aristocracy of the village gathered for dancing; here, over their wine cups, the older members discussed civic problems, the latest news from Washington, or messages from the Indian country. It was a common occurrence for these friends to spend long hours in friendly intercourse during which no subject was permitted to intrude that might dampen the friendliness and congeniality always prevailing in this social circle.[25]

Directly behind Mr. Chouteau's residence was the church lot, which occupied the entire block on Rue de L'Eglise, between Walnut and Market Streets. For many years the little old log church surrounded by "God's Acre" was the only place of worship. It was not until 1818 that Bishop Dubourg, the first bishop of the Louisiana Territory, replaced the log structure with a brick church[26] which, unfortunately, was destroyed by fire the following year. It was, in turn, succeeded by the stately old cathedral which still remains.

The home of Major Pierre Chouteau, brother of the Colonel, occupied the square fronting on Main Street and extending from what is now Washington Avenue to Vine and back to Second. Although his dwelling was neither so large nor so pretentious

24 Stoddard, Major Amos, *Sketches, Historical and Descriptive of Louisiana* (Philadelphia, 1812), p. 328.

25 Edwards, *op. cit.,* p. 286.

26 Rothensteiner, Rev. John, *History of the Saint Louis Diocese* (St. Louis, 1928), I, 272.

as that of his brother, it was built in the same style and of the same material. Old Madame Chouteau, the mother of Auguste and Pierre, lived in a long, low building on the corner of Main and Chestnut. Across the street from her home was that of Charles Gratiot, and on a cross street, south of Major Chouteau's home, the Cabanné family lived. As one journeyed on down the length of Main Street, the homes of Messrs. Sarpy, Yosti, Papin, L'Abbadie, Chenie, and Pratte, merchants and leading citizens of the town, came into view. Homes in those days served both as family dwellings and as stores or shops where furs and merchandise were bartered.

Outstanding among the names of the first French and Spanish traders and merchants were those of the Chouteau brothers, Auguste and Pierre, Manual Lisa, Gabriel Cerré, Joseph Robidoux, Jacques Clamorgan, and Charles Gratiot. These names have remained upon the merchant rolls of the city almost to the present day, followed closely by those of Messrs. Chenie, L'Abbadie, Sarpy, Papin, and Berthold.

The Chouteau brothers were representative of that class of merchants whose type seldom appears in the course of a century. In addition to the posts established by Laclede, these brothers had stations on the Osage River, the upper Missouri, the Des Moines River, and Lake Michigan. It is said that for forty years Pierre Chouteau controlled the trade of the Mississippi without any thought of being confronted by a rival merchant.[27] "The very genius of commerce inspired him, and the plans of this Indian trader, who got his earliest training among the Osages, on the border of Kansas, reached out wide like the arms of the Mississippi River."[28] His system included not only the Indians of the Osage country but those of the Cherokee, Chickasaw, and other tribes who might visit his trading posts.

Charles Gratiot, born in Lausanne, Switzerland, and educated in London,[29] became the leading merchant in the village of

27 Scharf, Thomas J., *History of St. Louis and County* (Philadelphia, 1883), I, 287.

28 *Ibid.,* p. 287.   29 Billon, *op. cit.,* I, 481.

Cahokia, Illinois. In 1782 he removed to Saint Louis and the transfer of his business tended to make Saint Louis the trade center of the west side of the river.[30] He was, through his association with John Jacob Astor,[31] well-known in New York, Philadelphia, and Montreal, and "better known in Paris, London and Geneva than on this Continent."[32] Manuel Lisa was a fur trader second to none. "He was upright, honest, a man of sterling worth, a competent judge of man and character and undoubtedly the best equipped man in every way, engaged in the trade on the Missouri at this time."[33] The Indians loved and respected him and brought to him their richest furs. During the War of 1812 he gave effective aid to his country by thwarting the English in their efforts to form a universal confederacy against the Americans.[34] All of these men, later close associates in the business and social life of Christian Wilt, were active in the commercial enterprises of the little town.

Saint Louis in its earliest days became a market for the fur trade, the arteries of which ran through that great wilderness mapped out, and in part explored, by Lewis and Clark. Hunters and traders found here regular employment, and each year they went, in ever increasing numbers, into the region about the headwaters of the Mississippi and northwest along the valley of the Missouri to barter guns, knives, cloth, trinkets, and brandy for the pelts of the otter, fox, and beaver. From Laclede's day down to 1850, Saint Louis was their favorite rendezvous; it became the Montreal of the Mississippi valley and the depot for the basins of the great rivers emptying into the "Father of Waters" from its source to the Gulf.[35]

30 Houck, *op. cit.*, II, 48.

31 Gratiot to Astor, September 27, 1812. Missouri Historical Society Collections; Porter, Kenneth, *John Jacob Astor, Business Man* (Cambridge, Mass., 1931), I, 276.

32 Scharf, *op. cit.*, II, 287.

33 Wagner, W. F. in introduction to *Adventures of Zenas Leonard, Fur-trader and Trapper, 1831–1836*, p. 21.

34 Manuel Lisa to General Clark, July 1, 1817. *Missouri Gazette*, July 5, 1817.

35 Scharf, *op. cit.*, I, 288.

Among the pelts handled by the traders were many fine furs, including those of the mink, the muskrat, the otter, and the beaver, as well as the coarser skins of the deer, the bear, and the buffalo. These inferior furs were used for lap robes, for rough coats and for other articles of wearing apparel. In addition to the skins, the traders also regularly brought into Saint Louis loads of bear tallow for making candles and soap and cargoes of buffalo tongue for use as food.[36] For forty years, from 1764 to the transfer of the Louisiana Territory to the United States in 1803, the richest peltries were brought to Saint Louis in ever increasing numbers. During the fifteen years previous to the Louisiana Purchase and including 1804, the annual average quantity and value of the furs, according to the records left by August Chouteau, Sr.,[37] were as follows:

			Value
Castors (Beavers)	39,000	lbs.	$66,820
Otters	8,000	"	37,100
Bear skins	5,100	"	14,200
Buffalo skins			
Raccoon, Wild cat	850	"	4,750
Fox skins	28,200	"	12,280
Martens	1,300	"	3,900
Lynx	300	"	1,500
Deer skins	158,000	"	63,200
			$204,750

The relative value of the peltries, determined in the early days, remained unchanged. There was little specie in Upper Louisiana and this deficiency induced the Spanish government to accept peltry as a medium of trade and as legal tender in payment of debt, except when that would have infringed upon the specific stipulations of a contract. For instance, a note of $100 was payable in peltry unless it was expressly stated that the payment should be made in *Spanish milled dollars*. Specification in contracts was the more necessary as one silver dollar

36 Chittenden, Hiram M., *The American Fur Trade of the Far West* (New York, 1902), I, 2.

37 Stoddard, *op. cit.*, p. 297.

was deemed equal to $1.25 in peltry.[38] Under the French monarchy the unit of value was the "livre", an old French coin equal to about 18½ cents of our money.[39]

Deerskins were taken as a standard for they were the least variable in price in spite of the fact they were abundant.[40] A pound of deerskin of the finest quality, which represented about twice the value of the "livre", was fixed by law at forty cents; medium, thirty cents; and inferior, twenty cents.[41] In disposing of his furs the Saint Louis trader brought his cargo tied in packs to the town, warehoused them, and secured receipts. These receipts or "deerskin" notes, as they were called, were accepted up and down the river.[42] A pack of skins contained ten buffalo robes, fourteen bear, sixty otter, eighty beaver, eighty raccoon, one hundred and twenty fox, or six hundred muskrat skins,[43] and weighed about one hundred pounds. Trade was thus made easy and computation accurate. According to Scharf, pelts constituted a much better and more uniform currency than the staple tobacco which was, at one time, the circulating medium of Virginia and Maryland.[44] Pelts were accepted even in payment of taxes for on Tuesday, March 19, 1805, the court of Common Pleas and Quarter Sessions in Saint Louis ruled that "taxes can be paid in shaved deerskins at the rate of three pounds to the dollar (33 1/3 cents) from October to April, *after that time cash.*"[45] Other things, such as whiskey, potash, maple sugar, salt, wood, venison, fish, or lead, might be taken in exchange or barter, but

---

38 *Ibid.,* p. 282.

39 Houck, *op. cit.,* I, 342 n.

40 Conard, Howard L., *Encyclopedia of Missouri History* (St. Louis, 1901), Article on Banking.

41 Scharf, *op. cit.,* p. 292.

42 Knox, *History of Banking in United States* (New York, 1903), p. 780.

43 Chittenden, H. M., *The American Fur Trade of the Far West* (New York, 1902), I, 38.

44 Scharf, *op. cit.,* I, 291.

45 Billon, *op. cit.,* II, 11.

fur was the standard of value from Mackinac, Detroit, and Prairie du Chien, all the way to New Orleans.[46]

The goods traded in exchange for furs were valued, not at their cost in the Eastern cities, but at their selling price in Saint Louis, and the peltries were valued at the current prices in the West. Cloth that might be sold in Saint Louis at sixty cents a yard, probably did not cost one half that, "including freight, interest, and insurance, while on the other hand, beaver worth $2 a pound in Saint Louis might bring twice as much in London and five times as much in Canton."[47] In Chouteau's reckoning the value of merchandise annually sent up the Missouri (not to speak of other extensive lines of commerce), during the fifteen years before the Purchase, was $61,250.[48] Among the different Indian tribes the returns varied. Brackenridge tells us that in 1810 the trade with the Osages yielded $30,000, showing on the outlay for goods a profit of 50 per cent measured in furs. With the Cheyennes commerce yielded a profit of 100 per cent, as was that with the Poncas. On the trade at the Arkansas Post with the Cherokees and Chickasaws, a profit of 150 per cent might be expected, on that with the Crows, 200 per cent, while that with the Sioux might be counted on for as much as a 300 per cent profit.[49] This variation in profitable returns might be due to the unequal number of members in the different tribes, or to the fact that the Indians shared their trade with both American and Spanish agents.

The articles of merchandise which the traders took with them into the Indian country were cheap and gaudy: red blankets, muskets, powder, shot, glittering trinkets, common blue and red strouding, beads, shawls of gaudy colors, mirrors, combs, flints and lead, knives of different kinds, kettles, copper, brass, and tin. But scissors, needles, thread, beaver, muskrat traps, and whiskey also went into the traders' packs. Although the United

---

46 Scharf, *op. cit.*, I, 291.
47 *Ibid.*, I, 289.
48 Stoddard, *op. cit.*, p. 298.
49 Brackenridge, *op. cit.*, p. 290.

States forbade the sale of liquor to the Indians, and though the missionaries waged an eternal warfare against this traffic, the strife was a useless one, for the free traders, who swarmed into the Northwest, deluged the Indian country with all kinds of liquor. This was the cheapest way to secure furs, and in self-defense the regular traders carried the outlawed "fire water" on their trading expeditions and evaded punishment as best they could.

One may get an idea of the prices at which articles were rated in the mountains from an extract from the bill of sale by which General William H. Ashley transferred his outfit to the firm of Smith, Jackson, and Sublette, near Great Salt Lake, July 18, 1826. The invoice included

gunpowder of the first and second quality at one dollar fifty per pound, shot at one dollar twenty-five per pound, three point blankets at nine dollars each, green ditto at eleven dollars each, scarlet cloth at six dollars per yard, blue ditto, common quality from four to five dollars per yard, butcher knives at seventy-five cents each, two and one-half point blankets at seven dollars each, tin kettles, different sizes, at two dollars per pound, sheet iron kettles at two dollars twenty-five per pound, beaver traps at nine dollars each, sugar at one dollar per pound, coffee at one dollar twenty-five a pound, grey cloth of common quality at five dollars per yard, thread assorted at three dollars per pound, worsted bindings at fifteen dollars per gross, beads assorted at two dollars fifty per pound, fourth proof rum reduced at thirteen dollars fifty per gallon, tobacco at one dollar twenty-five per pound, washing soap at one dollar twenty-five per pound, shaving soap at two dollars per pound.[50]

When the trading season opened in the fall all traders, except those representing the government, extended credit to the Indians.[51] That is to say, the articles offered on credit were given very high prices and the Indians were compelled to take the

---

50 Sublette Papers, Articles of Agreement between William Ashley, Smith, Jackson, and William Sublette on July 18, 1826, Missouri Historical Society *Collections.*

51 Brackenridge, *op. cit.,* p. 138.

goods at these high prices because they could not do without them. If the traders had not supplied the Indians with the necessities to enable them to support themselves, the latter would have suffered. But, by virtue of the excessive prices charged for the goods he furnished to the Indians on credit, the trader on reckoning his accounts at the close of trade in the spring felt that he had done a fairly good business if the Indians had repaid but half of the amount for which he had extended credit to them in the preceding autumn. The trappers and traders brought the pelts down the Missouri, usually in pirogues, to the landing place in Saint Louis at the foot of Market Street which led directly to the business district.

The business district was on Main Street, between Spruce and Pine, where in 1810, there were twelve general stones actively engaged in carrying on trade. In the summer of that year when Wilt opened his store in an old building which he rented from Mrs. Labadie, competition threatened to be keen. Directly across the street, just north of Charles Gratiot's home, lived Jacob Philipson, a friend from Philadelphia and a brother of Simon Philipson, the one-time partner of Hertzog.

Jacob Philipson had settled in Saint Louis in 1808,[52] opening his store opposite the Post Office where he sold "groceries and dry goods for cash at reasonable prices." In October of the following year, with a larger stock, he removed to the building just beyond the house of Charles Gratiot on Main Street,[53] where Wilt and Mussina found him when they came to open their new establishment; but in January, 1811, Philipson placed some of his goods with Mrs. Piscay on commission, and took the remainder of the assortment to Sainte Genevieve[54] where he remained only a short time. In the last month of 1814,[55] when war conditions made profit impossible, he sold his entire stock and closed out the business.

52 *Missouri Gazette,* November 10, 1808.
53 *Ibid.,* October 12, 1809.
54 Hertzog to Z. Mussina, May 4, 1811, Hertzog Letterbook.
55 Wilt to Hertzog, December 31, 1814, Wilt Letterbook.

Joseph Philipson, who came to Saint Louis a year before his brother Jacob, counted among his customers many of the early and prominent Saint Louisans. The names of Alexander McNair, the first Governor of the State, David De Launay, Inspector General of Militia,[56] Madame Labadie, one of the pioneer settlers, Mrs. Piscay, who opened the first girls' school in Saint Louis, the Chouteau brothers, Auguste and Pierre, are all found on the age-stained pages of his account books. These books record that Meriwether Lewis settled his account in full on August 22, 1809, a few days before he left for Washington on his last journey; that Frederick Bates, Secretary and often Acting Governor of Louisiana, paid four dollars for each of the two volumes of the *History of Virginia;* and that C. B. Penrose, member of the Board of Land Commissioners of the Louisiana Territory, purchased a silk shawl for sixteen dollars at the same counter.[57]

Whether Joseph and Jacob Philipson were partners in the mercantile concern is not clear, but they were interested in real estate and had acquired large holdings both in and around the city of their adoption. They were interested, too, in lead, which they sent to Pittsburgh, where Simon disposed of it to the best advantage. At times he was able to make a sale in Pittsburgh, at other times he consigned it to jobbers in New York City or in Philadelphia.

Simon remained in Philadelphia and acted as agent for his brothers who continued to operate in the West. Although he made several trips to Saint Louis, he did not establish his home there until 1821 after the financial panic in which both of his brothers lost heavily.[58] These three were shrewd men of busi-

---

56 Marshall, Thomas M., *Life and Letters of Frederick Bates* (List of Civil and Military Appointments, Oct. 1, 1810–Sept. 30, 1811) (St. Louis, 1926), II, 194.

57 Philipson Original Account Book.

58 We learn from William Drummond Stewart that he visited Saint Louis in 1830 and at that date found "Simon an agreeable old man who had an old wooden house on a square plot (called in Saint Louis *an island*) surrounded by streets. His abode contained an assortment of pictures and other objects

ness. They were capable of driving a hard bargain and were worthy competitors of the trained and experienced traders of early Saint Louis. They promised sharp rivalry to the new firm from Philadelphia, as was evident in their first deal, when they purchased the greater part of the invoice of goods that Wilt and Mussina brought to Saint Louis in the early spring of 1810.[59]

At the northeast corner of Main and Market, Bernard Pratte sold dry goods, groceries, liquors, iron, and steel. Pratte, while still a young man, came from Sainte Genevieve to Saint Louis, in 1793, to engage in business.[60] In May of the following year he married Emelie, the eldest daughter of Sylvestre Labadie and Pelagie Chouteau. His connection with the oldest and most respected families of this section, as well as his wealth and influence in the community, made him a formidable rival of the new firm of *Zachary Mussina*.

Opposite the building owned by Bernard Pratte, on the west side of Main Street, stood the old store of Hunt and Haukinson. Its gaudily painted sign "Hunt and Haukinson's New Cash Store" was, in the eyes of the children of the village, a veritable work of art, in front of which they gathered to gaze in rapt admiration. Here the Kerr brothers, Matthew and John, sold goods. They had come from Carlisle or Shippensburgh in the Cumberland Valley, Pennsylvania, about 1808,[61] and had opened a general store. Later they dissolved partnership and Matthew

either for use or vendu, but the house was never swept or dusted, save when a plume of ostrich feathers was called on to clean rare and curious articles which were stored here and which were exhibited at intervals for the satisfaction of hunters who visited this locality. He was most kind and hospitable to the extent of those commodities in which he indulged. His family consisted of Philippe, Louis, and Miranda. Philippe died in Lexington, Missouri, on the 24th of September, 1834, while returning from a trip to the Rocky Mountains. Louis, the youngest son, was drowned in Lewis Park in 1836 after having made an expedition with Sir William Stewart. Simon died in Saint Louis in 1841, a broken-hearted old man." William Drummond Stewart, *Edward Warren* (London, 1854), p. 182.

59 Hertzog to Wilt, March–April, 1812.

60 Billon, *op. cit.*, I, 466.

61 *Ibid.*, II, 243.

continued to carry on the enterprise alone. Each year he went East for his supplies and returned with a well chosen assortment which he sold at much lower prices[62] than those asked by the other merchants. This practice, although it made him unpopular among his associates, built for him a large and lucrative business. In June 1811, in company with Robert Moody, he removed to the house adjoining Charles Gratiot's, formerly occupied by Joseph Philipson. Their supply of goods included "cloth, blankets, cotton goods, hardware and glass", for in these pioneer days there was no tendency to specialize in any particular line of goods. Among the articles which they accepted in barter was corn, rated at twenty-five cents per bushel. During the War of 1812 Matthew Kerr and Christian Wilt, in partnership, attempted to furnish the American troops with supplies, but the association was not a happy or pleasant one and it was dissolved after a few months.

Berthold and Paul occupied the Valois house on the west side, between Market and Walnut. Berthold was born in the Italian Tyrol in 1789 and was only eighteen years of age when he emigrated to the American shore. After remaining in Philadelphia for a short time, he moved to Baltimore where he met René Paul, a native of Santo Domingo, who had been educated in Paris. In Baltimore the two men formed a partnership and moved to Saint Louis in 1809. For three years the Berthold-Paul Company carried on, but at the end of that period the association was dissolved. Berthold then joined his brother-in-law, Pierre Chouteau, Jr., and together they were able to engage the attention of those in need of the wares to be found on their shelves. The Berthold-Chouteau Company, which was organized in 1812, operated on a large scale, and in 1833, with John P. Cabanné and Bernard Pratte, became the western department of John Jacob Astor's American Fur Company,[63] an organization that for many years monopolized the fur trade of the Missouri country. It might be of interest to add that on January

62 Hertzog to Wilt, December 23, 1811.
63 Porter, Kenneth W., *op. cit.*, II, 693.

10, 1811, Berthold married Pelagie, the only daughter of Major Pierre Chouteau. For his bride he built on Main Street, between Market and Chestnut, the first brick house, not only in Saint Louis, but the first brick residence west of the Mississippi.[64] In this two-story building, which was made to serve as both store and dwelling, Berthold lived and carried on his business for several years.

Down on the northwest corner of Main and Almond was William Shannon who in 1808 had come from Sainte Gene-vieve, which was at that time a larger and more prosperous village than Saint Louis. However, the city at the mouth of the Missouri was reaching out in every direction and monopolizing all the trade within reasonable distance. Shannon, who was too shrewd a business man not to see the possibilities of the little fur-trading center, opened a branch store in the old stone house of Francois Benoist, and in 1809 added to his general assortment of dry goods and groceries a parcel of drugs and medicines. This, according to Houck, was one of the first drug stores in the area now known as Missouri.[65]

The United States Government, too, was operating in the field of trade and commerce.[66] General William Clark, acting United States Agent of the Indian Department, dealt especially in Indian goods. In September, 1810,[67] he offered for sale a quantity of bear's oil, Indian mats, feathers, and 100,000 pounds of lead. Later he put out the following articles:[68]

64 Billon, op. cit., II, 234.

65 Houck, op. cit., III, 83.

66 "In 1796, Congress made an appropriation for the establishment of a liberal trade with the Indians. It established factories carrying the usual line of Indian goods, to dispose of in exchange for furs at rates which would simply make the factories self-sustaining. In this way the Indian would get his goods at cost, and it was thought that he would patronize the factories in preference to the private trader." Chittenden, op. cit., I, 12–13.

67 Louisiana Gazette, September 19, 1810.

68 Ibid., March 21, 1811.

200 packs of shaved deer skins
32 packs of bear skins
6500 lbs. of buffalo, elk and deer tallow
2000 lbs. of mould candles in boxes

Patrick Lee, one of the "Irish crowd", as the McKnights and the Bradys were called, was not only a trader but an auctioneer, a broker, and a commission merchant, probably the first in Saint Louis. On July 10, 1810, he informed his intimate friends and the public in general that his store near the Post Office was well supplied with dry goods and groceries which he would sell at a very moderate price. He announced that he had "commenced the business of a Broker and Auctioneer in the town of Saint Louis" and promised "to execute with the greatest punctuality" the orders of such persons as addressed themselves to him. His "house and cellar", he said, "were well calculated for storing merchandise of every kind, and he was now ready to receive such goods or produce as might be committed to his disposal in private or public sale."[69]

Fred Yeizer, who, as captain in command of the gun-boat "Governor Clark", saw active service in the War of 1812, was a true son of the frontier for he dared to enter the commercial world with no knowledge of the rudiments of learning which, today, we consider absolutely necessary to success. His advertisement, as it appeared in the *Gazette,* read:

LOOK HERE!!

The subscriber has removed to the house adjoining Mr. Dongan's silver-smith store on Main Street. He has on hand a heap of whiskey, plenty of peach brandy, Linsey, country linens, cut and hammered nails, *cottons,* and cotton cloth, bed cords, etc., etc., which he will sell for *cash* or beef hides delivered at the store or at Squire Moorehead's slaughter yard.

N.B. *No credit* need be expected as the subscriber has (unfortunately) never learned to write.

F. YEIZER.[70]

69 *Ibid.*, July 10, 1810.
70 *Ibid.*, December 14, 1811.

Not only did these enterprising merchants carry on their business in Saint Louis but, in many instances, they opened branch stores in the surrounding towns where they disposed of their goods at fairly high prices. William Shannon kept both his Saint Louis and his Sainte Genevieve establishments in operation; H. M. Shreve conducted a branch at Sainte Genevieve in Mr. Newfield's new store, and at Saint Charles, in the house of Doctor Smith, Matthew Kerr displayed a large assortment of goods which he "offered at a low price, for cash."

Besides these general stores there were various shops wherein trades and crafts were carried on. It is interesting to find in this little frontier town tailors plying their needles. Because cloth was scarce and expensive, animal skins constituted the material from which the coarse outer garments were usually made. Bernard Lalande made coats for gentlemen at $4.50 each, and pantaloons at seventy-five cents each. "They were well made and in the latest fashion." On January 11, 1810, shortly before Wilt and Mussina came to Saint Louis, Pain and Armstrong opened a tailor shop near the Post Office. They carried on "Skin Dressing, Leather Pantaloon and Breeches making, and hoped from their peculiar attention to business to merit a share of the public patronage."[71] At the same time, they announced that they had "received from the Missouri Salt Works a quantity of salt which they would sell for cash or pork at market prices."

These were some of the men of Anglo-Saxon descent who fixed their residence in Saint Louis and gradually gained control of the larger mercantile interests of the town. They occupied the most prominent offices and determined public policies. While one finds little or no evidence of open antagonism between the French and non-French merchants, yet the former must have envied and distrusted the men of other nationalities who had usurped the control of the city founded by the French and long governed by the Spanish.[72]

71 *Missouri Gazette*, January 11, 1810.
72 Edwards, *op. cit.*, p. 278.

These early merchants, or "men of the Western World" as they loved to call themselves,[73] were obliged, in carrying on their business, to travel on horseback through the forests to New York, Baltimore, or Philadelphia to procure new stocks of goods. These stocks, nearly all imported, consisted of Indian goods, beads, and cotton goods from England, sheeting and blankets from Russia, coffee from Brazil, wine from Madeira, Lisbon, or Sicily, raisins from Malaga, rum from Jamaica, sugar from Havana, and steel from Germany, together with domestic articles and raw materials.

From Philadelphia these merchants sent goods to Pittsburgh in wagons, the freight charges sometimes reaching as high as seven to ten dollars a hundred weight. So rapidly did the commerce to the West grow, and so great did the traffic become, that in 1820 over three thousand four-horse freight wagons ran between Philadelphia and Pittsburgh transporting annually about eight million dollars worth of merchandise.[74] At Pittsburgh the owners loaded their goods on keelboats and traveled down the Ohio and up the Mississippi to Saint Louis.

Over the counter in his little store the Saint Louis merchant, as has been said before, bartered his goods for furs, lead, tobacco, and whiskey, while needles, pins, and sheets of writing paper served as small change.[75] Coins were rarely seen, the smallest being the Spanish milled dollar, which the merchant cut into halves or quarters. This was the earliest fractional currency. The merchants sometimes cut the quarters in two and made "bits", a bit being twelve and one-half cents.

Saint Louis afforded no stable banking facilities until the year 1837. Since the banks that were established in 1813 and 1817 were both failures, early business transactions were made on credit, except for those financed by bills of exchange on the government, offered as early as 1808 by Wilkinson and Price. In supplying outfits for the traders the merchant accepted credit and

73 Turner, Frederick J., *The Rise of the West* (New York, 1906), p. 68.
74 Turner, *op. cit.*, pp. 99–100.
75 Edwards, *op. cit.*, p. 295.

received in payment the traders' fur and peltry, usually in the spring. In extending credit the early merchants were very different from the modern, for the people of that time were more scrupulous in fulfilling their engagements. A man's personal or promissory note was accepted, but there was no fixed time for notifying endorsers and often two or three months passed before the notice was given.[76]

These merchants, as a class, were important, not only because of their numbers, but because they were men of intelligence, wealth, and enterprise.[77] They developed trade, speculated in land, opened and operated mines, founded manufacturing plants, and began weaving the fabric of society in the land of the West. Such were the men and such the conditions in Saint Louis in 1810, when the two merchants from Philadelphia, Wilt and Mussina, turned their faces westward to seek their fortunes on what was then the far western frontier.

76 Bolles, Albert S., *Pennsylvania, Province and State* (Philadelphia, 1899), II, 198.

77 Atherton, Lewis E., "Western Merchants", *Mississippi Valley Historical Review*, XXIV, 24.

CHAPTER III
MERCHANDISING ON THE FRONTIER
1810-1812

AFTER Mussina departed for the East to report, Christian Wilt was left alone in Saint Louis, and his first task was to find a suitable place for the consignment coming from Philadelphia. He visited the stores along Main Street and made the acquaintance of the older merchants, many of whom became his devoted friends. There were also young men—physicians, merchants, lawyers—who had lately come from the East, and who were glad to welcome another new comer to their midst. In this group was Edward Hempstead, ten years Wilt's senior. He had settled in Saint Louis in 1804, and in 1809, just a year before Wilt's coming, had been appointed Attorney General for the Territory of Upper Louisiana.[1] The acquaintance between the two young men ripened into a deep friendship, and when Mussina brought suit against Wilt in 1812, Edward Hempstead offered surety for the defendant. This bond of friendship was further strengthened by the marriage in 1819 of Charles Hempstead, Edward's younger brother, to Wilt's sister Rachel,[2] who came west in 1818 to be with her two brothers.

In looking about for an empty building, Wilt found that owing to the recent arrival of a large number of immigrants all houses were filled, rents ran high,[3] and every available place that might be suitable for business was already taken. When A. C. Dunn, who occupied Mrs. Labadie's store,[4] closed out his stock some time in the fall of 1810, Wilt rented the old building on the northeast corner of Main Street, between the streets now known as Pine and Chestnut. His next duty was to procure his merchant's license which cost him $10. This was an annual

1 Billon, *op. cit.*, II, 206.
2 *Ibid.*, II, 253.
3 *Missouri Gazette*, March 21, 1811.
4 *Louisiana Gazette*, January 21, 1811.

tax imposed by the laws of the Territory on all retailers of foreign goods but, in order that home industry might be encouraged, no tax was levied on the sale of merchandise produced in the district.[5] With his license duly signed by Jeremiah Connor, sheriff of the district of Saint Louis and acting collector and treasurer, Wilt proceeded to furnish his store which for him served both as a place of business and as a home. Here he kept bachelor's hall, cooked his own meals, and waited impatiently for Invoice No. 2 which Mussina finally brought back in July.

This cargo in Philadelphia was valued at $13,701, according to the following memorandum :[6]

JULY 23, 1811

(2nd Adventure)

Invoice (Philadelphia Goods)	$9332.52
Omitted 3 reams of sup. fine paper	13.50
Sundry Porterage	2.94
Indigo for Sadlery	77.35
Balance to Graham	29.04
Sutton's 2nd Bill (Pittsburgh articles)	505.43
24 cwt. bar Iron	180.00
Z. M. acct. from Cincinnati	500.00
Balance due Cook & Cresson	10.25
Tin Ware from A. Dunsett	10.58
5 Violins at Cincinnati	10.00
Wine at 8 months	125.00
	$10796.61
Sutton's 1st bill (Pittsburgh articles)	2841.06
	13637.67
Incidentals	63.33
	$13701.00

The great pile of dry goods, blankets, crockery, hardwood, gin, and other articles that came from New York, Philadelphia, and Pittsburgh almost filled the little store, and the young merchants opened their first permanent place of business with a

5 *Laws for the Government of the District of Louisiana, 1808–1810* (St. Louis, 1811).

6 Hertzog to Wilt, July 23, 1811, Hertzog Letterbook.

full line of merchandise, ranging from fish hooks to lexicons. They were ready to compete with the older mercantile establishments for a share in the Indian and local trade, and in that of the near-by settlements. They were also anxious to participate in fitting out the trapping and exploring expeditions, which were then preparing to depart for a winter in the mountains. Manuel Lisa and his Missouri Fur Company were at this moment gathering men and supplies for their journey to the headwaters of the Missouri, and the little town was alive with bustle and excitement. Indians stood in groups on various street corners, or gathered in front of Chouteau's house, watching with stolid indifference while voyageurs, trappers, boatmen, and traders went about their tasks, making purchases wherever they could get the cheapest and best articles, or bartering for traps, guns, cordelles, and tobacco.

The new store was well supplied with blankets, strouding, gaudy calicoes, knives, awls, kettles, guns, beads, trinkets, looking glasses, brandy, hatchets, powder, etc., which made up the cargo of every expedition going into the Indian country, and the youthful proprietors disposed of a large quantity of their goods to the Missouri Fur Company as well as to the individual trappers and coureurs-des-bois.

At the same time that the Missouri Fur Company was preparing for its winter expedition into the fur country, Wilson P. Hunt, formerly a merchant of Saint Louis and at this time leader of Astor's Overlanders, reached Saint Louis where he hoped to complete the preparations for his journey into the Oregon country. With his party of thirty voyageurs Hunt had journeyed from Montreal to Mackinac where he was joined by Ramsey Crooks, who had left Saint Louis in June. From Mackinac, the whole company came in canoes by way of Green Bay, the Fox and Wisconsin Rivers, to Prairie du Chien, and from there dropped down the Mississippi to Saint Louis, which they reached on September 3, 1810.

Ramsey Crooks was a young Scotsman who, several years earlier, had been in the employ of the Northwestern Company and later had engaged in traffic with the tribes of the Missouri[7] with whom he managed to carry on well at his own personal risk. In his visits to Saint Louis he met Wilt, and they formed a lasting friendship. Into this friendship was admitted Joseph Miller—young, handsome, energetic—who some years before had come from Baltimore to try his luck in the West. He was an interesting youth, who had received military training and, at one time, had been an officer in the United States Army. But he had resigned his commission and had gone as an independent trader to the western plains and along the headwaters of the western rivers,[8] where he spent his days in pursuit of the wild animals of the region. Hunt had induced Miller to become one of the partners of the Astoria expedition, and it was, perhaps, owing to the influence of these two friends that Wilt furnished a large part of the goods and provisions for the men, seventy in number,[9] who made up the party that headed for the Pacific Coast in March, 1811.[10]

The extent of Hunt's purchases at Wilt's store may be measured by the drafts drawn on John Jacob Astor, the promoter of the expedition. During the winter Hertzog sent to the Farmers and Mechanics Bank of New York several notes which were promptly paid. In the early part of the spring months, just before his final departure for the West, Hunt gave Wilt three notes. One was for $400, payable in fifteen days, another, for $600 at sixty days, and still another for $1165.55 due on June 2, 1811. At that time John Jacob Astor did not have unlimited

7 Irving, *op. cit.*, p. 122.

8 *Ibid.*, pp. 125–26.

9 *Louisiana Gazette*, March 11, 1811.

10 The *Louisiana Gazette,* March 14, 1811, carried an interesting account of the little band of daring adventurers who feared neither the elements nor the wild Indian although they knew that several of their predecessors had met with more than ordinary hardships. "William P. Hunt," records the *Gazette,* "left this place last Monday, with a well-equipped barge, to join his associates at the Otto village, to proceed on his expedition to the Columbia River. His party amounted to about seventy ablebodied men, nerved to hardship" (March 10, 1811).

financial credit, for in presenting these bills through Messrs. David and Philip Grimm of New York, Hertzog wrote:

Should you have perfect confidence in the standing of Astor, would request you to have the two larger (notes) discounted at the bank and remit me the proceeds. Have received from Astor payment of several drafts on him in the course of last winter and have always heard him spoken of as of the finest respectability.[11]

The drafts were duly honored by the Farmers and Mechanics Bank of New York, but payment was not made until the date at which each successive note became due.[12]

On March 10, the day before he left for the Pacific,[13] Hunt gave Wilt another draft on Astor for $200, at eight months, "for supplies furnished to his hands going up the Missouri."[14] This draft was not presented at once because the financier would honor such paper only at the date of maturity. However, Hertzog had the draft in his possession and had no reason to worry about its value.

After the Missouri Fur Company and the Overlanders had left Saint Louis, the young merchants, Wilt and Mussina, looked to the home trade and, although their establishment was regarded as a "dear store", they succeeded in attracting a goodly portion of the local patronage. This may have been a tribute to the pleasing personality of the young proprietors, or an evidence of the preference of the Saint Louisans for articles of quality. The volume of business for the first year, which ended in March 1811, was most satisfactory. While complete records are lacking, various notes, statements, and the letters of Wilt reveal the extent to which the young men were themselves responsible for the working of their concern and how they entered into the commercial life of their adopted city. The sales for January, February, and up to March 10, amounted to $6408.48. Of

11 Hertzog to Messrs. David and Philip Grimm, March 30, 1811.
12 Hertzog to Wilt, June 8, 1811.
13 *Louisiana Gazette,* March 11, 1811.
14 Hertzog to Messrs. David and Philip Grimm, April 23, 1811.

this total, $3146 was for cash and $3262.48 was on credit.[15]
The April receipts which were forwarded in May were equally
encouraging. During this month[16] Wilt wrote to Hertzog, and
enclosed drafts and notes as follows:

Philipson's Draft dated May 13	$ 990.92½
Bank Notes	600.00
Lucas, Bills of Exchange dated May 23	300.00
Hunt " " " " " "	100.00
Chouteau " " " " " "	590.92
On May 28 he forwards Clark's draft	800.00
Clark's Bank Note, May 28	100.00
	$3481.84½

The Philadelphia partner was delighted. In order that the
promise of so auspicious a beginning might be realized in the
future course of the business, he wrote a long letter of advice
to Wilt, from which we quote:

Make an extensive acquaintance in the towns about and deposit with
safe hands (some of) your goods on commission. That is, give (the)
goods at a high limited price—they to have what they get over. . . .
If Cahokia is a good place of business, make an acquaintance there;
Smith[17] might do at Sainte Genevieve, Cultivate carefully, your up-
state river business and endeavor to keep an eye on great things in
preference to little matters. Get the good will of the German settlement[18] up the Missouri. Find a good young man if you can to assist
you in business, you have too much for one person to do.[19]

Later Hertzog wrote, "On the whole, my anticipation of sales
to the amount of $200,000 annually does not appear extravagant
if we are not drawbacked by losses or misfortune."[20]

15 Hertzog to Wilt, April 23, 1811.

16 Hertzog to Mussina, May 23, 1811; Hertzog to Wilt, May 28, 1811.

17 Smith was a lad whose father kept a tavern on Arch Street, Philadelphia. He came West with his brother to establish a distillery which was
subsequently opened near Herculaneum, Missouri.

18 Probably Saint Ferdinand. There must have been a large number of
German settlers in and about Saint Louis because Joseph Philipson adver-
tised both German and English Bibles for sale, as early as November 10,
1808.

19 Hertzog to Wilt, April 23, 1811.   20 Hertzog to Wilt, May 2, 1811.

So pleased was Abraham Wilt with his son's success that he gave Hertzog $1500 which was to be invested in the firm for Christian who had, on January 8, 1811, reached his majority. With this amount of capital, and in consideration of his services as manager of the business in Saint Louis, Wilt became an equal partner with Hertzog and Mussina.[21]

Early in March, 1811, Mussina prepared to go East for the fall goods. That he might have a cargo to take with him on his eastward journey, he sent Saint Cyr up the Mississippi to collect a load of lead from the Indians near Prairie du Chien.[22] Hyacinth Saint Cyr, Jr., was an experienced boatman.[23] His sister, Helene, was the wife of Nicholas Boilvin,[24] an Indian trader who dwelt near Prairie du Chien and for whom the Indians had the greatest respect. This sage gentleman had won the confidence of the red men, and it was probably because of young Saint Cyr's family connections that Mussina and Wilt selected him to negotiate for lead at the mines on the Mississippi. He succeeded in collecting a considerable quantity which was in readiness when Mussina started toward Philadelphia.

Up to that time the partnership had not received Mussina's share of the capital; yet his membership in the firm had never been questioned. Before leaving Saint Louis, Mussina arranged after some unpleasant bickering with the Philipson brothers that they should pay the amount called for in the note which they had given him for his services. The note was dated May 10, 1810, and was due in one year. The Philipsons failed to meet his demand, but because he felt sure that they would keep their word and pay the amount when it fell due, he was satisfied that from May 1811 he would be considered a bona

21 Hertzog to Wilt, June 27, 1811.

22 Hertzog to Wilt, March 20, 1811.

23 Houck, *op. cit.*, II, 12. Hyacinth was born in Saint Louis in 1786. In 1800 he and his brother, Leon, received grants of land in Missouri from the government in consideration of losses sustained by their father, Hyacinth Saint Cyr, Sr., while in the employ of the United States.

24 *Ibid.*, I, 357; State Historical Society of Wisconsin, *Collections* (Madison, 1856), II, 122.

fide partner and entitled to a share in the profit realized. He left Saint Louis about the first of March and took with him two boats of lead, furs and other products of the Western country, which he either sold or left on commission with the agents of the firm, who were stationed here and there in the towns along the Ohio. He was advised to bring back Invoice No. 3, which Hertzog had already purchased. It is quite apparent that this event marked the date when all partners of the firm assumed equal footing.

Left alone the second time, Wilt "busied himself about many things." He had been instructed to pick up bargains in real estate with the injunction to pay in goods. When Joseph Philipson offered the Meriwether Lewis tract in payment of the last of the three notes given the previous spring, Wilt readily acquiesced.[25] This land was located about six miles northwest of Saint Louis on a creek called Marie Castor, and measured about 3000 arpents. It was part of a 4850 arpent tract which had originally been granted by the Spanish government to Joseph A. Hortiz who sold it to Pierre Chouteau, Sr. He in turn disposed of it to Meriwether Lewis. The land was then sold at public auction for $890.[26] Thus on October 27, 1810, it passed into the possession of Joseph Philipson. Wilt considered this tract a most desirable piece of property, because it afforded a suitable site for a distillery, which he and Hertzog expected to build in the vicinity of Saint Louis. The remaining land was to be divided into a number of farms of convenient size and upon these the partners hoped to establish a colony peopled by farmers who came in from the East.[27] After some months of vacillation, Philipson refused to complete the bargain without an additional sum of $600,[28] to which arrangement Wilt refused to assent, and the land remained in Philipson's possession.[29]

25 Hertzog to Wilt, March 30, 1811.
26 Original Deeds, p. 287, City Hall, Saint Louis.
27 Hertzog to Wilt, June 27, 1811.
28 Hertzog to Wilt, June 11, 1811.
29 Hertzog to Simon Philipson, July 20, 1811.

Another opportunity to secure cheap land presented itself when, on the first Monday in March, Auguste Chouteau, the administrator, offered at public sale the Iowa estate of Julian Dubuque who died sometime in 1809. The tract covered some 75,852 arpents which was divided and sold in smaller lots of 6000 arpents each at twenty cents per arpent.[30] Wilt investigated and found that the Indian title acquired by Dubuque had expired at his death. When the Land Commissioners refused to confirm its continuance, he cautiously refused to invest. Later, Wilt purchased large holdings in what is now the heart of the business section and the residential districts of the city of Saint Louis, as well as extensive tracts in other sections of the state. Among these possessions were listed:

Lot ....Main and Locust Street;
Henderson's Lot ....Opposite side of street;
Tract (640 acres) ....About three and one-half miles southwest of the town of Saint Louis, in the prairie called Barriere de Noyer;
204 Acres ....Situated in the town of St. Ferdinand;
New Hartford tract (640 acres) and
Labadie land (400 acres) .....Situated on the Illinois side of the river.[31]

It was on the land purchased in Illinois that Wilt eventually constructed his distillery and his saw mill. In all his land ventures he sought the counsel and advice of his friends, General William Clark and Judge Silas Bent. The latter had been deputy-surveyor for the Territory of Louisiana but at that time was acting judge of the Saint Louis Court of Common Pleas and Quarter Sessions.[32]

To carry on his merchandising it was necessary for Wilt to gather funds to secure bargains in the Eastern markets. He set to work, as did all the Saint Louis merchants of that day, to

30 *Louisiana Gazette,* Notice of Public Sale, November 5, 1810.

31 Original Deeds, City Hall, Saint Louis.

32 Marshall, *op. cit.,* II, p. 190 N.

barter groceries and dry goods for lead, furs, beeswax, saltpeter, and hemp. These articles were shipped down the Mississippi to New Orleans, or up the Ohio to Pittsburgh, thence to Baltimore, New York, and Philadelphia, where they were sold for cash or exchanged for articles of merchandise. The prices in these markets rose or fell as the supply and demand varied. On February 14, 1811, the *Gazette*[33] printed the following prices of produce in the New Orleans Market, as of January 2, 1811:

Flour, Western Country, bbl...9 to 10 dollars, but on the rise of the river waters will probably decline to 6 or 7 dollars.
Wheat ....None
Lead, lb. ....8 to 8½ cents
Flaxseed, lb. .... None
Saltpeter, lb. ....37½ cents to 43 cents
Red River Cotton, lb. ....17½ cents to 18 cents
Sugar, Country Muscovada, lb. 8½ cents to 9 cents
Sugar, Havana White, lb. .....12 cents to 13 cents
Sugar, Brown, lb. ....10 cents to 11 cents
Flour, Atlantic, bbl. ....12 to 13 dollars
Coffee, lb. ....25 cents
Tea, Imperial, lb. ....130 cents
Tea, Hyson, lb. ....100 cents
Freight to Liverpool on cotton. 4 cents per pound

In the late spring of the year 1811 prices dropped. Hemp-rope was a drug on the market and sold at 11 cents per pound; spun yarn from Kentucky and Ohio brought from 12 to 13 cents per pound; saltpeter, 14 to 15 cents; feathers, which formerly brought from 40 to 50 cents per pound, were selling for 20 to 25 cents; beeswax was worth only 25 cents a pound and would not sell readily for even that low price. Furs, too, varied in value but these were always convertible into gold. In April, 1811, the hatters' busiest season, otter brought $2 and $2.50, while beaver bought in Saint Louis at $2, sold in Philadelphia for $3.85 on 60 and 90 days. Beaver, for hats alone, meant wealth for both fur dealer and hatter, as well as high wages for felters and other minor laborers employed in preparing the furs.

33 *Missouri Gazette,* February 14, 1811.

I think you need not fear giving $2 for any quantity of respectable beaver, [wrote Hertzog from Philadelphia]. Deerskins are dangerous on account of the worm, besides they require a judge to tell the quality. Some are out of season, some too much injured by shot, and some too light of weight. A parcel allowed to be of good quality was sold here two weeks ago at 25 cents a pound.[34]. . . The muskrats will not bring 6 cents, which is mortifying, as the best are worth 37½ cents. Wish you would never send raccoon again as they are said to be worth not 12½ cents, and the carriage comes to that, I suppose. Beaver, my boy, send me till your back cracks. Otter, though we make a profit on them, are not in that regular demand as the other. Yet as you become a better judge send handsome ones picked up cheap which must, and always will, answer.[35] Send up the river by every opportunity. Pack them smooth and flat in barrels or casks.

In order to do this Wilt contrived a press that made the packs as "solid as a cheese or a madder."[36]

During the spring and summer Wilt did as he was told and collected parcels of furs which he sent on at every opportunity. Some of his beaverskins were sold in Philadelphia at $4 on two and four months credit; others at $3.50; the otter at $2.50; the muskrats at 20 cents. In September Moses Scott[37] reached Philadelphia where he was to do his fall buying. He brought with him from Wilt another shipment of furs. Hertzog wrote concerning the sales:

Have the little ones (muskrat skins) yet of a former parcel, cannot get anything for them. The breed of muskrats in your country cannot be good. The best sell here for 45 cents.[38]. . . Am gratified to find you improve in your judgment of beaver, etc., but regret you have not the courage to attach all the good beaver you could get at $2. I think it will continue to sell well now. If you can, buy it very superior, at

34 Hertzog to Wilt, May 13, 1811.

35 Hertzog to Wilt, July 18, 1811.

36 Hertzog to Wilt, May 4, 1811.

37 Moses Scott came to Saint Louis in the winter of 1810–11 and opened a store in the north part of the old John B. Becquet house on Main between Myrtle and Elm Streets. Billon, *op.cit.*, p. 272.

38 Hertzog to Wilt, September 26, 1811.

$2.25, DON'T MISS IT.[39] . . . The profits depend largely on the quality. This is better than sending a boat up the river with lead. These furs have eaten neither lard, fish, fowl nor beef. Perhaps you can send on in the same way an additional quantity but send in care of George Anshutz, Jr., instead of George Sutton.[40]

George Sutton, a member of the Pittsburgh firm of Sutton and McNickle, had for some time acted as agent for the Saint Louis firm but was now being replaced.[41] As representative, he received the furs and lead sent up the Ohio from Saint Louis, and disposed of them in Pittsburgh or sent them on to Philadelphia. Likewise, wagonloads of supplies to be sent to Saint Louis went to him where he was stationed in Pittsburgh. He paid the wagoners, stored the goods brought in for the western store, filled orders for Pittsburgh articles to supplement and complete the Philadelphia assortment, and, when all was ready, loaded the flats going back to Louisiana.[42]

As Mussina could best be used in the East to assist in selecting goods for the western trade, and since business was once again growing rapidly, Wilt in the autumn of 1811 engaged an agent in each of the large towns along the Ohio and Mississippi Rivers. To them he entrusted all business transactions and sent his lead and furs to be sold or bartered on commission. William Steele in Lexington, Andres Dunsett[43] and John Nelson[44] in Cincinnati, accepted large quantities of lead to barter for Kentucky and Ohio products; John Baird[45] in Nashville had Georgia cotton to exchange for peltries, crude lead or Philadelphia goods; Charles H. Robbertus,[46] who was at the same time agent for John Jacob Astor, took care of cargoes sent to New Orleans.

39 Hertzog to Wilt, June 13, 1811.

40 Hertzog to Wilt, September 26, 1811.

41 Hertzog to G. Anshutz, August 13, 1811.

42 Hertzog to G. Sutton, April 20, 1811.

43 Hertzog to Wilt, July 20, 1811.

44 Hertzog to Wilt, December 2, 1811.

45 Hertzog to Z. Mussina, May 10, 1811.

46 Hertzog to Wilt, May 4, 1811.

Abraham Bird,[47] agent at Bird's Point near the mouth of the
Ohio, loaded and unloaded Wilt's flats from Saint Louis or his
keels going up the Ohio to Pittsburgh or up the Mississippi to
Saint Louis.

Land speculation and merchandising were but two of the
many projects that called for Wilt's attention, or filled his
thoughts in the spring of 1811. The levee along the Mississippi
at the foot of Walnut and Market Streets was lined not only
with the flats coming up the river and keels going down, but
with canoes, pirogues, barges, and other types of craft then
afloat on the inland waters. All were piled high with merchandise of every sort, and boatmen were busy preparing to carry
their cargoes; some were to go up the Mississippi to settlements
rapidly developing into towns or cities, others farther on
through land drained by the Missouri; many more were destined
for New Orleans, and still others for Cincinnati, Lexington,
Louisville, or Pittsburgh. Boats were individually owned and
operated, and a shipper, who was so unfortunate as not to own
his own means of transportation, was dependent upon a chance
vessel, the time of departure of which was determined by the
prompt or tardy completion of its load.

The transportation of goods on the rivers was both dangerous
and difficult. The boats, for the most part, had to be propelled
by oars and settling poles, or drawn by hand and by grappling
hooks from one root or over-hanging tree to another, or towed
by the long cordelle or towing lines, where the shores were sufficiently clear of woods and underbrush to permit the men to
pass along the banks. New sandbars and reefs were constantly
being formed, while logs and brush, torn from the heavily
wooded banks, continually built new obstructions along the
river's channel.[48] Consequently, the sharpest lookout had to be
maintained, and the pilot was both skillful and lucky who completed his trip without permitting his boat to be caught on a
planter, or dashed on the bank at a bend of the river. Navigation

47 Wilt to Bird, October 23, 1812, Wilt Letterbook.
48 Irving, op. cit., p. 127.

by night and on foggy days was hazardous in the extreme and was avoided as far as possible. It was a happy moment when the patroon, whose destination was Saint Louis, brought his load safely to dock at the foot of Market or Walnut Street.

Wilt foresaw the commercial possibilities of a line of barges between Saint Louis and Pittsburgh, and another connecting Saint Louis with New Orleans. Even the expense of the wharfage dues of two dollars, which was imposed by the town on every boat of five ton capacity,[49] did not deter him from carrying out his project. He looked forward to the day when his boats would ply up and down the waters on scheduled time. It would then be possible to dispatch four or five loads in the time which formerly sufficed for only two. However, there was little inducement for a crew to complete a trip speedily, for in sending boats down the river the patroon and hands were provided with everything necessary for the passage, and when their destination was reached, each received a stipulated sum of money. It, therefore, mattered little, to the crew at least, how much time was consumed on any expedition.

The patroon not only controlled and directed the crew but was often commissioned to sell his cargo along the way, or to consign the goods to agents in towns, where the Saint Louis merchants had representatives, who could either sell the cargo or barter it for flour, vinegar, rags, or other products of the section. On returning from Pittsburgh the barges were scheduled to bring large shipments, in order that the Saint Louis stores might always have a full assortment of "seasonable goods."

Freight, at three cents a pound, could be easily solicited from the other merchants of Saint Louis, who were continually watching for opportunities to ship parcels of beaver and furs to the East. General Clark, who was ever solicitous for the success of any project that might further the interests of his adopted city, promised Wilt a share in the transportation of government

49 Proceedings of Trustees of Town of Saint Louis, August 10, 1810 to March 3, 1823. City Hall, Saint Louis. (Wharfage ordinance was passed February 25, 1811 and repealed August 28, 1812.)

and Indian goods to and from the West. Moreover, along the rivers a great deal of freight could be collected, when it became known that Wilt's boats were running as regular packets. A wise regulation, forbidding the acceptance of any perishable articles that might delay the boat, was adopted. Wilt's system of organized river transportation was finally inaugurated in the spring of 1811[50] by Joseph Morin and Vincent Bouis, both experienced and registered boatmen.

Late in March, Bouis as patroon on Wilt's boat, *Endeavor,* left Saint Louis with a cargo of lead, shot, and furs.[51] The furs were destined for Philadelphia, but Bouis was instructed to sell his lead and shot along the way, put the funds thus received into the hands of Sutton when he reached Pittsburgh, and return at once with Invoice No. 3, which Mussina had brought to Pittsburgh, where it had been stored in Sutton's warehouse.

In the meantime, Mussina came from Philadelphia to Pittsburgh to attend to the disposition of whatever remained of the cargo that Bouis was bringing from Saint Louis, and also to supervise the reloading of the boat for her return journey.[52] After waiting in vain several weeks for Bouis' arrival, Mussina took a flat loaded with some of the goods of the Third Invoice and went down the river. Instead of pushing on rapidly, "for the water was high and in fine order," he "brought to" every night for fear of passing Bouis, seemingly without thought of the fact that unless he made haste, the season for the profitable selling of some of the articles he was carrying would be over. He also overlooked the loss in time and money to the two keels which, with a large crew, waited at the mouth of the river. These boats had been sent from Saint Louis by Wilt to trans-ship the goods coming from Philadelphia.

Mussina's cargo included spades, scythes, shovels, sickles, weed-hooks, whiskey, rifles, and iron. The scythes were Rhode

50Hertzog to Wilt, March 30, 1811, April 6, 1811.
51 Hertzog to Wilt, May 13, 1811.
52 Hertzog to Wilt, April 6, 1811–May 4, 1811.

Island products which had had an amazing sale among the farmers of the East, and there seemed little doubt that the "jolly haymakers of Louisiana would prefer them to those imported from England."[53] The rifles had been made in Pennsylvania and answered well the needs of Missouri. From the earliest colonial days, shot and firearms had been manufactured in America. The best shot made in the Mississippi Valley was that prepared in Kentucky and Tennessee. Sizes running from twenty balls to the pound up to a hundred balls, and ranging in price from fifteen dollars to one hundred dollars per pound, were common in any shop displaying an assortment of ammunition.[54] Guns and pistols were usually made by artisans in their homes, and good gunsmiths were everywhere highly esteemed.

One Cramer who came from Lancaster, Pennsylvania, to live in an obscure place in Illinois, was famous "as the maker of pistols and guns." Brackenridge says that a pair of plain pistols made by Cramer had been sold for two hundred dollars, and that one hundred and fifty dollars had been offered for one of his rifles. John Smith T, that famous character in the early days of Missouri, was no mean gunsmith and was proud of his accomplishment. He kept in his workshop two Negroes who labored continually manufacturing flint lock rifles and pistols.[55] The firearms in the consignment going to Wilt were not of the expensive type. Mussina paid eleven dollars each for twenty rifles[56] which he purchased at a shop owned by Gunther, a trader in Lancaster, at which point the wagons stopped on their way from Philadelphia to Pittsburgh.

Pig iron was one of the articles most needed in the new country, but it was difficult to get it transferred to Pittsburgh from the mines of Center County, Pennsylvania. When Mussina's boat left for Louisiana in May, 1811, only two tons had been

53 Hertzog to Wilt, March 20, 1811.

54 Clemens, James Jr., *Travels on an Inland Voyage* (New York, 1810), pp. 17–18.

55 Houck, *op. cit.*, III, 74.

56 Hertzog to Wilt, July 20, 1811.

hauled in and these, with other articles, were ready to be taken
to the West.

Messrs. Lyon Mussina, brother of Zachary, and Patterson
kept a general store at the little mining town of Aaronsburg,
Center County, Pennsylvania, and they exchanged groceries
supplied from Philadelphia for bar iron purchased from the
iron masters, John Mitchell and Joseph Miles of Milesburg.
When it could be done, Mussina and Patterson sent wagonloads
of iron down to Pittsburgh or had it ready for the teams sent
from Pittsburgh by Sutton and Anshutz, agents of the firm.
The wagoners were reluctant to make the trip to the mines with
little or no cargo, and to return with a heavy load of metal which
called for powerful draft horses and for wagons stoutly built.
Thus it was not easy to get an adequate supply of the metal from
the mines at any one time. In July, 1811, when the fourth invoice was being prepared for the West, Anshutz had only about
$800 worth in storage, and that in spite of Hertzog's admonition
that "Mussina and Patterson are as anxious to have the iron
delivered as I am, and you cannot oblige me more than by taking pains to get it to hand as fast as you can fetch it."[57]

During the winter months, when the hauling season was dull
and idle wagons "tolerably plenty", and when the farmers had
little to do, teams could be supplied more easily. In February,
1812, David Kennedy, one of the regular and trusted teamsters
on the Philadelphia-Pittsburgh route, contracted to haul iron for
three months for $50 a ton. His wagons, with those supplied by
Anshutz, were to bring not less than thirty tons to Pittsburgh
before the spring. But at the appointed time when sixty tons
should have been available at Pittsburgh, for there was plenty
of iron at the mines awaiting transportation, only a small quantity was at hand. At this date times were hard, and money was
not plentiful. The price of iron rose from $100 a ton to $105,
and carriage or freight from $50 to $53.33½. To make matters
even worse, the sales at Pittsburgh were dull on account of the
opening of forges and furnaces in the towns along the Ohio. All

57 Hertzog to Anshutz, Jan. 14, 1812.

through the long summer conditions remained the same. The gathering of the bountiful harvest of that year kept all the farmers engaged in the fields, and as late as August twenty-fifth no iron had been brought to the warehouse in Pittsburgh. In the following March (1813), when war was raging along the frontier and the wagons were being pressed into service by the United States Government for the transportation of supplies and ammunition to points in the Mississippi Valley, and along the Lehigh, the hauling of iron from the mines to Pittsburgh was virtually discontinued and no cargoes for Wilt were forthcoming.

Whenever there was more pig iron or bar iron than was needed for the western store, Anshutz sold the surplus and used the funds for purchasing glass, crockery, casting, and nails. If these articles were not needed, the funds were placed to the credit of the firm. But in the summer of 1811 funds were needed in Pittsburgh to complete Invoice No. 3, part of which Mussina had taken with him when he went down the river seeking Bouis and the "long-winded boat."

The account of Bouis' trip from Saint Louis to Pittsburgh is an interesting commentary on river traffic. Mussina finally met him just above Cincinnati. After sending his own boat on its way to the mouth of the Ohio, instead of journeying to Pittsburgh with Bouis, Mussina went on to meet his family in Cincinnati. Here, after arranging their passage on a boat bound for the East, he secured a horse and rode back to Pittsburgh to settle with Bouis. The latter had succeeded in bringing his boat to dock about the end of June, after a dilatory journey of four months. We can imagine the chagrin and indignation of Wilt, who was waiting for the supply of spring goods with which to stock his store. Hertzog wrote of this loiterer, Bouis, in no complimentary terms. "From the whiskey, meat, lard, flour, etc., we find charged in his bill", he remarked, "we conclude he was always eating and drinking. No wonder they were so slow! Has he not sold muskrat for 15 cents which cost 25 cents? It is likely he has put money into his pocket."[58] Be that as it may, Mussina reloaded the *Endeavor* with the remaining goods, provided Bouis with what was necessary for his return trip, and ordered him not to purchase anything on the way unless at his own expense. Bouis left dock in Pittsburgh, bound for Saint Louis, on July 6, 1811. He was met in Cincinnati by Dunsett, Wilt's agent at that point, and requested to carry a consignment of cordage which Wilt required. Bouis, however, refused to take the extra pack and complained that he had no room.[59] This untoward act aroused suspicion. Dunsett immediately informed his employer in Saint Louis, and Wilt concluded that Bouis was carrying freight on his own account and determined, should he find sufficient proof, to sue Bouis for damages. Somewhere between Cincinnati and the mouth of the Ohio River, however, the ship struck a sand bar and went down. Although Bouis escaped drowning, the flannels, stroudings and bales of mackinac, which could not be replaced at any price, were all lost. The whiskey, iron, stoves, and the remainder of the ironmongery were apparently also lost. The crew managed to save the frying pans and the large saws.[60]

News of the wreck was a severe blow to the young merchant in the frontier village. His hope of large sales with high profits was suddenly swept away. He promptly offered a reward of fifty dollars[61] for the return of the boat, which was found during the latter part of August.[62] The blankets and flannels had rotted so badly that they could not be sold. Sparke and Henderson, artisans who had been sent from Philadelphia to open a red lead factory in Saint Louis, and who had arrived there early in July, arranged to put all the hardware on sale after they had polished it so as to make it appear almost new. Wilt was obliged to sell these articles at a low price, but in spite of the discount, the

58 Hertzog to Wilt, July 9, 1811.
59 Hertzog to Wilt, July 20, 1811.
60 Hertzog to Z. Mussina, July 27, 1811.
61 Hertzog to Wilt, August 15, 1811.
62 Hertzog to Wilt, September 26, 1811.

profit was still worth while. The loss, as reckoned from the invoice, was at first estimated at $3721,[63] but after the boat and heavy articles had been recovered, it was found that $1400 would cover the entire loss.[64] To sue Bouis on his return, July 20, 1811, would have been useless, even had there been proof of the violation of his trust. He was already in Wilt's debt and the simplest way out of the difficulty was to dismiss him from the service, which was immediately done.

A few weeks after Bouis started on his eventful journey Morin, with a load of lead and shot, left Saint Louis in another boat of Wilt's line,[65] the *Mary,* so named after Wilt's sister. Morin was an experienced river pilot but his progress up the Ohio was slow and tedious. Spring rains had increased the height of all streams emptying into the Mississippi, and the boat was exposed to frequent dangers from contact with floating trees, logs and reefs, as well as to other perils encountered during the flood season. Morin reached Pittsburgh on June 20, 1811, and found the greater part of Invoice No. 3 still waiting to be transferred to the West. Mussina had taken one load (mostly Pittsburgh articles), when he set out to find the *Endeavor,* but much still remained. The consignment from Philadelphia alone consisted of eight 3000 pound wagonloads. Each load was charged six and one-half dollars for freight, and the entire invoice, not counting land carriage, totalled $14,329.73.[66]

Morin loaded the *Mary* with as much as he thought she could carry, took with him Joseph Henderson, one of the men going out to establish a red lead factory, and started homeward.[67] While the assortment was a large one, many necessary articles had been omitted or secured in limited quantities. English linen, Lustra and Irish linen, for example, could not be found in the

63 Hertzog to Wilt, July 27, 1811.

64 Hertzog to Wilt, February 24, 1812.

65 Wilt's line consisted of Endeavor, Mary, Sparkler, Dolphin, Betty, Redbird, and Enterprise.

66 Hertzog to Wilt, August 29, 1811.

67 Hertzog to Wilt, July 9, 1811.

eastern markets; ironmongery was scarce and expensive; tea was selling at $1.85 a pound, and Russian sheeting at $18; Mackinac blankets, one of the most essential articles for the Indian trade, were not for sale on the Atlantic Coast nor were they to be had in England, where at this time they were manufactured only on special orders.[68]

Virtually all the goods required for the Indian trade were imported. Cotton goods from American plants compared favorably with the European output, but American woolen cloth, blankets, and shawls, which were indispensable for the trade in which Wilt was interested, were inferior in quality. Cotton cloth, sheeting, muslins, woolens, blankets, guns, cutlery, awls, traps, trinkets, ironmongery, and beads came mostly from the factories of England; from China came tea and rice; the West Indies sent coffee and cocoa. But the Embargo and the Non-Intercourse Act having interrupted our foreign commerce, the amount of these goods on the market was small, and prices rose in proportion. In May, 1810, however, Macon's Bill No. 2 restored our commerce to its status before the Embargo and tonnage of 127,000 was added to our merchant marine in that year. Our exports rose from $52,000,000 to $67,000,000, and our customs receipts from $7,000,000 to $12,750,000.[69] While the greater part of our foreign trade was carried on with Great Britain, the English government would not desist from the impressment of our sailors or the seizure of our ships. Nothing daunted, the American merchantmen carrying a high insurance, ran the European blockade and brought back products of the looms and forges of Germany in lieu of the manufactured goods of Yorkshire, Manchester, and Birmingham, while the prices of these articles soared often to an advance of one hundred per cent.

It is little wonder, then, that our merchants were overjoyed at a report in March, 1811, that the French Emperor had given

68 Hertzog to Wilt, May 13, 1811; May 2, 1811.

69 Adams, Henry, *History of the United States of America* (New York, 1921), V, 290.

up all "American ships and property and allows free trade with France and the countries in alliance with her, and if, as many anticipate, England takes off her Orders-in-Council and blockade, we shall once more have foreign trade, which has long been stagnant and is really very desirable."[70] But England did not rescind her orders, and in May, speculating on the non-importation of all English goods by fall, the eastern importers began to withdraw their own goods from the market.

Among the articles that reached Saint Louis in the limited consignment of the summer of 1811, Wilt found drugs and medicines; and on October 12th he inserted the following advertisement in the *Louisiana Gazette*.[71]

Just received from Philadelphia, Genuine Patent and Family Medicines, which are celebrated for the cure of most diseases to which the human body is liable, prepared only by the sole Proprietor, T. W. Dyott, M. D., grandson of the late Dr. Robertson of Edinburg. (Price one dollar and fifty cents). One of the most efficacious medicines ever offered to the public, for the speedy relief and cure of obstinate coughs, colds, consumption, the whooping cough, asthma, pains and wind in stomach, removing habitual costiveness, sickness at the stomach, dysenteries, colera morbus, severe gripings, the summer bowel complaint in children, etc. etc.

Dr. Robertson's Vegetable Nervous Cordial or Nature's Grand Restorative (Price—one dollar and fifty cents) is confidently recommended as the most efficacious medicine for the speedy relief and cure of all nervous complaints, impurities of the blood, etc.

Dr. Robertson's Celebrated Gout and Rheumatic Drops (Price— two dollars), a safe and effectual cure for the gout, rheumatism, lumbago, stone and gravel, sprains, bruises, and all kinds of green wounds— the cramps, pains in the head, face and body, stiffness in the neck, chilblains, frozen limbs, etc.

Dr. Robertson's Celebrated Patent Stomach Bitters (Price—one dollar) which are celebrated for strengthening weak stomachs, increasing the appetite and a certain preventive and cure for fever and ague, etc. etc.

70 Hertzog to Wilt, March 31, 1811.
71 *Louisiana Gazette,* October 12, 1811.

Dr. Robertson's Infallible Work Destroying Lozenges, a medicine highly necessary to be kept in all families, (price—fifty cents).

Dr. Dyott's Anti-Bilious Pills—For the prevention and cure of Bilious and Malignant Fevers. (Price—25 cents—large boxes 50 cents.) These pills, if timely administered, will remove the causes which commonly produce Yellow Fever, Bilious Fevers, Ague and Fevers, Cholic Pains, Flatulence, Indigestion Costiveness, Hipochondrial and Hysteric Complaints, Stranguary, Gravel, Rheumatism and Gout.

Dr. Dyott's Patent Itch Ointment—For pleasantiveness, safety, expedition, ease and certainty, is infinitely superior to the other medicines for the cure of that most disagreeable and tormenting disorder, the Itch. (Price—50 cents per box).

The Restorative Dentifrice—For cleansing, whitening, and preserving the gums. (Price—50 cents per box).

Since these invaluable Medicines were first discovered, upwards of Seven Hundred Thousand Persons have experienced their happy and salutary effects, many of whom from the lowest state of their disorders. A supply of the above medicines just received and for sale by Christian Wilt, St. Louis; where pamphlets containing certificates of cures, etc. etc., may be had gratis. Take notice that each and all the above genuine medicines are signed on the outside cover with the signature of the sole proprietor.

T. W. DYOTT, M.D.

This announcement is interesting not only because of the infinite variety of diseases any one of Dr. Dyott's patent medicines might cure, but also because it discloses the thousand-and-one ills to which the people of the West were subject in the days of high waters, undrained swamps, poor sanitation, and lack of proper medical care.

When these goods were started for the West, land carriage on freight from Philadelphia to Pittsburgh had advanced from 4½ to 6½ cents per hundred pounds, an added expense that the goods must carry when they reached their destination. Hertzog advised Wilt to raise prices:

On all these goods clap a handsome advance. Take care of moths. Calicoes are also run out. You will have to take care of your British goods. The assortments are so run out that many articles are not at all procurable, which ones they are you will easily know, both dry goods and ironmongery, particularly such as are not fabricated in this country. What Clark's clerk told you is true, by the non-intercourse law all goods arriving from Great Britain or its dependencies are seizable. Manufacture will spring up in this country of course, but prices will certainly be high, so I would wish you to hold on for a good advance.[72]

A little later Hertzog warned, "appearances here are for war."[73]

After the *Endeavor* and the *Mary* had turned down the Ohio headed for Saint Louis, Mussina, without waiting to send on two loads of goods that had just come in from Philadelphia, left Pittsburgh for the eastern coast. When he reached Philadelphia he was irritable and quarrelsome. He was worried because the Philipsons had not yet settled their account; in consequence, he owned no stock in the western venture, nor could he expect a share in the profits of the firm, in spite of the fact that his name was written large on the front of the Saint Louis store. After several days of ill-humor, he proposed, in the presence of witnesses, that he withdraw from the firm and that he be paid a salary for the time he had served the company. Hertzog accepted his offer without, however, agreeing on the amount of salary. Apparently satisfied with the new arrangement, Mussina set about collecting material for the Fourth Invoice, and Hertzog notified Wilt of the change in the personnel of the firm, and advised him to change the name of the establishment in Saint Louis.[74] Mussina visited all the wholesale houses in the locality, but could get few articles needed in the Western trade.[75] The importers either held back all goods from the market or asked so exorbitant a price that few could buy.

So sharp was the speculation among the Philadelphia wholesale merchants during the summer months that by the first week

72 Hertzog to Wilt, June 11, 1811.
73 Hertzog to Wilt, Aug. 8, 1811.
74 Hertzog to Wilt, May 23, 1811.
75 Hertzog to Wilt, July 9, 1811.

of September many firms had been driven into bankruptcy. Among those who were forced to the wall were Edward Pennington, Joseph Latimer, Jr., John Wall, Snowden & North, and Jacob Clarkson.[76] Hertzog and Mussina had done business with each of these in turn.

In Invoice No. 4, which Mussina was ready to take to Saint Louis early in July, 1811, there was not a bolt of stroud, flannel, calico, blanket, or coarse cloth. Ironmongery was as scarce and as dear as woolens, but there were liquors, mackinaws, vermilion, indigo, and innumerable other articles that had been picked up earlier in the season. Liquors were selling high in both Philadelphia and New York. Lisbon wine brought $1.67½ a bottle; sherry, $2. Although there was little Madeira on sale, and French wine was not to be found on the market, still several barrels of Lisbon, Madeira and a pipe of sherry had been sent to Saint Louis with the other supplies.[77] Prices of groceries kept pace with the advance in other commodities. An inferior grade of coffee was sold at auction and brought sixteen cents cash;[78] good green coffee was selling at eighteen cents per pound. Listed with the Pittsburgh articles we find such things as country stockings, linsey, cow bells, horse bells, and broad axes. The axes sold at $3.50 apiece.[79] Hertzog wrote confidently:

I expect the goods will find a good market. One thing I am sure of, that goods bought here now, and taken on, will not lessen the prices, for everything is dear, even what is not scarce, but many articles are not to be had at all.[80] Yet, the necessities of the dry goods people compel a great deal into the market which would otherwise be held back, thus all there is appears, and no doubt if Congress does not settle with Great Britain the next session there will be great advances on British goods. No guess as to the measure Congress will adopt.[81] . . . The two invoices together of this season, of May and

76 Hertzog to Wilt, September 12, 1811.
77 Hertzog to Anshutz, July 27, 1811.
78 Hertzog to Wilt, August 13, 1811.
79 Hertzog to Wilt, August 29, 1811.
80 Hertzog to Z. Mussina, October 12, 1811.
81 Hertzog to Wilt, October 31, 1811.

July, or as I call them, Nos. 3 and 4, will amount, with the Pittsburgh disbursements, to more than $22,000, and have not much
doubt but it will bring double the sum of which, if you can contrive
to send me through the fall ten or twelve thousand, I shall be able
to provide you an early assortment for next spring.[82]

A short time before he had written:

I regret that we are not able to make an addition of $3000 worth of
woolens which have not enclosed to you, but as they are not to be
had we must comfort us with getting a higher price for those we
have. . . . The quantity and assortment are both respectable and I
hope you will find them well adapted to your market and make rapid
sales. You will find, perhaps, too much of some articles which you
will warn me in forwarding next goods as I calculated on picking
up occasional bargains. You have well-considered invoices, lists of
articles for next spring, summer and winter. Think we will keep our
store assorted by sending on a season beforehand, by which we shall
gain much in advance prices by selling while others are out as will
pay the interest.[83] . . . I believe you know my plan to establish a
house in Pittsburgh. It is indispensable to us. Z. longs to live here
and we cannot long depend on him and besides between his ill-will
and his vanity he has done some of our business in no very good
stile. I calculate Andrew[84] for this part, where I mean Z shall establish him this spring, be with him a few months and then he come
here.[85]

Mussina continued his buying. His plan was to finish loading
the wagons the first week of July and send them to Pittsburgh
or Wheeling, where he was to meet them, buy a boat and push
on to Saint Louis. This, according to Hertzog, was a simple
matter as there were few goods on the market. From Saint Louis
Mussina was to take a suitable cargo to Prairie du Chien, form
a connection for the firm with Blondeau, an Indian trader and
later a sub-agent for the Sacs, bring back a load of lead to Saint

82 Hertzog to Wilt, July 23, 1811.
83 Hertzog to Wilt, July 18, 1811.
84 Andrew Wilt, brother of Christian.
85 Hertzog to Wilt, July 23, 1811.

Louis and either take a load of red lead down to New Orleans with beaver and whatever else was at hand, or take horse to Pittsburgh and be back in the East by January, 1812. When Hertzog proposed that Mussina stop on his way back and establish a house at Pittsburgh, the latter did not take kindly to the proposition. Hertzog's reason for choosing Mussina was that he might have some reliable person in Pittsburgh to send goods regularly to the mouth of the Ohio, and at the same time keep the western store handsomely supplied with Pittsburgh articles.

The invoices of Philadelphia articles for the season of 1811 were Nos. 3, 4, and 5. No. 3 was valued at $14,329.75; No. 4, at $9331.44; No. 5, which was sent on later in the fall, amounted to $2542.67, making a grand total of $26,203.84. This amount did not include carriage or other expenses incurred at Pittsburgh. These shipments, together with the remnants of the earlier invoices, constituted a supply of goods not exceeded in quality or assortment in any of the stores of the Middle West. Wilt hoped that fortune would assist him in collecting $1000 per week for at least one hundred weeks. Hertzog's advice was to

take in money on all occasions. That is, don't let your customers quit you for other stores. We can sell as cheap as any of them. This I do not mean you to apply so much to retail as to wholesale, which ought to be your forte. Hope you will have a larger and better store than the present when you receive the next goods, which is pretty good assortment of plain articles. Not much fine goods and shall help the assortment this coming trip.[86]

On Thursday, July 18, 1811,[87] Mussina left for the West. In parting, Hertzog assured him that they would settle their account and adjust their difficulties to the satisfaction of both on Mussina's return the following spring. This pleased Mussina and he departed in good spirits. However, when he reached Saint Louis and found that the sign on the front of the store read, not

86 Hertzog to Wilt, June 8, 1811; Aug. 29, 1811.
87 Hertzog to Wilt, July 20, 1811.

"ZACHARY MUSSINA", but "CHRISTIAN WILT", he was furious. Although he was ill and hardly able to travel, he returned on horseback to Philadelphia, instead of going on to Prairie du Chien to establish the branch store. When Mussina reached Philadelphia empty-handed, without lead, furs, or funds, Hertzog was greatly distressed because he expected that this expedition would furnish him with the money he so much needed. It was, indeed, a bitter disappointment. He attempted to settle with Mussina but without avail. It was then that he determined to make Andrew Wilt, the nineteen year old brother of Christian, the firm's representative in Pittsburgh, and immediately prepared to send him the following spring to the Louisiana Territory to learn the details of the western trade. Andrew was ready to depart in April, 1812.[88]

Unhappy, and hoping to outwit Hertzog, Mussina by secret inquiries learned the date of Andrew's departure for Pittsburgh and timed his own departure so that he would reach the western points and collect all debts before Andrew arrived.[89] Taking without leave one of Hertzog's finest riding horses, Mussina set out accompanied by Lawrence Brown, one of Philadelphia's bonnet makers. It was thought improbable that this gentleman was aware of Mussina's mission or that he was in any way implicated in Mussina's plans.[90]

As soon as Mussina reached Pittsburgh he went immediately to John Spencer and induced him to turn over the balance of money due the firm. Seeing nothing unusual in this request, Spencer handed over the funds. Encouraged in his mischief, Mussina attempted to force George Anshutz to pay him the amount still owed to the firm, but this time his victim was more wary and refused to comply with the demand.[91] The day before Andrew reached Pittsburgh Mussina left for Cincinnati, where he was unsuccessful in his attempt to obtain a settlement of

88 Hertzog to Wilt, March 25, 1812.

89 Hertzog to Wilt, April 18, 1812.

90 Hertzog to Andrew Wilt, April 18, 1812.

91 Hertzog to Lyon Mussina, April 21, 1812.

accounts from Dunsett and Hoffler. In Louisville he was more fortunate and prevailed upon John Nelson to give him what he had left of the balance due on the firm's shot and lead. The funds thus collected had been intended for Andrew, who was to use them for the purchase of articles displayed in the different towns through which he passed, articles to complete the spring supply which he was carrying to his brother, Christian.[92] When Mussina reached Saint Louis in July, 1812, in order to intimidate Wilt and oblige him to pay $4000 which he claimed as his due, Mussina took out a writ of replevin of $35,000 on the store. The deputy sheriff seized Wilt's store and goods.[93] Wilt retaliated with a counter-replevin, and Edward Hempstead, a lawyer, later Missouri Territory's first representative in Congress, offered to go security for Wilt. The sympathy of most professional and business men was with Wilt. The extensive capital he was managing, his integrity in all business dealings, his correct and modest deportment, as well as his youth and inexperience, interested the worthiest and most intelligent citizens of the territory. Major Penrose, member of the Board of Land Commissioners, who was at that time on business in the East, promised Hertzog that he would render Wilt every service in his power, and Hertzog added that "his influence may be useful to us as he is well connected here." Honorable Frederick Bates encouraged Wilt to hope that the court would "squash the proceedings on the grounds of illegality."[94] Hertzog immediately sought legal advice on the question. According to the opinion of an eminent jurist of Philadelphia, Mussina had used the wrong means of securing justice. In a letter to Hertzog the lawyer said:

If Mussina had any claim, it was against you. The personal property of Wilt and yourself is not liable for your private debts. The idea that Mussina entertains, by his having secured a writ of replevin, supposes the whole property repleved belonged to himself,

92 Hertzog to Andrew Dunsett, May 12, 1812.
93 Hertzog to Sutton, June 13, 1812.
94 Hertzog to Wilt, June 18, 1812.

for the object of the replevin is not to compel the payment of a debt that one may owe, but to recover a specific property which another has in his possession. Even if Mussina had a claim against you, individually, he has mistaken his remedy. He might perhaps, by the laws of the Territory, have issued a foreign attachment against you, but the sheriff is unquestionably responsible for the acts of his deputy. The law is very clear on the subject. The case of Hazard vs. Israel decided in the Supreme Court of Pennsylvania—1st Benny's Rep. 9240, is a case in point. . . . Arbitration is, perhaps, not as advisable as a decision in a court of law, but the circumstances of this case and the situation of the parties with reference to the laws of the Territory, must govern your opinion on the subject.[95]

In anticipation of a lawsuit, Hertzog sent Wilt the following story of the organization of the partnership:

In the spring of 1810 Mussina determined to leave the Philipson Company in whose employ he had been for some years and proposed to Hertzog that they enter a partnership. The articles were signed on February 24, 1810. At Mussina's request the sums were not inserted until settlement with the Philipsons lest the sums vary, but it was understood that Mussina's share was to be $5000—Hertzog's $10,000 with Mussina drawing one-third of the profit. An additional article provided that at any time thereafter, Zachary might put in half the stock and draw half the profits. The articles stated *specifically* and *absolutely* that the purpose of the partnership was to open and establish a store in Louisiana.[96]

After the formation of this partnership the first invoice, amounting to $13,841, consisted of groceries taken from Hertzog's own store, and of dry goods bought at wholesale houses or at auction for cash, or for credit on short terms. These goods were accordingly packed and forwarded to Saint Louis in the spring of 1810. Instead of opening a place of business and selling his goods as a regular merchant, Mussina sold at a sacrifice, the greater part of the stock to the Philipsons who gave three promissory notes on which, up to the present, April 22, 1812,

95 Hertzog to Wilt, June 6, 1812.
96 Hertzog to Wilt, June 6, 1812.

they had paid only a small amount. Of the subsequent events, Hertzog wrote:

After sending on Invoice No. 2 in September, 1810 my anxiety became very great, lest any misfortune should happen to the consignment for since the stock of the two invoices was all mine the loss would be all mine. It seemed that since Zachary had no money invested and had incurred no risk it was but fair that there should be a reduction from his share of the profits. In pursuance of these considerations, I wrote Christian for his opinion on the subject and the letters arriving while Zachary was in Saint Louis, he (Zachary), read the letters and ever after was a changed man. When he returned to the East, he was dissatisfied, unhappy and discontented. At first he desired to go into the dry goods line, fancying he could rival I. Moss and others who had amassed a fortune in the wholesale business in Philadephia but later in the presence of witnesses, he declared that he did not wish to be considered a member of the firm but wished, rather to be on salary. As the unexpected request, to be on salary, abrogated any necessity for a settlement or a deduction, it was gladly accepted, and with Zachary's full knowledge, measures were taken to change the name of the firm in Saint Louis, his only comment on the matter being that no debt could be collected unless Wilt in Saint Louis employed a clerk but this remark went by unnoticed.

Since the difficulty could not be adjusted outside the courtroom, Mussina employed Rufus Easton and William C. Carr, two very able lawyers. Easton[97] had come West in 1803 to assist General William Henry Harrison, Governor of Indiana, who with the Indiana judges, was preparing to draft laws for the "District of Louisiana". He had studied law in the office of Samuel Kirby of Litchfield, Connecticut, and proved himself an able assistant in the compilation of the legal code for the new territory. In 1804 President Jefferson appointed him one of the judges of the Louisiana Territory, and in 1805 he became first postmaster of Saint Louis, which office he held until 1814. William Carr,[98] a Virginian by birth, had in 1805 gone to Saint

97 Billon, *op. cit.*, II, 203.
98 *Ibid.*, II, 201.

Louis where he opened a law office. For many years he continued to be prominent in both legal and political circles of the West.

Wilt entered a counter-suit with Edward Hempstead as his lawyer and Pierre Chouteau as one of his securities.[99] Lawsuits in those pioneer days were expensive luxuries. This fact is written large in the early history of the country and the suit in Saint Louis proved no exception. Edward Hempstead, Wilt's lawyer, asked $1000 as his fee. They arranged that $400 should be paid when the case opened, and agreed that should "its cause be gained," another $600 would be added.[100] This amount was not decreased when a change of venue transferred the case to Philadelphia. The attorneys for Mussina, Easton and Carr, asked a like compensation. McNair, the sheriff, placed his fee at $150. To this demand, however, Wilt did not acquiesce because he believed it too high for the replevying of the store and goods, but McNair persisted because his demand was backed by a decision of the court of common pleas at a previous session. This decision permitted a sheriff to have 10 per cent of the value of the goods involved in a replevy.[101] In spite of this backing, a Philadelphia lawyer declared that neither a Philadelphia attorney nor a Philadelphia sheriff could demand such exorbitant payment for professional services.

It was the consensus of opinion among the pioneers of Louisiana that no good could come from a lawsuit, and before the case was called, Mussina's lawyers advised a compromise. Time for adjusting the matter was not given, because Mussina left abruptly for the East.[102] When he reached Philadelphia, he consented to place the dispute in the hands of a board of arbitrators. The members of the arbitration board included Thomas Mifflin, Peter Wiltberger and William Bethel. Both parties agreed that whatever decision the board handed down would be accepted as

99 Wilt to Hertzog, July 19, 1812.
100 Wilt to Hertzog, August 2, 1812.
101 Wilt to Hertzog, November 3, 1812.
102 Hertzog to Wilt, June 13, 1812.

final and without appeal, except under a considerable penalty. As a preliminary measure, bonds were issued in which it was agreed that both Mussina and Wilt would withdraw their respective[103] challenges and that the suits would be dropped. After this had been done no more was heard of the proceedings in Saint Louis.[104]

The certificates of the discontinuance of these suits, Mussina *v.* Wilt and Wilt *v.* Mussina, together with the depositions of Sparke, Andrew Wilt, Major Wilson, and Demun, were sent to Philadelphia that the arbitrators might decide the merits of the case.[105] At the meetings of the board neither of the parties to the suit was to have an attorney, but, before presenting the facts, Mussina was permitted to ask advice of his lawyer, Henry Broslasky.[106] The first meeting of the Board was held November 14, 1812, and two other meetings followed in quick succession. On November 18, a fourth meeting was held and the verdict was in favor of Mussina who was given an award of $7000. This was obviously unjust, since no consideration was given to the $2000 that had previously been paid to him.[107] According to the decision, the entire loss to Hertzog totaled $9000. "There was foul play in this somewhere," said Hertzog. Close study of the men who rendered the judgment led Wilt to believe that politics had influenced the decision. His reason for so believing was that the board of arbitrators was composed of Federalists, and Hertzog was a good Democrat.[108] Hertzog's lawyer took immediate steps to set aside the unjust decision, and during the first week of January Hertzog appeared before the Supreme Court of the State of Pennsylvania where the judge, after examining the evidence, set aside the "unjust and improper reward."[109] This

103 Wilt to Hertzog, September 13, 1812.

104 Hertzog to Wilt, July 23, 1812.

105 Hertzog to Andrew and Christian Wilt, October 20, 1812.

106 Hertzog to Andrew and Christian Wilt, November 18, 1812.

107 Hertzog to George Anshutz, November 30, 1812.

108 Wilt to Hertzog, March 13, 1813.

109 Hertzog to Lyon Mussina, January 19, 1813.

arrangement permitted the case to come before a jury in the
regular courts.[110] When a commissioner was sent on to Saint
Louis to make inquiries in behalf of Mussina, Hertzog's interests were ably upheld by Major Penrose and Honorable Frederick Bates. The case dragged on for three years, at the end of
which time Mussina and Hertzog agreed to compromise and the
dispute was ended. The letters do not give the terms of the
compromise, but there is no doubt they were more favorable
to Hertzog than was the decision of the arbitrators.

The whole matter was a sore trial to the young merchant of
Saint Louis, who during all these anxious weeks carried on his
many projects. Wilt feared, moreover, that his name and reputation had suffered throughout the towns and the countryside,
and that the effect on his business might prove disastrous, but
the War of 1812 was threatening, and he was aware that there
would be heavy demands for goods of all kinds, especially those
needed for the soldiers and for military equipment. He hoped
that the unfortunate incident with Mussina would be forgotten
in the excitement and turmoil that the war might bring in its
wake; and since he had a large and useful assortment of goods
in his possession, and boats that would bring him new consignments, he planned to amass profits which would help to revive
his sinking spirits and enable him again to compete on favorable
terms with his fellow merchants.

110 Hertzog to Wilt, January 25, 1813.

CHAPTER IV
PROGRESS IN LEAD MANUFACTURE

IN the early days of exploration and discovery, when precious metal was the objective of all quests, there was found in abundance throughout the province of Upper Louisiana neither gold nor silver, but lead. Among the most noted of these deposits were the mines at Prairie du Chien, the "Spanish Mines", and the mines of southeastern Missouri. The Prairie du Chien mines in the Northwest Territory were situated about seven hundred and fifty miles above Saint Louis, measured by the meanderings of the Mississippi, and six miles east of the river. The mine field was some eighty-four leagues in length with an average breadth of three leagues.[1] In 1810 the tract where the mines were most productive was still in the possession of the Sac and the Fox tribes, the original owners of the soil. Even before the coming of the white man these Indians knew of the presence of lead in the region between the Wisconsin and Illinois Rivers, but they began to appreciate its value only after the French had taught them the use of firearms. In spite of the fact that the Indians were poor miners, the annual yield was estimated at from 20,000 to 40,000 pounds.[2] The ore lay at no great depth in the Galena limestone and the red men collected it either by scraping from the surface or by sinking shallow shafts from which it was hoisted in deerskin bags. Afterwards the Indians melted the ore on log heaps, a process so wasteful that much of the metal remained in the ashes. This waste was eagerly bought up by the enterprising white men who made large profits on small investments.

The "Spanish Mines",[3] or Diggings as they were called, embraced 148,176 arpents of land, near what is now the city of Dubuque, Iowa. It was claimed by Julian Dubuque through a

1 Schoolcraft, *A View of the Lead Mines of Missouri* (New York, 1819), p. 62.

2 *Ibid.*, p. 62.

3 Houck, *op. cit.*, II, 79.

grant from Carondelet, the last Spanish Governor of Louisiana, but the Indian title was granted only for Dubuque's life. The mines of southeastern Missouri included among others, Mine á Breton, Mine á Renault, Shibboleth, Old Mines, and the Vallé Mines. These were known to the white men from the early French days.

Prior to 1700 outposts had already been established on the eastern bank of the Mississippi at Vincennes, Kaskaskia, Fort Chartres, and Cahokia where the settlers were actively engaged in agriculture and in the profitable trade of bargaining with the Indians for furs and peltries. But across the river and to the west lay a great tract shrouded deep in the mysteries of the virginal forest, rich in mineral wealth and alive with fur-bearing animals. It was not long before adventuresome spirits crossed into the vast region beyond the Mississippi, among whom was Francois Renault, representative of the Company of Saint Phillipe, "a subsidiary of the Royal Company of the Indies." Monsieur Renault, who left France about 1720, brought with him two hundred miners, numerous laborers, and the necessary equipment for carrying on mining operations. On his westward voyage he stopped at Santo Domingo where he purchased five hundred Negroes who were to be employed in the mines which he hoped to locate on his grant.[4] This tract included "two leagues of ground at the mine called Mine de Monsieur La Motte, the front looking toward the northeast, and the prairie of said mine making the middle part of the two leagues." Renault found, not gold or silver but rich deposits of lead. Understanding the value of his find, he gathered the members of his company and set them to work. His furnaces were constructed of the brick he had brought from Paris and upon which his name was stamped.[5]

The only outlet for the product of the mine was the Mississippi, and on its western bank at a strategic point near the "Diggings" a town grew up, which Renault called Sainte Gene-

4 *Ibid.*, I, 282.
5 *Ibid.*, I, 281–282.

vieve. This was the first permanent settlement in the present
state of Missouri. The town became the depot for the lead from
Mine La Motte, and later for that from Mine á Breton, Old
Mines and Vallé; as well as for the iron from Iron Mountain,
one of the greatest mineral deposits found in America. All these
minerals poured into the little village and thence were shipped
via New Orleans to France and to other parts of the world.
Thus a thriving center had been established, whence came inspi-
ration for other and more daring projects.

Schoolcraft tells us that so numerous were the miners who
flocked to these lead mines of Missouri, that in 1818 the surface
of the hills was completely perforated and that, while most of
the pits had not been continued more than twenty or thirty feet
below the surface, there were so many of these openings that
"there was scarce ground left undisturbed for the safe passage
of a traveler who was continually kept in peril by unseen excava-
tion or falling-in pits."[6] The only instruments used by the early
miners in digging the lead were a pick, a wooden shovel, and a
sledge hammer. In smelting the ore the pioneer white men made
little improvement on the process used by the Indians. In 1810,
according to Stevens,[7] these miners built a stone furnace on the
side of a hill, an arched entrance at the bottom, with the top
open to the weather. Three large logs, four feet long, were rolled
into the furnace, while small logs and huge pieces of wood were
piled around. The ore, in great lumps, was thrown on top of the
wood. A fire was lighted in the evening, and the following morning there was melted lead in the hole dug at the entrance of the
arch. Usually six thousand pounds of ore were used at one firing,
and the first smelting yielded about three thousand pounds of
lead. The scorched metal and ashes or slag were put through
the furnace again and gave up twenty-five to thirty per cent
more lead.

6 Schoolcraft, H. R., *Journal of Tour into the Interior of Missouri and
Arkansas* (London, 1821), p. 4.

7 Stevens, Walter B., *St. Louis, the Fourth City, 1764–1909* (St. Louis,
1909), p. 266.

Around the rich lead deposits a settlement grew rapidly for the mines became the mecca, not only of regular miners but of adventurers, smelters, merchants, and of gamblers of every sort. In consequence, it was necessary to formulate a code of laws by which mining claims might be governed. There is extant the manuscript copy of the rules which the Vallé brothers put into effect for the government of their holdings.

The Vallés, Francois and Jean Baptiste, held important government posts under both the Spanish and French regimes. In 1796 they received from Don Zenon Trudeau, the lieutenant-governor of Upper Louisiana, a grant of the Mine La Motte, and in 1800 they began work. Since the section was rich in mineral they, with Jean Baptiste Pratte and St. Jemme Beauvais, merchants of Sainte Genevieve, laid claim to two other leagues adjacent to the mine. The grant was recommended by DeLassus, the governor of Upper Louisiana, and the matter was presented to Intendant Morales at New Orleans by Reverend James Maxwell, parish priest at Sainte Genevieve, who had power of attorney to represent the petitioners. A survey of the land was made and the title and claim confirmed.[8]

It may be interesting to interrupt this recital in order to discuss briefly the location and extent of the Vallé possessions. The Vallé mines run diagonally across Saint Francois and Perry counties from northwest to southeast. In their extension south they present a remarkable network of veins, some of which spread over an area of about fifteen hundred feet in length by five hundred in breadth. These are examples of mines of a more permanent character than are to be found in the northern lead region. In Saint Francois County there are numerous shafts and more of the same type in the Perry area. Of all these, only two are less than fifty feet deep; six exceed one hundred ten feet, and one reaches a depth of one hundred seventy feet. They extend out in all directions. It is estimated that the Vallé Mines produced about ten million pounds of lead from 1824 to 1834, and about as much more in the next twenty years.

8 Houck, *op. cit.,* I, 352 n.

The estimates of the production are based upon very uncertain data, no records for the most part having been preserved of the lead mined and smelted.[9]

The Vallé brothers did not reside at the mines but that they looked after their own mining interest is manifested by the regulations under which all "peaceable persons were permitted under contract to work on the land of the subscribers." These ordained:

1. There will be allowed to each Digger twelve feet around his hole (viz) inasmuch as—the local situation will permit in the place where he shall have made his hole and each lot shall be sunk five feet in three days from the taking of his tool in the lot.

2. Each Digger shall have or hold but one lot at a time on which he shall work and to facilitate the Diggers he will be allowed six days without working his lot and still hold it but after the expiration of that time the hole shall be forfeited and therefore any other Digger shall have the right of taking and working the same.

3. No one shall have the right of holding any lot without the consent of the proprietors and for improper conduct will be prohibited its privilege.

4. No one shall have right of buying mineral from the Diggers without giving notice to the proprietors and the purchaser shall become himself responsible for the debts due by the Diggers or Vendee.

5. Each Digger shall deliver his mineral well cleaned at the furnaces of the proprietors, and it will be optional with the proprietors to give four hundred pounds of lead or twenty dollars in cash for each thousand pounds of mineral.

6. The proprietors reserve to themselves the privilege to alter or amend any of the foregoing rules and, by giving thirty days' previous notice to stop the digging.

7. Any person making a discovery one hundred yards from where mineral has been reached shall be entitled to twenty-five feet ground all around his hole.

9 Missouri Geological Survey Reports, "Dr. Litton's Report," *Annual Reports of the Geological Survey of Missouri, 1853–1854* (Jefferson City 1856), II, 35–37.

8. All lots that the proprietors may put hand to work will not be forfeited.
9. All the difficulties between the Diggers concerning the diggings is to be settled by arbitration according to our Rules, and each Digger hath the right to go into his neighbor's hole at any time to see if he drift on his lot.
10. No person shall have the right to build on our ground except for the purpose of digging.
11. The proprietors reserve the Southeast quarter of Section Five in township thirty-eight North of Range five east and forbid anybody to dig on it.

VALLÉ'S MINE—5 December, 1826.

(Signed) VALLÉ & VALLÉ[10]

In their attempt to respect human rights and to insure justice these canons put to shame many codes of present-day industrial organizations. Their articles of arbitration might have been used, at a later time and in a larger sphere, as a model of the adjustment of difficulties, not among miners of various nationalities, but among the nations of the world.

There were other men besides the Vallés who owned and operated mines in Missouri. John Smith T, as has been noted above, claimed the mine Shibboleth, one of the richest in Upper Louisiana. During 1811, a year of high production, the miners collected and brought to Smith's furnaces 5,000,000 pounds of ore from which 3,125,000 pounds of bar and pig lead were produced.[11] Moses Austin, too, was interested in lead mining. He came to the West from Connecticut, where he was born the year after Saint Louis was founded. In December, 1796, he visited Louisiana and in May, 1797, "obtained from the Spanish government a grant of land three miles square which included the Mine á Breton."[12] The terms of the grant obliged him to introduce certain improvements in mining and to manufacture some of his lead for commercial purposes. Accordingly, he sank

---

10 This manuscript is in the possession of J. Felix Vallé of Sainte Genevieve.

11 Schoolcraft, *op. cit.,* p. 116.

12 Barker, Eugene, ed., *Austin Papers* (Washington, 1924), pp. 1–2.

the first lead mine shaft in Louisiana. It was not unlike those used in European countries. He erected a reverberatory furnace for smelting lead, began the manufacture of sheet lead, and in 1810 built a shot tower at Herculaneum. He kept a force of forty or fifty men[13] employed at his furnaces and mines and was, at the time of our story, one of the most conspicuous and important men in the mining region.

Almost immediately after establishing his store on Main Street, Wilt turned his attention to the lead industry, for lead was an indispensable article in the western wilderness. Its uses were many; not least among them was its acceptance as legal tender in business transactions, because there was little or no "hard money" in circulation. The merchants of Missouri gathered great boat loads of the metal, sending them east either by way of the Ohio or down the Mississippi to New Orleans, where the lead was loaded on ocean-going vessels bound for some port on the Atlantic Coast. It was valued at from $11 to $16 a ton and, when it reached its destination, it could be bartered or sold for goods. Early in the spring of 1811, Wilt engaged Hyacinth Saint Cyr to undertake an expedition up the Mississippi[14] to the mines at Prairie du Chien to collect a quantity of lead which he intended for the Philadelphia market.

Going into the Sac and Fox country, Saint Cyr took an assortment of goods to be exchanged for lead, but Wilt cautioned him not to compute the value of the lead at more than three cents a pound, so that a profit might be made on the cargo when it was sold in Philadelphia or New Orleans. Saint Cyr could not make satisfactory trades with the Indians, and Wilt planned that Mussina, when he came to Saint Louis from Philadelphia with a cargo of goods in August, 1811, should be sent up the Mississippi to Prairie du Chien to establish there a permanent branch house under the supervision of Blondeau, an Indian trader and later a sub-agent for the Sacs.[15] This plan was frus-

13 Houck, *op. cit.*, I, 371–72.
14 Hertzog to Wilt, March 20, 1811, Hertzog Letterbook.
15 Marshall, *op. cit.*, II, 86 n.

trated, however, for we know that Mussina severed his relations with the firm early in the spring of the year. In May, 1811, after Saint Cyr's return from Prairie du Chien, Charles Lucas,[16] who had just returned from school in the East, arranged with Wilt to go up the Mississippi to negotiate with the Indians for their lead.[17]

In his expedition to the Prairie, Lucas was more successful than Saint Cyr but owing, undoubtedly, to the influence of British agents, who were active at that time in instigating the Indians of the Northwest against the Americans,[18] he was unable to procure as large a quantity of the metal as he had hoped.

From this time until after the war the supplies of crude lead or lead ashes brought down the Mississippi from the Prairie du Chien mines greatly diminished. As this ash supply was rich in lead, Wilt placed great store by it; when it was cut off, he was forced to apply for lead to the south Missouri mines. Much pig lead was sent from Missouri to Philadelphia dealers, who converted it into shot of all sizes. John Wetherill, Baker, Gratz, and Dr. Strong, manufacturers of lead, were importing great cargoes; Gratz[19] received 4000 pigs in one consignment,[20] and

16 Charles Lucas was the second son of Judge John B. C. Lucas. In 1805 when he was but thirteen years old, he came to Saint Louis with his father's family. The young man had attended Jefferson College in Philadelphia for five years and on his return home in 1811, he studied law in the office of Colonel Easton. Lucas joined the volunteer troops in Saint Louis at the opening of the war and later assisted in organizing a company of Volunteer Artillery, of which he was elected captain. They were sent to Portage des Sioux which was located on the west bank of the Mississippi about six miles above the mouth of the Missouri, where the war parties of the savages must pass in an attempt to attack Saint Louis. When the war was over, Charles Lucas was elected to the Legislature and some time afterward was appointed United States attorney for the territory. On September 27, 1817, when only twenty-five years old, he was killed in a duel with Colonel Thomas H. Benton. Billon, II, 215.

17 Hertzog to Wilt, May 13, 1811.

18 Manuel Lisa to Governor Clark, July 1, 1817, *Missouri Gazette,* July 5, 1817.

19 Probably Michael Gratz, merchant. *Pennsylvania Archives,* 3rd Series, XV, 213.

20 Hertzog to Wilt, June 27, 1811.

smaller parcels were arriving continually. At this time, however, the market became so flooded with British shot that the Philadelphia shot factories were obliged to suspend operations.[21] As a result of this influx the price of pig lead dropped from $15 to $8.50, then to $8 a ton. Hertzog realized that there would be financial loss in further exploitation of the crude ore, but foresaw possibilities in the manufacture of red lead.

In April, 1811, Wilt received from Hertzog a letter outlining a plan for establishing a red lead factory in Saint Louis. He was advised to secure either Chouteau's or Sanguinette's lot, opposite the market, on which to erect a factory, and Hertzog sent two men from Philadelphia, Joseph Henderson and John Sparke, to carry on manufacturing operations. Wilt undertook to secure a mine, as such an investment would probably prove more economical than buying lead; Herculaneum seemed to be a desirable site for storing and shipping the metal. Hertzog discussed the type and the cost of buildings—these to be of logs—and castings for machinery, the former to cost two or three hundred dollars, the latter about fifteen hundred. He saw the possibilities of large sales along the Ohio River[22] and, since Pittsburgh had five glass factories all using red lead, he was confident that a trade might be established with these firms where the red lead might be sold or exchanged for glass. He wrote to Wilt:

Trade with Philipson for a few boat loads of his lead ashes, for we expect to be able to make some red lead this year and at the rate of two tons a week. . . . We must fill Tennessee, Kentucky, and Ohio full of it and send the remainder to New Orleans and around here. This non-import law is the thing.[23]

Henderson left Philadelphia by stage May 30, 1811,[24] and journeyed to Pittsburgh where he was to secure tools and castings for the machinery of the new plant. He was a capable soap-

21 *Gazette*, January 24, 1811.
22 Hertzog to Wilt, April 30, 1811.
23 Hertzog to Wilt, May 13, 1811.
24 Hertzog to Wilt, June 3, 1811.

maker, in addition to his other talents, and while waiting for Sparke, his companion, he was "to make a boil at Pittsburgh for the joint account of the firm and if the business should do as well as the lead, he was occasionally to make a boil in Saint Louis."[25] Zachary Mussina, who was to meet Henderson in Pittsburgh, was instructed to assist in the sale of the soap. Although there is no record of the outcome, it probably was a success, for during the War of 1812 Henderson made soap in Saint Louis for the United States troops and for agents in the factories located along the upper Mississippi.

Henderson, with Morin, sailed from Pittsburgh on the *Mary,* one of Wilt's boats. They left the Pittsburgh dock on June 20, 1811, with the balance of Invoice No. 3 and reached Saint Louis the latter part of July. Sparke, however, was not ready to leave Philadelphia until June 12. On that day he, his wife and four children, and Mr. Henderson's wife and child, left Philadelphia for Pittsburgh, going as part of the cargo of two wagon loads of goods. A trip by wagon between these two cities usually took a month; one by stage was made in about twenty days, but neither mode of travel was pleasant in the day of springless wagons and ungraded roads.[26] The little group left Pittsburgh about the middle of July on the *Sparkler,* another of Wilt's boats, and on August 2 reached the mouth of the Ohio where Morin, who had returned from Saint Louis, was waiting to take them up the Mississippi to their new home.

By prearrangement with Hertzog, both Sparke and Henderson were to be allowed $9 a week from the time of reaching Pittsburgh until the works in Saint Louis were in operation, or were ready to open.[27] After that they were to receive one third of

25 Hertzog to Wilt, May 23, 1811.

26 Travelers were in continual danger from the condition of the roads, and could hardly escape the overturn of the stage, which often happened twice in one day. "When not in sloppy plains", writes one traveler, "we had to walk over slippery rocks which hurt our feet, while wild briars scratched our faces." (Quoted from Bishop Du Bourg's letter to Reverend Brute, November 13, 1817.) Rothensteiner, *op. cit.,* I, 263.

27 Hertzog to Wilt, May 13, 1811; and May 23, 1811.

the profits.[28] When they reached Saint Louis the red lead factory building was not yet begun. Wilt had been unable to secure either Sanguinette's or Robideau's land and instead had purchased, on August 1, 1811, Charles Hempstead's lot at Main and Locust, where he planned to build both store and factory.[29] The factory was to be constructed of logs and to consist of only one large room where two furnaces were to be installed. The main door was to open toward the Mississippi so that the ashes from the furnaces, instead of being left in great heaps about the building, could be more easily taken out and thrown into the river. On each side of the room were to be two openings which could be closed by great solid wood shutters, such as were commonly used on buildings at the time. As no upper story was necessary and as the bare ground would serve for floor, little time would be required to complete the building. Wilt, Sparke, and Henderson hoped that at least a load or two of red lead would be ready for the Philadelphia market before the winter of 1811 set in. The first estimate of the cost of the factory building was $420, but before all was ready for operation the expenses had mounted to $2000. This was caused by Wilt's change in plans. Instead of using logs, he built the factory of rock. While rock was ready to hand on the factory lot, it required not only a longer time to cut and quarry but was, in consequence, a more expensive building material than logs.

Unforeseen difficulties, moreover, loomed at the very outset. The city fathers objected to the presence of a lead factory within the limits of the Corporation, much to the disgust of Hertzog who protested that Saint Louis officials were more particular than were the Philadelphia Trustees who had never "thought of prohibiting a lead factory within their boundaries."[30] The difficulty was amicably settled and the building proceeded. In August the country was swept by one of those terrible epidemics of fever that follow a year of high water, and most of Wilt's workmen

28 Hertzog to Z. Mussina, May 23, 1811.
29 Hertzog to Wilt, August 29, 1811.
30 Hertzog to Wilt, August 15, 1811.

were obliged to give up their work. The winter weather put a stop to all operations, and it was not until March, 1812, that everything was in readiness to begin the manufacture of red lead.

That a supply of ore might be on hand when the factory was finished, Wilt urged young Lucas to redouble his efforts and to secure from the Indians as much as he could gather. Lucas was successful in his dealings with the red men, but British intrigues made his task a difficult one. He secured not only pig lead but lead ashes, which were cheaper and which contained large quantities of lead. He sent two boatloads from Prairie du Chien to Saint Louis, and in due time Sparke smelted the lead ashes. A little later Lucas reported to Wilt that he had a great quantity of lead or nearly 10 tons ready to send down the Mississippi.

In anticipation of the success of the red lead business and realizing that Lucas' consignments, though large, would not be sufficient to keep the men steadily at work, Wilt, in November, employed John Honey, a half-brother of Thomas F. Riddick, to furnish him with lead from Herculaneum.[31] Honey came to Louisiana from Virginia a few years after the Purchase, and in 1808, when only nineteen years old, was appointed by Lewis, "Clerk of the court of common pleas, Quarter Sessions, and of Oyer and Terminer of the District of Arkansas." At the same time, he held the offices of treasurer, recorder, and judge of the probate court of the same district. In 1809 he was back in Saint Louis, and when Riddick resigned from the Board of Land Commissioners to attend to his private interests in Kentucky, Honey was unanimously elected to his place. On May 17, 1811, he was appointed coroner of the district of Saint Louis.[32] His official duties, although numerous, took little of his time. He became interested in the lead and shot business at Herculaneum and contracted to furnish Wilt with lead for the factory in Saint Louis. At this time, the lead at the mines was

31 Hertzog to Wilt, November 4, 1811.
32 Marshall, op. cit., II, 135.

selling at four cents. Since exchanging goods for lead was cheaper than paying cash for the metal, Wilt opened a store for that purpose at Herculaneum with Honey in charge.

Herculaneum, which is about thirty miles south of Saint Louis, is situated on a high bank of the Mississippi, at the mouth of Joachim Creek. It contained in 1811 twenty houses with two hundred inhabitants and in business enterprises it boasted "one store, an excellent blacksmith shop, a hatter, and two shot towers; J. N. Macklot's in the south part of town and Moses Austin's on the bluff at the northern end of the village."[33] Since it was not far from the mines, there would be no difficulty in bringing lead to the village and, as it was situated on the bank of the Mississippi, it offered direct shipment to Saint Louis at a nominal freight. Thus the cost of transportation, which was an important problem to the young Saint Louis manufacturer, was virtually solved. With Honey in charge at Herculaneum, Wilt proposed to open a branch store in Sainte Genevieve.

Sainte Genevieve on the Mississippi, thirty miles below Herculaneum, had been from the earliest days the shipping port of the lead from the mines of that section, and it was still the depot of the outgoing cargo. Just at this time, however, so much of the metal had been poured into the village that it had become a drug on the market and the merchants refused to accept it in exchange for goods. Here was Wilt's opportunity; he chose P. Falconer as his agent in Sainte Genevieve to open a branch store where lead could be exchanged for goods which were marked so as to yield a good profit. Falconer and J. G. Comegy came to Saint Louis in 1809, with a consignment of goods from the Falconer-Comegy store in Baltimore, and by the fall of 1811 they had sold out their stock. They were preparing to return to Baltimore when Comegy fell a victim of the fever that was then raging throughout the Saint Louis district. Falconer would not leave his friend alone among strangers, and it was while waiting for Comegy to recover that he engaged with Wilt to take charge of an assortment of dry goods and

33 *Louisiana Gazette,* March 21, 1811.

groceries in Sainte Genevieve where the goods could be readily exchanged for lead.[34]

With regular supplies of lead from Prairie du Chien, from Sainte Genevieve, and from Herculaneum, Wilt hoped to collect at Saint Louis, before the winter set in, not less than 300,000 pounds of crude material which would later be converted into bar, red and white lead. He aimed to corner the lead market of the western country. The price of the metal at the mine was low, and since he had a large consignment of goods to exchange for it at high prices, this seemed the moment to push his plan into effect. During the years 1805 and 1806, according to the United States report, the annual importation of white lead alone was five million pounds. As a result of the Non-Intercourse Act the amount of white lead brought into the country from England was limited, and Wilt had, therefore, no fear that he would overstock the country with the crude and manufactured lead; on the contrary, he was troubled lest he might not be able to produce even one-half of the amount needed for the market.[35]

Pittsburgh would buy the manufactured product of the Saint Louis factory, while Philadelphia would consume vast quantities of the crude lead. In Pittsburgh, in 1811, there were several glass factories in full blast, while a number of potteries were carrying on an ever increasing business, and both glassmakers and potters needed the red lead in the manufacture of their wares.[36] Bakewell & Company, on the southeast corner of Grant and Water Streets,[37] was the largest glass house in Pittsburgh. Their factory was built in 1808 and here the first successful flint glass made in America was manufactured. In the pioneer days of glassmaking Benjamin Bakewell met with difficulties that would have disheartened a less determined man. His furnace

34 Hertzog to Mussina, May 4, 1811, quoting from Wilt's letter, March 21, 1811.

35 Hertzog to Wilt, December 2, 1811.

36 Hertzog to Z. Mussina, June 10, 1811.

37 Bakewell, B. G., *The Family Book of Bakewell* (Pittsburgh, 1896), p. 70.

was badly constructed, his workmen incompetent, opposition to the training of apprentices met him at every turn, raw materials were hard to get, and though costly, were of inferior quality. In 1810 he replaced the old furnace, which held six 20-inch pots, by a ten-pot furnace properly constructed. He could then offer glass of all sizes and kinds in exchange for the red lead of the Saint Louis plant, which began operations in the spring of 1812. Wilt accepted Bakewell's offer, since there was great demand for glass for the new stores and homes that were being built both in Saint Louis and in the growing settlements of the surrounding country.

In Philadelphia, Gratz dealt in the wholesale and retail trade of the crude lead which for some years past had been brought in great cargoes from the mines of Upper Louisiana. The firm of Strong and Whetherill, in the manufacture of their white lead,[38] used large consignments of the raw material, while Beck and Lammot, at South Water Street, used great quantities of the bar lead in the manufacture of shot.[39] Paul Beck was early engaged in the manufacture of shot and it is said that he built the first shot tower in the United States. He became one of the leading merchants and philanthropists of his day, supported all worthy causes and gave generously of his wealth to every benevolent institute founded in Philadelphia during his life. Beck and Lammot employed thirteen men at their factory, and from 1811 to 1816 the output of the plant was two and one-half tons a day.[40] They regularly demanded and consumed large consignments of the crude lead from the Saint Louis firm.

38 White lead was used extensively in the manufacture of paint. In Kentucky, Ohio, and western Pennsylvania, where paint manufacturers were opening plants, the proprietors offered to buy the output of the Saint Louis white lead furnaces at the Philadelphia price, which in the fall of 1811, was $16 per cwt. At that time, prices in the eastern markets for both crude and manufactured lead were high. Crude lead brought $27 per cwt; bar was quoted at $9 per cwt; red at $11 and $12, while Whetherill was selling white lead at $17 per cwt.

39 Hertzog to Wilt, September 12, 1811.

40 Hertzog to Wilt, November 11, 1811.

In the summer of 1811, according to the Philadelphia *Aurora,* war was imminent. Naturally, the demand for large quantities of ammunition sent the price of lead to a high level. The members of the Saint Louis firm knew that they had not sufficient lead on hand to meet the demand in the event of hostilities with Great Britain, but they felt that, at the moment, the Non-Intercourse Act was a sufficient safeguard to their new undertaking.[41] In order to deter others from entering into competition with them, however, and to check merchants from importing lead from England, Wilt prepared to distribute 300 tons of crude and bar lead among the principal cities of the United States. Should war be averted by the rescinding of the Orders-in-Council and by a settlement with England, then the American manufacturer would be compelled to rely upon Congress to protect his infant industry by placing duties and prohibitions on lead imported from foreign countries. In order to make assurance doubly sure, Hertzog addressed to the Honorable Adam Seybert, Representative from Philadelphia[42] and member of the House Commerce and Manufactures Committee, a letter dated November 18, 1811, from which we take the following excerpt:

I have undertaken to establish at Saint Louis a factory of red lead and litharge, which articles we calculate on making in sufficient quantities to supply the United States. Having some time past had a tolerably extensive trading house there and finding we can trade in pig lead to advantage, have actually engaged two men who understand the business and who have wrought at it in this city who are now on the spot preparing the necessary works which are nearly completed. We propose making four tons per week at first, and to extend the supply with the demand, which at present do not know how to estimate, and would thank you if you can conveniently be informed at the Treasury, to state the supplies of two or three former unrestricted years. The expense of getting it brought around to our cities will not exceed that of bringing in pigs. Our factory is on the eve of completion and in a letter just received from my partner and nephew, Christian Wilt, dated Saint Louis, October 28,

41 Hertzog to Wilt, August 8, 1811.
42 *Annals of Congress,* 1809–1810, p. 680.

he writes 'expect to send you by spring a load of red lead and maybe some white' so that the prospect for us is sufficiently flattering at present. One only fear presents itself that in case of renewal of trade with Great Britain, they may pour in quantities and ruin us by either underselling or by preventing our selling altogether.

To solicit your care and protection of this infant establishment in your official capacity is the object of this letter.[43]

In writing to Adam Seybert for protection for his red lead factory in Saint Louis Hertzog knew that his appeal would be favorably received, for Seybert believed that our "infant industries should be fostered and protected."[44] Early in 1810 the Pennsylvania Congressman said:

Our manufacturing establishments must be regarded as so many infants who need a mother's care to bring them to maturity . . . protection from the government is absolutely necessary.[45]

The factory, begun in the fall of 1810, was not finished until March, 1812. When the building was ready the furnaces were immediately installed and the smelting of the lead started. Sparke calculated that they could make four tons of the red lead a week, but Henderson, who during his leisure moments had studied Aiken's *Chemistry* and Nicholson's *Dictionary* in an endeavor to "discover some valuable processes for making sundry profitable articles",[46] worked out a new formula by which the red lead might be manufactured through the use of heat alone, without the need of pounding, grinding, and washing. He believed that with this new discovery the weekly output need not be limited to four tons, but that the quantity manufactured could be regulated according to the demand of the market. Unfortunately, however, after several attempts to produce the red lead according to Henderson's new method had failed, it was necessary to build a mill for washing and grinding the lead.

43 Hertzog to Seybert, November 18, 1811.

44 Seybert on January 9, 1810, *Annals of Congress*, p. 1175.

45 *Ibid.*, April 18, 1810, p. 1891.

46 Hertzog to John Sparke, March 30, 1812.

During the winter, when the weather did not permit outside work on the mill, Sparke, Henderson, and their helpers busied themselves indoors smelting the crude metal into pig lead.

In March, 1812, they had 38,000 pounds of bar lead ready for shipment. Henry W. Drinker,[47] who was taking his own cargo of 62,000 pounds to Philadelphia and had offered to take Wilt's consignment, left Saint Louis on March 14, 1812,[48] with bar lead and furs and reached New Orleans on May 23. He wrote at once to both Wilt and Hertzog that he was shipping the lead by sea. To do this was a dangerous venture and would require a high insurance, for on April 4, the *Aurora* announced that Congress had passed a ninety-day embargo. This act did not hinder coastwise trade but the presence of British frigates in the adjacent waters made passage by sea perilous.[49] Unfortunately, Drinker did not find a freighter that would carry his cargoes to Philadelphia and for safekeeping he stored Wilt's furs and lead with Chen and Relf, merchants of New Orleans. A year later, May 2, 1813, Benjamin Morgan, acting as agent for Wilt, examined the furs and found them still safe and in good order but subject to New Orleans charges until the war was over. To Hertzog the manner in which Drinker had carried out his business transactions merited contempt. He wrote:

It would have been vastly in our favor had they (the furs and bar lead) been entrusted to any other than that drone, Drinker, who neglected two opportunities of shipping them to me which were

47 Drinker, a close Philadelphia friend of Wilt was a young man of excellent qualities and made a deep impression on John Bradbury, the English scientist, who accompanied Hunt on his journey to Astoria. Bradbury at this time was recuperating in Saint Louis from an illness which attacked him afer his return from the West. He relates in the story of his travels how Drinker frequently visited him in his illness, and "created in me a strong attachment", also how Drinker intrusted to him a cargo of 3000 pounds of lead to be sold in New Orleans or stored for his account.

48 Hertzog to Andrew Wilt, April 9, 1812.

49 Hertzog to Wilt, April 4, 1812.

presented before the declaration of war, viz., Chandler Price's ship and a ship consigned to Wardner and Company.[50]

In the spring of 1812 prices in the eastern markets for both raw and manufactured lead, according to the Philadelphia quotations, "were flattering". Red lead sold at $10.50 per ton, white at $16, orange mineral at $20, litharge at $14, and crude at $10.[51] No red lead had been made in Saint Louis, but a few weeks after Drinker left Wilt sent to New Orleans another load consisting of 360 cwt. of bar lead. This was sold at $8 per cwt. A little later 50,000 pounds more floated down to the southern city, where the price was 6½ cents per pound. At the same time Wilt sent up the Ohio 11,000 pounds of pig lead on which he paid freight at 1½ cents per pound. Hull, the patroon of the boat which carried the bar lead, offered to sell the cargo free of commission or to barter it for produce.[52] In exchanging lead for the different Mississippi Valley articles he used the following prices listed in the Price Current published in the *Louisiana Gazette,* May 2, 1812 :[53]

ST. LOUIS PRICE CURRENT (THE PRODUCE OF OUR TERRITORY) MAY 2, 1812

Article	Per	Prices D. C.
Bacon	lb.	$ .10
Butter	"	.25
Beef	"	.08
Candles, dipped		.20
Candles, moulded		.25
Coal	bushel	.16
Flaxseed	"	1.00
Feathers	lb.	.50
Flour, superfine	bbl.	9.00
Flour, fine	"	8.00
Flour, horsemills	"	7.00
Furs, Otter	skin	2.00
Furs, Fox	"	.50
Furs, Muskrat	"	.30
Furs, Raccoon	"	.30

50 Hertzog to Wilt, May 2, 1813.

51 Hertzog to Wilt, April—1812.

52 Wilt to Hertzog, July—1812.

53 *Louisiana Gazette,* May 2, 1812.

Furs, Beaver	lb.	2.50
Gun powder	"	.50
Grain, wheat	bushel	1.00
Grain, rye	"	none
Grain, oats	"	.50
Grain, corn	"	.75
Hemp	"	6.00
Hempseed	"	3.00
Hog's lard	lb.	.10
Hides, beef	skin	2.50
Honey	gal.	1.00
Hops	lb.	.37½
Horns, Ox	plenty, no demand	
Horns, Buffalo	" " "	
Leather, sole	lb.	.37½
Plank, or boards, Oak	100 ft.	3.00
Plank, or boards, Ash	"	3.00
Plank, or boards, Cotton	"	2.50
Plank, or boards, Walnut	"	3.50
Plank, or boards, Cherry	"	4.50
Lead, pig	cwt.	4.25
Lead, bar	"	6.00
Lead, sheet	"	14.00
Peas	bushel	1.25
Pork, fresh	cwt.	3.50
Peltry bear, black	piece	2.00
Peltry bear, white	"	from 5. to 50.00
Deer, shaved	lb.	.20
Deer, buffalo robes	piece	3.00
Rice, upland	cwt.	3.00
Salt	50 lbs.	2.00
Shot—all sizes	cwt.	7.50
Sugar, Maple	lb.	.20
Starch	"	.12½
Soap	"	.12½
Tallow, beef	"	.12½
Tallow, deer	"	.12½
Tallow, buffalo	"	.12½
Tobacco, leaf	cwt.	4.00
Tobacco, carrot	"	10.00
Wax, bees	"	.20
Whiskey	gal.	.62½
Wool	lb.	.50

These articles found ready sale at the Saint Louis store for either cash or barter. In order that there should be no delay when the red lead was placed on the market, Wilt engaged a competent man in each of the larger towns of Ohio where he had no regular agent. These representatives agreed to buy, at a stipulated price, from the Saint Louis factory in quantities of 100 pounds, or to take the cargo on commission with the Pittsburgh price as the standard of selling.

As the spring advanced into summer, signs of war in the East became more threatening. Neither the Delaware River, which carried ships to the wharves of Philadelphia, nor the Mississippi, which controlled the maritime commerce of New Orleans, was blockaded, but British vessels patrolled our coast in ever increasing numbers, making it extremely difficult for American sails to put into port. Congress had been sitting behind closed doors for several days and people were waiting anxiously for the result of their deliberations, when on June 18, 1812, war was declared.[54] It was not until nearly a month[55] later that the news reached the frontier border of the Mississippi Valley, where it was received with demonstrations of great joy.

It is safe to conclude that those engaged in any enterprise that furnished supplies for soldiers, ammunition, or other war-time commodities, had good reason to anticipate excessive profits. These merchants of the West were no exception to the general rule, and we may assume that they made every effort to gather not only supplies of clothing and provisions for the troops going up into the Indian country to protect the settlements along the frontier, but also a store of lead which could be converted into war materials.

54 Hertzog to Christian and Andrew Wilt, June 18, 1812.
55 Wilt to Hertzog, July—1812.

CHAPTER V
WAR TIME EXPERIMENTS

THE year 1812 was for Christian Wilt one of great uncertainty and anxiety. In February his letters were full of confidence and eager anticipation, for the rumors of war then prevalent foreshadowed a sharp rise in the price of goods with which he was fairly well supplied, and the lead business promised quick and certain returns, but as the year grew older he had many disappointments.

According to the Price Current for July 11, 1812, about a month after war had been declared, the prices of lead and shot in Philadelphia[1] and New York[2] were very encouraging.

In Philadelphia		*In New York*			
1812			*1810*	*1811*	*1812*
Pig Lead per cwt.	$10	Pig Lead per cwt. .	$ 9.00	$ 9.50	$14
Bar " " "	11–12	Bar " " " .	12.25	11.25	15
Red "	12–14	Red "	11.00	11.00	16
White " (dry) .	21	White " (dry) ...	15.50	15.00	25
Ground	27	Ground, per "	16.00	17.00	26
Orange Min.	20				
Litharge	16	Litharge " cwt. ..	15.00	14.00	18
Shot	13	Shot per ton	$230.–240.	225.	13.50 cwt.
Vermilion (best)	3	Sheet Lead per cwt.	12.50	13.00	13

Hertzog urged the rapid completion of the factory and an early delivery in the East of a cargo of the red lead, for

the quoted prices assure us of a fortune if the works are rightly pushed but if we dilly dally until a peace is patched up, we must work the harder and make the less. According to these prices we can pay 25 per cent insurance. You can see (by the list) that lead is rising but owing to hostilities, the sea risk increases. Insurance at any rate is hardly obtainable but notwithstanding all this, get all the lead you can collect, but to compete with foreign importations it is necessary that your Saint Louis produce is equal to that of the British.[3]

1 Hertzog to Wilt, July 11, 1812, Hertzog Letterbook.

2 Mings' *New York Price Current,* for July 7 and Oct. 6, 1810, and July 6 and October 5, 1811.

3 Hertzog to Wilt, July 11, 1812; July 23, 1812.

Some months before this letter came, Wilt sent Charles Lucas up the Mississippi for a supply of lead. Lucas took with him dry goods and provisions which he was to exchange for the ore. In June the Indians in that section, instigated by the British traders, became restless and reports reached Saint Louis that the Sacs, Foxes, and Puants, together with several other tribes held council, and that 10,000 of them voted to join the British standard.

To this council the Missouri Indians had been invited, but through the influence of Manuel Lisa they were induced to remain neutral. In a letter to General Clark, Lisa said that more than a year before the war broke out he had

gained intelligence that the wampum was carried by British influence along the banks of the Missouri and that all the nations of the great river were excited to join the universal confederacy then setting on foot, of which the Prophet was the instrument and British traders the soul.[4]

That the British incited the Indians against the Americans there is much evidence. Stoddard says that the British by presents and misrepresentations invited the Indians to plunder the property of the American traders and to drive them from their stations or trading posts.[5] As early as 1807 some 2000 Indians visited Amherstburg where they were armed by the British and supplied with provisions and ammunition.[6] The western tribes, according to C. P. Lucas, embraced the British cause because the English had befriended them and the Americans had not.[7] However that may be, the most probable cause of the Indians' bitterness toward the Americans was the "white man's desire for land in the West."[8] Here between 1803 and 1806 by a series of

4 *Missouri Gazette,* Letter M. Lisa to General Clark, July 5, 1817.

5 Stoddard, *op. cit.,* p. 302.

6 Kellogg, Louise Phelps, *The British Regime in Wisconsin* (Madison, 1935), p. 271; Beers, Henry P., *The Western Military Frontier 1815–1846* (Philadelphia, 1935), p. 25.

7 Lucas, C. P., *The Canadian War of 1812* (Oxford, 1906), p. 81.

8 Goebel, Dorothy B., *William Henry Harrison, a Political Biography* (Indianapolis, 1926), p. 107.

treaties the Indians were obliged to cede to the United States millions of acres of land in what is now Ohio, Indiana, Illinois, and Missouri. This loss of their hunting grounds created dissatisfaction[9] and unrest among the western tribes and at the least provocation they were ready to take up arms against the intruders.

Since the danger at Prairie du Chien seemed real, Wilt notified Lucas to return at once. When several weeks passed and he did not come, his family began to fear that he had been killed by the Indians. In July Lieutenant Pryor[10] went up to Prairie du Chien to ascertain the true attitude of the Indians and reported, upon his return, that they were peaceably disposed, but that Lucas was not at the trading post. Pryor learned, however, that twenty days before he reached the Prairie, Lucas had gone with two hundred Renards, to secure a raft on which to float down his lead.[11] It was believed that his Indian companions would protect him should any hostile tribe attack. In September, much to the joy of his family and his employer, Lucas reached Saint Louis with planks, cedar posts, pickets, and some lead.[12] He had succeeded in disposing of the flour and whiskey which he had taken with him, but the remaining goods he left with Michael Brisbois, a prominent Prairie du Chien trader, and a man whom the Indians both feared and respected.[13]

Lucas had made friends among the red men and was anxious to return to the Prairie for he had found a rich trading territory some distance north of that point. He believed that the British traders[14] would not venture so far west during the war and that he would, in consequence, have the field virtually to himself. But the danger of attack in going up the Mississippi was daily growing more serious. Captain Nathaniel Pryor, stationed at

9 *Ibid.*, p. 107.

10 Nathaniel Pryor was a sergeant in the Lewis and Clark expedition. He was promoted for his faithfulness on this journey. Marshall, *op. cit.*, p. 220.

11 Wilt to Hertzog, August 2, 1812.

12 Wilt to Hertzog, September 6, 1812.

13 Wilt to Hertzog, September 27, 1812.

14 *Ibid.*

Fort Madison,[15] reported that some Wisconsin Indians gathered on Rock River were examining every boat for Americans, while the British and French Canadians were allowed to pass unmolested; thus the Indians, following the example of Great Britain, applied the right of search. All goods for the United States were plundered and the traders captured and often slain.[16] Wilt, because of these conditions, decided to close the account of the Prairie adventure and attempt nothing further in that quarter until peace was established. The returns had not been all that he had anticipated. Because of the comparatively small amount of lead procurable, only a small portion of the goods had been bartered; in addition, there were some bad debts incurred by the Indians and white men that would never be collected, and the proceeds from the unsold goods would be long in coming to hand.

Again danger lurked on every side. Not only was the passage up the river a hazardous undertaking but, even with the assurance of friendship on the part of the Indians, there was constant peril of an attack. In September the Puants raided the town of Prairie du Chien and burned all the American property they could find. Many of the traders lost stores of valuable goods. A heavy loser was Major George Wilson, acting agent for John White & Co., who held licenses to trade with the Sioux, the Fox, and the Sac along the waters of the Mississippi. James McFarland,[17] another active Indian trader, whose field was the district on the Mississippi above the mouth of the Missouri, also lost heavily through the destruction of his property. By good fortune Lucas' goods were safe, as the Indians disturbed neither Brisbois nor his household. The government's vacillation in the conduct of Indian affairs, together with the continued Indian depredations along the frontier, caused great dissatisfaction throughout the Middle West. "The government should certainly

15 Fort Madison in Iowa on the upper Mississippi. Earlier it was called Bellevue.

16 Kellogg, *op. cit.,* pp. 278–79.

17 Marshall, *op. cit.,* II, 203.

send relief to our frontiers and attack the savages in their villages," wrote Wilt;[18] and Bates in a letter of July 31, 1812,
said:

Our 'Red Brethren' must get some paternal admonishings before
they learn to deport themselves like members of a decent family. It
does appear to me that we carry the patriarchal notion too far.
These wretches whom we so familiarly class as brothers take no
pride in the alliance. Divested of what few virtues they might have
possessed as savages, without having acquired anything but the
frauds and the hypocrisy of civilization, it is very fond in us to
imagine that they will be governed, restrained and impelled by
motives similar to those which influence ourselves—austere and
haughty justice will alone answer.[19]

The news of the declaration of war and the President's proc-
lamation reached Saint Louis on July 9, 1812. Volunteer companies were immediately organized and virtually every able-
bodied man in Saint Louis enrolled for service. The militia was
reorganized under an Act of Congress, approved June 4, 1812,
providing for the government of the Missouri territory. Among
the first to volunteer were Wilt, Lucas, Henderson, and Sparke.
Many of the mechanics and workers enlisted, and for the operation of his plants, Wilt was obliged to depend upon the few
workmen who would remain and upon the Negroes he could
engage or buy. It cost relatively little to buy southern Negroes;
the expense of clothing them was small and the pay of a white
man at $15 a month for three years would easily purchase a
Negro slave. To be sure of some help when his men were called
into service,[20] Wilt hired a black boy at twelve dollars a month
for ten months, hoping, in the meantime, to procure two eighteen
year old lads from Maryland, where they were selling at four
hundred dollars apiece,[21] while at Saint Louis they were worth
five hundred.

18 Wilt to Hertzog, September 13, 1812.
19 Marshall, *op. cit.*, II, 229.
20 Wilt to Hertzog, September 27, 1812.
21 Wilt to Hertzog, September 6, 1812.

Henderson's attempt to make red lead with heat only, without grinding and washing, had as stated before, been unsuccessful, and the failure had necessitated the building of a mill, a stable, and a lead house, all of which delayed manufacture until the following August. By that time Wilt complained that the "war puts a stoppage to our lead business for the moment, as we cannot get hands to complete the mill house which I hoped to see going in a week, as nothing is wanting but the floor and bracing, and the selecting and levelling of the stones."[22] While the building was in progress, Henderson and Sparke calcined the lead, and in August they had 60,000 pounds ready[23] in spite of the fact that Henderson was ill the greater part of the summer. In September, when word of the attack on Prairie du Chien came, several of the militia companies prepared to march, but fortunately, neither Sparke nor Henderson was at that time, called to the colors and they continued their work at the factory. The work on the mill, however, advanced so slowly that Hertzog in Philadelphia complained:

Our good times will come by and by, though Heaven knows our disappointments and sufferings have been heavy enough. . . . It is absolutely necessary to spur the red lead men on. Raising the building etc., has taken more time than they ought. Do for goodness sake, let us begin to draw something out of it. Send me on via Pittsburgh also crude lead of good quality. Patent shot laid in low will do well, as the price here now is $15.[24]

In November he wrote:

Could you have been able by this time to have sent off any red lead by way of the River Ohio and Pittsburgh it would stand a good chance of making us a handsome profit. Pig lead, I fancy, would do still better as the white lead people cannot get supplies and I suppose it will bring rather more than red lead at present. If any boat starts for Pittsburgh after the receipt of this, be sure to put some on board and let Anshutz send it on to me unless it brings $13.50 in

22 Wilt to Hertzog, September 13, 1812; Nov. 3, 1812.
23 Wilt to Hertzog, August 16, 1812.
24 Hertzog to Wilt, November 3, 1812; November 30, 1812.

Pittsburgh. This is now the time. The same lead in spring may not answer as it is not impossible a peace may take place, in which case instead of gaining three or four dollars per cwt., we may lose *half a dozen*.[25]

In order that lead of some kind might reach Hertzog for the eastern market, Wilt asked William Steele of Louisville,[26] to whom he had sent 10,000 pounds[27] of pig early in the summer, to forward the supply to Pittsburgh at the first opportunity. This was done.

It was early in October, 1812, that the horsemill was ready, and before the twenty-third of the month Sparke and Henderson had ground enough lead to make five tons of the red. On the fifteenth of November, Henderson had colored 33 cwt., which was the first red lead manufactured west of the Mississippi. According to the opinion of the other workmen, it was very superior in quality.[28] In December, when the weather was too cold to permit the men to grind the lead, they kept themselves busy calcining so that they might have a large supply on hand when mild days would permit them to use the mill.

Hertzog wrote again to Wilt urging him to send lead to Philadelphia as soon as possible for if peace were declared, he insisted, prices would sink and the firm would suffer a real loss. The white lead manufacturers of Philadelphia, and Beck and Lammot, makers of shot, were possible customers, and Hertzog was anxious to secure their trade.[29] He quoted the price of pig lead at $15, and urged that since the white-lead people had little or no lead on hand, they would gladly pay that price. Beck and Lammot's patent shot, too, was selling at $15 per cwt.; red lead was quoted at $16 in Philadelphia, but an invoice would bring only $14. Since all these prices included the freight, Hertzog

25 Hertzog to Christian and Andrew Wilt, November 10, 1812.

26 Wilt to William Steele, September 19, 1812.

27 Wilt to Hertzog, January 23, 1813.

28 Wilt to Hertzog, November 22, 1812.

29 Hertzog to Wilt, December (no date) 1812.

advised Wilt to choose the most advantageous—that is, the cheapest way of forwarding.

Difficulties between Sparke and Henderson, which had existed for some months, now became acute. Wilt looked upon Sparke as an indolent laborer, and of course, not dependable, but Henderson, he believed to be an honest fellow and a good workman. According to the terms made before the men came to Saint Louis, they were to be partners in the business and each was to receive one-third of the profits. After the manufacture of the red lead had begun, however, these terms were not satisfactory and it became necessary to make other arrangements. Wilt proposed that each man work alone and that each be allowed $20 per ton for the finished lead. In this way time lost would be the individual workman's loss and not that of the firm. But Sparke was not satisfied that the two men should work on an equal basis. He said he understood, when he entered into the partnership, that he was to be the director of the factory and Henderson only a helper. But Henderson was the better worker and since manufacture had begun worked diligently. In nineteen days he had calcined 48,000 pounds so it was highly improbable that Wilt would permit any hardship to fall on him.[30] In spite of his dissatisfaction, Sparke accepted Wilt's proposition and in January began washing his share of the lead. By February 26, 1813, he had finished coloring his first batch, but the quality did not equal Henderson's. In March his second parcel, containing 8400 pounds, was finished and was better than the first. At that time the two men had 30,000 pounds of the red lead manufactured and 5000 pounds more calcined. This, with what Honey had sent up from the mines, made a total of 80,000 pounds of crude and manufactured lead on hand at the Saint Louis factory.

Hertzog ordered that the red lead be packed in barrels of 4, 5, or 6 cwt., so that the transportation would be cheap and safe. Wilt found the greatest difficulty in supplying the men with these strong kegs as rapidly as they were needed. The iron hoops were brought from Pittsburgh but the staves were made in Saint

[30] Wilt to Hertzog, February 13, 1813.

Louis by hand, a long and slow process. There were few coopers in the new country and these, when engaged, would not work steadily. Wilt, however, secured the services of two who promised to work by the day and to work faithfully.

The working-day was from "sun up to sun set," which during the course of the year made a day of varying length. In the summer time, when the sun rose very early, the day was long, but an hour for breakfast, from six to seven, was allowed and again the day was broken by a full noon hour, from twelve to one. This practice continued in Saint Louis until some carpenters, in 1840, started a movement advocating a working-day of ten hours. Wages varied with the kind of labor performed. For common services the pay was about $11.25 a month. Flatboatmen, who rated lowest in the labor scale, received about $8 a month.[31] The amount of wages that Wilt offered his coopers is not recorded, but they left his employ after working a short time. He decided then to give up the making of kegs in his own factory and in May made a contract with the Warners[32] who promised to supply him with kegs at fifty cents apiece.

In April, 1813, word again reached Saint Louis that the Indians were assembling at Prairie du Chien in preparation for an attack on Fort Madison. The militia was ordered to march at once. This time Sparke and Henderson were called out and on April 27[33] they started for Prairie du Chien with their company of artillery commanded by Captain Charles Lucas. Instead of going to the Prairie Captain Lucas occupied Fort Lookout, situated on an island just below Portage des Sioux,[34] to await an attack from the Indians. Dixon's[35] Indian allies had gathered at Prairie du Chien eager to go down the Mississippi to attack the settlement, but Dixon persuaded them that there were no armies

31 Stevens, W. B., *St. Louis—One Hundred Years in a Week* (St. Louis, 1909), p. 8.

32 Probably Jabez Warner, who evidently was a cooper.

33 Wilt to Hertzog, April 24, 1813.

34 *Missouri Historical Review,* October, 1931–June, 1932, p. 285.

35 Sometimes spelled Dickson. Robert Dickson, a British trader, led the Sioux against the Americans during the War of 1812. Beers, *op. cit.,* p. 89.

in that direction, only helpless women and children. Instead he led his warriors against Harrison at Fort Meigs.[36] Thus was the danger averted for a time. The red lead men could be spared better at this time than later in the season, for the supply of crude lead at the factory was low and Honey's parcel of 40,000 pounds at Herculaneum could not be brought up the river until the boats that carried troops to the Portage had been released and made available for private work.

At this time Hertzog questioned Honey's ability to conduct the business at Herculaneum, but Wilt replied with a spirited defence of his friend:

I have no reason to withdraw my good opinion of him [Honey]. He appears to me a very honest man indeed, and is generally believed so. . . . I think him better calculated for Herculaneum than any other man I know, he has acted as a clerk of the Court which tends to awe the miners who are generally an abandoned set and always at law. But knowing Honey to have some smattering of the law, they fear opposing him, and besides this, he has gained their confidence. He has applied for a Commission in the army and the government has recommended him for a post. As to the business at Herculaneum he wishes an augmentation of his salary and he agrees to find a suitable store and cellar for $700 which I shall allow him. The government has recommended him for the army. He is related to the Pirots of your place, merchants.[37]

While Henderson and Sparke were fighting the Indians, the men left at the factory were kept busy grinding and washing the calcined lead so that it would be ready for coloring when the two soldiers returned. The latter were back in Saint Louis before the twenty-ninth of May. They found 30,000 pounds of lead ready to be colored, although the mill had been idle for some days because the horses got out of the stable and could not be found in the prairie back of the village. Henderson went to work immediately after his return and in three weeks colored 33,000 pounds. At the same time he made 7 pounds of vermilion

36 Kellogg, *op. cit.*, pp. 296–97.
37 Wilt to Hertzog, May 29, 1813.

out of 1½ pounds of red lead. This could be disposed of as easily as pure vermilion and found a ready market at $5 a pound.[38]

In early August, 1813, an outbreak of the Indians in the North once again caused great alarm in Saint Louis. Henderson and Sparke left the factory, and Wilt closed his store.[39] On August 8 they were all on their way up the Mississippi, but the alarm proved false and within a very short time they were back in Saint Louis.[40] On Wilt's return, he found another offer for lead from Bakewell. This time the Pittsburgher offered him 12½ cents for the crude lead in Saint Louis. The eastern price was 15¾ to 16 cents, with the prospect of an even higher level should the war go on, and in consequence, a higher price for the crude lead in the West.

When the new year of 1814 dawned, Wilt was troubled because of the great scarcity of crude lead, its high price and his lack of funds to purchase it. Owing to the cold and snow the miners were doing little at the Missouri mines, nor could they, until spring, attempt anything on a large scale. No lead was expected from the mines on the upper Mississippi, although it was certain that an expedition would go north in the spring to establish a fort at the Prairie, since rumor had it that Dixon had left the country and gone over to Mackinac with all the Indians he could muster. Should the Indian mines be opened, Wilt could count on the 12,455 pounds that Brisbois had promised to send in payment of a note that he owed. But when the American troops were driven out and Prairie du Chien fell again into the hands of the British, this hope was shattered.

Some new lead deposits in southern Missouri were being unearthed, but none produced any large quantity, although one "discovery"—the name applied to any considerable body of ore found in the Missouri field—promised an abundant supply. It was located in the dry bed of a river which had once emptied

38 Wilt to Hertzog, June 19, 1813.
39 Wilt to Andrew Wilt, August 7, 1813.
40 Wilt to Hertzog, August 14, 1813.

into the Missouri. Pierre Chouteau, Sr., who owned the land, went with his four sons to inspect the lead. They agreed to give $1200 to the boatman who made the discovery should the deposit prove as fruitful as it had been reported,[41] but the outcome of the investigation is not recorded.

The scarcity of lead induced the miners and merchants to speculate, and the price rose accordingly. In December, 1813, lead was quoted at 5½ cents;[42] on January 20, 1814, it had jumped to 7½ cents.[43] William Smith, later of Smith and Von Phul, who needed 2000 pounds to complete a boatload, offered Wilt 7 cents for what he had collected at Herculaneum. When Wilt refused, Smith offered Philipson and Cabanné 12 cents[44] which they likewise refused, because they were preparing to send three boat-loads of pig lead up the Ohio and were willing to pay any price to secure the 100,000 pounds that they needed to complete their loads.

In order to compete with other merchants and to be sure of a supply of the raw material, Wilt decided to open a store at the mines near Herculaneum, with Cameron in charge, but Cameron enlisted for the spring campaign on the upper Mississippi, and William Bates finally organized this new venture. For some years Bates had been about the Missouri mines and knew the business thoroughly. In 1811, with James Bryant, a son-in-law of Moses Austin, he made a contract to work a "Lead-Mine-Land," a piece of United States property, which adjoined the mineral tract of Austin at Mine á Breton, in the district of Sainte Genevieve.[45] This experience having taught Bates the details relating to all lead transactions, he was familiar not only with the miners and speculators, but with the different qualities of the raw material.

41 Wilt to Hertzog, October 2, 1813.
42 Wilt to Hertzog, December 4, 1813.
43 Wilt to Hertzog, January 20, 1814.
44 Wilt to Hertzog, February 12, 1814.
45 Papers of Frederick Bates. Lease dated October 26, 1811. Missouri Historical Society, Saint Louis.

Bates began his new task at once and by June, 1814, he had collected 11,000 pounds at the mines and had agreed to purchase from a Mr. Mason 40,000 pounds at 6 cents per pound. Mason wanted cash, but Wilt would not permit Bates to contract on those terms for he could not "bind himself to pay in silver, not knowing whether he would be able to procure so scarce an article."[46] Wilt, however, was willing to pay half the purchase price in cash, and this Mason accepted. At Herculaneum, Honey secured 80,000 pounds from James Willkinson at 7 cents, but prices continued to rise from 7–7½ to 8 cents, and in December, 1814, lead was selling at 9½ cents a pound at both Herculaneum and Sainte Genevieve.[47]

These prices were reflected in the advance of lead prices in the eastern markets. In March, 1814, red lead sold in Pittsburgh at 15 cents a pound, and in Philadelphia at 21 cents.[48] In May the New Orleans price of pig lead was 9–9½ cents,[49] and in July it had reached 10–10½ cents.[50] This was an opportune time to dispose of the bar lead that Wilt had sent down by Macklot earlier in the year. Wilt instructed Morgan, his agent, to sell the lead or send it around by water to Hertzog in Philadelphia, where it could be disposed of at the advanced prices. It was at this time that Cromwell, who represented Bakewell, Page and Bakewell of Pittsburgh came to Saint Louis to contract for Wilt's red lead. He offered 12½ cents a pound for ten tons, but Wilt refused because the Pittsburgh price had then reached 21 cents. Later, however, he agreed to sell to Cromwell 23,000 pounds (all he had on hand) at 13 cents, for even at this quotation the red lead would net a good profit, assuming the cost of the lead per pound in Saint Louis to be 5½ cents; the manufacture, the wood for firing the furnaces, and other expenses, 1½ cents; and the freight 3 cents. Wilt took in payment a draft on

46 Wilt to William Bates, October 6, 1814.
47 Wilt to Hertzog, December 31, 1814.
48 Wilt to Hertzog, March 19, 1814.
49 Wilt to Hertzog, May 28, 1814.
50 Wilt to Hertzog, July 28, 1814.

Pittsburgh for $3190.60 with no responsibility for transportation of cargo. This he considered a good bargain as it eliminated all risk of the river voyage; it put into his hands funds of which he was in dire need; and it gave him a handsome profit on his red lead.[51] The red lead carried by the *Enterprise* was also sold to Bakewell for 15 cents a pound. For the pig lead he gave 13 cents. These prices were so encouraging that Hertzog urged Wilt to enlarge his furnaces, or to build another, in order to make, running at full capacity, a total of eight tons per week, instead of the meager two tons that they had been able to turn out previously.

Wilt felt that if there was to be any further expansion in the red lead plant, the new furnaces and mill should be built at New Hartford, where his shot tower was under construction, where transportation costs from the mines to Saint Louis could be saved, and where fuel could be more easily obtained. Wood was the only available fuel. The farmers from Vide Poche (Carondelet) brought their green wood in charettes and sold it at six "beets" (bits) a load, but a sufficient supply for the furnaces could not be obtained in Saint Louis from this source. In December, Sparke took all the factory hands across the river to Wilt's land on L'Abbe Creek, where they cut 100 cords of wood which provided fuel for at least several weeks.

The factory was too small for the two sets of furnaces already installed, and the lot on Locust with the store, the mill, the factory, and the lead house, was already crowded. The horse-mill was not equipped to grind more than two tons a week, and constant repairs were needed to keep it in running order.[52] Seven men were required to operate the plant; two for the mill, one for washing the lead after it was ground, one to keep a supply of split wood as fuel for the furnaces, one for calcining, and two for the coloring furnace.[53] The men were unwilling to work Sundays, and when they attended the furnaces at night, the

51 Wilt to Andrew Wilt, April 2, 1814.
52 Wilt to Hertzog, April 2, 1814.
53 Wilt to Hertzog, December 16, 1814.

added expense to the firm was great.[54] The coloring furnace, oblong in form with a wall separating it in the middle, had a fireplace at each end, and thus it might more properly have been called two furnaces. Not more than two batches of about four tons in each furnace could be colored in six days.

During the entire war Wilt was beset with many difficulties and worries. Laborers were few because of the frequent army drafts; lead could be secured only in limited quantities; and Cromwell, when he was in Saint Louis, warned Wilt that the Pittsburgh glassmakers would build their own red lead factory if they could not get the red lead at their own price. Now word came that the glassmakers were preparing to make red lead on a large scale. This was distressing, but he found consolation in the knowledge that an eastern factory, so far removed from the source of raw material, could hardly undersell a western plant situated almost in the heart of one of the richest lead districts in the country. However, to avoid incurring loss, Wilt planned to send a boatload of red lead to Pittsburgh every month.

Accordingly on Sunday, February 14, 1814, the *Missouri Packet* took as freight at 3 cents a pound, Wilt's cargo of 24,966 pounds of red lead, and 2012 pounds of pig lead (French weight) priced at 6 cents, together with 7 barrels of saltpeter weighing 1913 pounds at 25 cents a pound, 2 barrels of old brass and copper weighing 209 pounds. The lead and copper alone were valued at $2154.79½.[55]

On April 23 the *Betty*, which Wilt had sold to Mr. Thomas for $500, took the 23,000 pounds of red lead that was going to Bakewell, and at the same time 54 packs of shaved deerskins weighing 5454 pounds for Hertzog. The cost of the skins was $540 plus $31.12½ for cartage and packing.[56]

54 Wilt to Hertzog, December 31, 1814.

55 Wilt to Hertzog, February (no date) 1814.

56 For transportation to market furs were securely packed in bundles weighing about one hundred pounds each, and so wrapped as to protect them from the weather and from any accident on the river. It was a costly and perilous undertaking to move the heavy cargoes that were sent down the Missouri, Mississippi or Ohio rivers. It is said that General Ashley offered

When the *Betty* left Saint Louis there was little crude lead at the factory, nor could any be secured except with cash. Money in Saint Louis was very scarce, owing in a large measure to the inability of the United States to pay its troops, who in turn, were unable to pay the merchants to whom they were indebted. Wilt was one of the storekeepers to suffer greatly through the depletion of the national treasury. According to the annual report of January, 1814, the treasury had disbursed thirty millions during the previous fiscal year and needed forty millions for the current year. Acting Secretary of the Treasury, William Jones, looked with "alarm at the prospect of borrowing thirty millions",[57] for the failure to recharter the Bank of the United States had left the government without financial machinery or a sound bank note circulation. Revenues were inadequate to meet wartime expenditures, and the treasury was on the verge of bankruptcy and unable to pay the troops. The situation naturally caused deep concern among all business men, but was especially disturbing to the merchants of the West.

On July 9 Wilt sent James Maze down the river in the *Red Bird* with 11 packs of deerskins, and Moses Austin of Mine-à-Breton promised that he would take 16,000 pounds of red lead to Pittsburgh. Wilt expected that before the first of August his own boat, the *Captain Porter,* which was being built in the port of Saint Louis, would be ready for use, but in this he was disappointed. Even when the boat was finally ready, he was unable because of the low water in the Ohio, to launch it until the following spring. Before that time James Maze returned from Pittsburgh, and on Monday, October 10, 1814, he departed again with 93 kegs of red lead. Because they could be secured through barter, furs were always part of any consignment of goods going East, and this load contained 283 bearskins in 14 packs, 127 pounds of beaver, 17 otterskins, in addition to 3

a dollar a pound to any one who would insure him against loss during the transportation of his furs on the long journey to Saint Louis from the rendevous where the Indians brought their pelts. (Chittenden, H. M., *op. cit.*, I, 39–40.)

57 Adams, *op. cit.*, VII, 385–86.

barrels of saltpeter, and 12 kegs (1000 pounds) of white lead,[58] which Wilt priced at not less than 35 cents a pound.[59] The white lead of Saint Louis was of a superior quality and was the first white lead made in the Louisiana Territory. In November Wilt sent 40,000 pounds more of the red lead to Pittsburgh, and later in the month Hunt took 28,000 pounds to the East.[60]

During the early summer, when the factory had little crude lead on hand, Henderson rebuilt the furnaces. As soon as they were finished he began the manufacture of white lead. Nearly a year before, in March, 1813, the first real attempt to manufacture white lead had been made. The pots were set, but an almost insurmountable difficulty arose when an attempt was made to collect a quantity of dung for use in the process of heating the crude lead. At the same time Wilt succeeded in gathering a sufficient quantity to make about 1000 pounds of white lead.[61] There were no heavy teams kept in Saint Louis, and the people, Wilt complained, exposed the dung to all weather where it lost its strength. He wrote:

The inhabitants use no straw to litter their horses. We intend trying grass as a substitute. You know that when rotting it somewhat burns. Of course, the heat it contains must equal that of dung. The cost will only be the cutting and hauling. Henderson thinks he can work it by steam by a plan different from any yet invented. This plan is to make the white lead without dung, which cannot be procured in sufficiently large quantities, and to use strong lye instead of vinegar.[62] His ideas are good but time will tell. Bulan of Pittsburgh manufactured some white lead by boiling, but did not succeed in making it white.[63]

58 Wilt to Hertzog, October 22, 1814.

59 Wilt to Andrew Wilt, October 15, 1814.

60 Wilt to Hertzog, November 5, 1814.

61 Wilt to Hertzog, March 20, 1813.

62 Vinegar or acetic acid is used in the manufacture of white lead by the old Dutch process. Bezanson, Anne, *Wholesale Prices in Philadelphia 1784–1861* (Philadelphia, 1936), p. 145 n.

63 Wilt to Hertzog, May 29, 1813.

"If he succeeds," Wilt wrote later, "Henderson will be able to turn out one hundred tons annually." And he added, "hope to God he may succeed."[64] During the summer, while the furnaces were being repaired, Wilt collected enough lead to make 50,000 pounds of red lead, and within a short time Henderson had calcined and colored 36,000 pounds of this quantity.

At the opening of the year 1815 crude lead was still scarce. The price at Sainte Genevieve was 9½ cents,[65] but as the United States had not yet paid the troops, Wilt had not been able to collect sufficient funds to purchase the ore. He decided to convert all the crude lead he had on hand into red lead, and drop the manufacture of shot until he could collect money to buy enough crude lead to supply both of his factories. This would mean no loss as both shot and red lead, which was of ready sale, were quoted in Philadelphia at 16 cents a pound.

The *Captain Porter,* the barge which Wilt had built and which he declared to be "the best boat on these waters," left Saint Louis March 7, 1815, with 58,583 pounds of red lead, some beaver and deerskins.[66] A veritable fleet of boats carrying pig lead had already left Saint Louis, others were preparing to follow, and with such a quantity of the metal in the market, prices would necessarily drop.

Wilt advised his brother Andrew in Pittsburgh to sell the cargo of the *Captain Porter* directly from the boat, to reload her with flour, and to send her direct to New Orleans where the returns for her load could be invested in sugar at $8 to $9 per cwt. He hoped that the bar lead, which Drinker had taken down, and which was still in New Orleans, might be sold to the United States for Jackson's army and the money used to buy the Southern produce that he needed in Saint Louis.[67]

On May 14 Captain Andrews' boat dropped down the river from Saint Louis, carrying 31,464 pounds of red lead, 6 kegs

64 Wilt to Hertzog, July 24, 1813.
65 Wilt to Andrew Wilt, January 7, 1815.
66 Wilt to Hertzog, March 13, 1815.
67 Wilt to Andrew Wilt, February 27, 1815

of white lead weighing 940 pounds, and 156 pounds of the first quality of beaver, 65 pounds of shaved deerskins, and 294 raccoons.[68] The white lead was sold along the Ohio at not less than 20 cents, and the red lead at 16 cents a pound. However, before Captain Andrews reached Pittsburgh the price had fallen to 12 cents, but even at that price Wilt could still sell at a profit.

As the spring wore on the speculation in crude lead ceased, and the price dropped, probably because of the report that the lead trade at the Mississippi mines was to be revived. In March the price had fallen to 6½ cents at Sainte Genevieve, and later at Herculaneum to 5 cents, with a possibility of its going down to 4 cents. Taking advantage of the drop in price, Wilt invested all the money he was able to collect in lead for both the shot and the red lead factory.

Later in May the Zanesville, Ohio, glassmakers proposed to contract for Wilt's red lead at the market price, a proposition worthy of consideration.[69] Bakewell, too, offered to make a contract to take the red lead and quoted a price of 10 cents, but Wilt would consider nothing less than 12 cents per pound, for pig lead in Saint Louis was worth 6 cents. The freight to Pittsburgh would be at least 3 cents, and the manufacturing could hardly be done for less than 2 cents. After some bickering Bakewell accepted Wilt's terms.

Wilt realized that in order to fulfill these contracts the factory must be kept in constant operation. For this laborers were absolutely necessary, but it was difficult, because of the increased militia drafts to keep men at work, particularly during the spring and summer. Henderson had gone with the spring expedition, and Harry Cauld, the colored man, who was the only person able to calcine and color the lead, now that Henderson was away, became ill of lead colic and died April 16, 1815. Wilt looked upon this as a terrible calamity, not alone because of the loss of his helper, but because of the difficulty he would experience in hiring hands for the factory as his "countrymen were very ap-

68 Wilt to Andrew Wilt, May 8, 1815; Wilt to Hertzog, May 15, 1815.
69 Wilt to Andrew Wilt, May 29, 1815.

prehensive of there being danger in the work."[70] The only person he had left to help was the negro boy, Stephen, and he was put at the coloring furnace soon after Cauld died. He, too, became ill but recovered and was able to go on with the work until more helpers were found.[71] All during the summer the furnaces were kept going, but Wilt thought it advisable not to send any red lead up the Ohio until all the pig lead that had gone up in the spring (in expectation of war prices) had been sold, or until the owners had been obliged either to sell at reduced prices or to leave their lead stored in Pittsburgh.

Since the eastern markets, early in 1815, were glutted with lead, Wilt proposed to open a warehouse for the red and white lead in New Orleans. He had retailed in Saint Louis 1000 pounds of the white lead at 37½ cents a pound, and since foreign goods were not coming into the southern port, the price there should be not less than 75 cents. But Messrs. Hepburn and Pleasants, his agents in that city, reported that unless the Saint Louis lead could be sold for less than the lead imported before the blockade, they could effect no sales. There is evidence that little was done in the lead business at New Orleans, probably because of the military operations in and about the city.

When the Indians were "handsomely drubbed" and fully subdued, Wilt hoped that business would revive and that this would cause "the western country to thrive immensely" and grow in population, in trade, and in wealth. He was confident that a large share of the increase in trade would flow to his establishment and he would thus be repaid for his patience in enduring the misfortunes of the preceding troublous years.

In April, 1813, shortly after the red lead factory began operation, Wilt had written to Hertzog:

Were I not afraid you might think we have too many irons in the fire, I would mention to you a proposition of Honey. He has offered to establish a shot factory to consist of three partners, himself, us, and young Mickau [St. Amand Mickau] who makes Mack-

70 Wilt to Andrew Wilt, April 17, 1815.
71 Wilt to Hertzog, April 24, 1815.

lot's shot and who, Honey says, is the best hand to cast shot of any in the territory. He says he can have a lot of about 2 acres with a rock on it, presented to him if he builds a factory on it. This place is on the Mississippi, about one mile above Austin's factory and on the same rock. We should have to build with logs to make it high enough (which are handy) to drop shot, and dig a well about 17 feet deep. He allows it would cost $1500 to establish it and that he could work at all times, which Macklot and Austin cannot on account of particular winds. He says Macklot can make 300,000 per annum and charges 2½ cents per pound for making. He says we could get a portion of the lead from all the mines in the vicinity. The yield in 1811 from the Shibboleth mine alone was 5,000,000 pounds of ore, which gave 3,125,000 pounds of lead. This supply alone would insure metal for the tower. The road from Shibboleth being so much better than the roads from the other mine, Honey thinks we would have done well to have established our red lead factory there and wood is so much cheaper. I think in time it may do to attack this business, as in times of peace we can draw all our lead for the factory here, from the Spanish mines and the store at Herculaneum would make perhaps enough for the shot factory. Have told Honey I would consider upon it but at present could not think of engaging in new business.[72]

In July, 1813, Macklot, who in 1809 had built at Herculaneum the first shot tower in the Missouri territory, offered to sell his establishment for $15,000. He assured prospective buyers that a person having enough capital to keep 100,000 pounds of lead always on hand could make from $20,000 to $25,000 a year by sending shot to Pittsburgh and other Ohio towns.[73] It was the consensus of opinion that Macklot had made money in the shot business because, although he was deeply in debt in 1809 when he went to Herculaneum, by 1813 he had paid up all his obligations and had invested money in Negro slaves. To have a number of slaves on one's plantation was considered a sign of prosperity and Macklot's wealth was estimated at $25,000, a veritable fortune in those pioneer days. Although he

72 Wilt to Hertzog, April 17, 1813.
73 Wilt to Hertzog, July 31, 1813.

claimed that he did not have sufficient capital to carry on the business as it should be conducted, there was a more important reason for his giving up the shot tower. His health had failed and when, early in the spring of 1813, one of his little children died, he could no longer be persuaded to remain in the town. Macklot's property at Herculaneum, according to Wilt, was not worth $15,000, but he was anxious to buy a suitable site for the erection of a shot tower, as he felt that it would make a good investment. He informed Hertzog:

I now approve of the shot tower as it certainly appears to me more safe and profitable than even merchandise at the present quotation of goods, and for many reasons even more promising than the manufacture of either white or red lead. First, because of the improbability of manufacturing the white lead in sufficient quantities to make it worth while unless Henderson's new plan should succeed; second, our experience in realizing little profit from the red lead, and third, judging from the returns Macklot drew from his shot, the business must be a profitable one.[74]

Although Macklot had been successful, Wilt felt confident that he could carry on the business to even better advantage. Linen for bags had cost Macklot 37½ cents to 50 cents a yard, and for all other imported articles he had paid in like proportion; his boxes cost 50 cents apiece. Wilt could get the goods for the shot bags from the eastern markets with the consignments for his stores at much lower rates than Macklot had paid, and his boxes also would cost less than Macklot's. Moreover Macklot had manufactured shot for other people and had made little profit from it. Because of the heavy expenses incurred in the conduct of his business, he had been able to ship to the eastern firms only a small quantity each year. For several years past shot had been bringing from $11 to $14 a cwt., in the eastern markets, and Macklot thus missed a source of income that would have brought him lucrative returns. With a "capital then of $10,000 and with no misfortune or ill luck before us", Wilt calculated that a shot tower would clear itself in a year.

74 Wilt to Hertzog, January 15, 1814.

Instead of accepting either Macklot's offer, or the two acres John Honey offered for sale, Wilt purchased from Jonathan Kendall in August, 1813, the New Hartford tract containing 640 arpents in Jefferson County.[75] An execution bond had been taken out against the property, and since Kendall was in need of money to meet his obligations, he sold the land for $800.[76] Before purchasing, Wilt consulted several of the leading men of Saint Louis who "allowed the place was a handsome one, abounding in springs some of which would serve as a site for a distillery and the bargain a good and cheap one." The little town of New Hartford, now known as Illinois Station, was two or three miles nearer to the Richwood mines than Herculaneum,[77] and since the transportation of lead from the mines to the town must be considered, this shorter distance was of no small moment. The wagoners with their heavy loads drawn by slow, patient ox-teams would choose the route to the nearer town, provided always that they could get the same price for their lead and find the goods as cheap as at Herculaneum. A new road from the mines to New Hartford was built, and the young prospector envisioned his new town as a busy place rivaling in trade and commerce, not only Herculaneum, but the other towns along the Mississippi.

On the new purchase was a rock fifty-seven feet high, which was suitable for a shot factory, and Wilt estimated that two buildings, one on top and another at the base of the rock, with a deep trench along the bottom of the cliff, could be built for $3000. In September, 1813,[78] the plans were complete. The lumber for the building was brought up the river from Sainte Genevieve. In November Septlivres hauled 1000 feet of flooring planks; 1000 feet of planks one inch wide and 500 feet, 1½ inch, from Depestre, De Mun & Co., who charged $3.50 per thousand feet but were willing to wait until spring for payment.

75 Original Deed Book, K, p. 375, Saint Louis City Hall.

76 Wilt to Hertzog, August 28, 1813; Oct. 9, 1813.

77 Wilt to Hertzog, July 31, 1813.

78 Wilt to J. N. Honey, September 25, 1813.

With the help of four hands, Barlett, the carpenter, promised to have the work finished in two months but the "plans of mice and men gang aft agley" and the building at New Hartford was no exception.

In the early spring the heavy timber for the factory was all cut, ready to be hauled; "three hands were framing and a good deal of digging was already done."[79] In early June, Wilt expected to raise the factory "in three weeks or less from this time, and hope to be ready for shot making in a month after the raising."[80] But one detects a tone of disappointment and almost of reproach in his letter to Andrew, when he said: "We commenced raising the shot tower last week and should have got up the first story which is the most difficult, in a day, had you sent me the blocks ordered. As it is, the first story was nearly raised but since then nothing has been done for want of hands."[81]

The following month brought more disappointment, for so many "men have been drafted will be a hindrance to the finishing of our shot tower as soon as it otherwise would have been done. It would have been done in two or three weeks. I shall, I hope, be able to send a little to Pittsburgh in the fall." Later in the month the tackles or blocks, as he called them, reached Saint Louis, "but they were a disgrace to the maker. The wood is shrunk and twisted and one of the sheaves will not turn. The rope also appears to be too large for the blocks. The pees are broken and the iron powdery."[82] Yet "hope springs eternal in the human breast," and on the last day of the old year, with the task still unfinished for want of building material and disappointment in workmen, Wilt, "hoped to be ready in the course of two weeks if we have lead."

According to specifications, the lower part of the main building, which was built on top of the rock, instead of being made of logs, was frame: that is, twelve upright posts each thirteen inches square were placed so as to form a tower 30 feet square. This made for solidity and durability. The upper part of the building ran narrower. The entire structure, 53 feet high, was weather-boarded from the base of the rock up to the roof, which was shingled. There were two doors, two windows, and a wooden floor. Here the smelting and casting of the lead was carried on. At the base of the rock an eighteen foot trench was dug and filled with water into which the melted lead was dropped from the tower through copper sieves. The fall from the top of the tower was 150 feet, which was deeper than either Macklot's or Austin's and permitted the formation of more perfect buck shot and bullets. Another building was erected at the bottom of the hill where the shot was polished, sorted, and packed for shipment. The cost of erection, not including material, was $700.

The cost of manufacture was trifling and the equipment inexpensive, but trifling or expensive, everything had to be brought by boat from the eastern markets to the new plant. The first order for equipment included the following items: 300 pounds of white arsenic, which was an essential in making shot (on an average three pounds of the oxide was required to make 1000 pounds of lead but the amount used depended upon the size of the bullets to be made); shot irons or flat sheets of iron, which were perforated with a set of uniform sized holes through which, from the top of the tower the melted lead was poured into the water beneath; a keg of black lead, a better and more effective quality than that used for stoves; and punches, which were much like shoe punches. The latter were used to make holes in the deerskins through which the sorted shot was sifted. The punches were assorted according to the different sized shot, the numbers varying from 0, which was larger than BB, to No. 12; these punches lasted only about a month and it was necessary to have a large assortment on hand. A drying pan, too, was needed which must be 4½ by 3 feet and 4 inches high, and edged with thick wire.[83] The pan had not come on July 3, 1815, nearly a year after Wilt had ordered it, and with some annoyance he

83 Wilt to Andrew Wilt, September 10, 1814.

wrote Andrew: "You have neglected sending me the drying pan invoiced for September 10 last. It would seem that my best way is to get such things here and pay three prices for them."[84] A shot stamp with the different numbers was used to mark the bags containing the different sized shot. The empty bags were stamped with the name of the firm and after they were filled the number of the shot was added. The blacking used in stamping was made of lampblack and linseed oil with a little turpentine.

To provide bags for shot offered little difficulty, but to provide boxes proved a real problem. Able carpenters were, according to Wilt, not to be had in or about Saint Louis. At New Hartford, where lumber was valued at $2 per hundred, Honey contracted for some boxes which would hold 300 pounds (English weight), at 10 cents apiece. In addition to the expense for boxes, Honey was responsible for the board of the carpenters who were making them. Wilt wrote: "Cannot you arrange the boarding of the hands by giving them provisions? Bread and meat is sufficient."[85]

Saint Amand, Macklot's shot maker, who was to direct the manufacture of the shot, was to receive a salary of $500 a year for his services.[86] Ten hands were to be employed at $3 a week and each one was expected to manufacture, bag, and box 500 pounds a day,[87] but owing to the scarcity of hands, Wilt succeeded in hiring only two men besides Saint Amand.

In manufacturing shot Macklot procured the lead according to French weight, and returned it in shot, according to English weight,[88] charging 2¼ cents per pound for the finished product. Wilt calculated his expenses per 1000 pounds from $6.75 to $10, and he determined to meet this expense, as Macklot had done, by the difference between English and French weights. The shot going to Philadelphia and Pittsburgh was packed according to

84 Wilt to Andrew Wilt, July 3, 1815.

85 Wilt to Honey, June 12, 1815.

86 Wilt to Hertzog, June 5, 1815.

87 Wilt to Hertzog, January 15, 1814.

88 Wilt to Hertzog, January 15, 1814.

size, in bags of twenty-eight pounds each, and all bags of the same number were packed in one box. The boxes were then strapped with thongs of bullhide at the ends to prevent them from bursting.

With a capital of $10,000, Wilt calculated the output should be 600,000 pounds per annum. New Orleans offered a large buying market. There shot had been bringing from $11 to $13 per hundred. In Pittsburgh and Philadelphia, prices were slightly higher. In Saint Louis, Wilt retailed 10,000 pounds a year at 12 to 16 cents per pound, and his profits on his own manufactured product should, according to his reckoning, be $7000 per annum. The dream, a roseate one, did not materialize immediately.

In September, 1813, lead sold at 4½ cents;[89] in December, it was 5½ cents;[90] January, 1814, found it at 6 cents and later it rose to 7 and 7½ cents.[91] On February 12, 1814, Wilt wrote:

Lead has been so scarce and continues (to be) that I am not able to procure any let alone for merchandise. Smith pays cash for all the lead he buys and is one of those who wishes to rule the market and let no other than himself get any. He intends doing as much with lead and furs. . . . He has funds, as he is connected in his lead purchases, with people in Lexington. But business being so dull, I have been unable to get any cash and to barter any quantity of goods for lead is out of the question.[92]

There was expectation that lead would come from the Spanish mines on the Mississippi, but these hopes were blighted by the failure of the United States troops at Detroit and Fort Meigs, a defeat which meant that these mines would be unprotected from the attacks and depredations of the red men.

In March, 1814, Wilt followed Honey's suggestion and opened a store at the southwestern Missouri mines in order to

89 Wilt to Andrew Wilt, September 20, 1813.
90 Wilt to Hertzog, December 4, 1813.
91 Wilt to Hertzog, January 15, 1814.
92 Wilt to Hertzog, February 12, 1814.

procure the lead he so much needed.[93] At the same time he allowed Honey to contract for 50,000 pounds at 7 cents.[94] During
the years 1814 and 1815 there was little or no money in the
country, and the demands of military service left the mines idle,
thus causing an acute scarcity of lead. As a consequence, prices
soared. In April, 1815, Wilt wrote "I have no shot yet tho' I
expect to hear of some being made. If I had lead would make it
into shot and send it to you. My case is desperate, having no
money to buy with."[95]

Two new discoveries of lead had been made in the early spring
of 1815, and dealers hoped that the supply would now be plentiful. But in spite of the new mines, lead continued scarce and the
following spring the supply was still greatly reduced, and the
manufacture of shot had not yet begun.

Wilt wrote to Honey who was directing the work of the shot
tower at New Hartford, "I am almost tired of disappointment,"
but still not losing faith, he added, "it will go on regular as clock
work when started. Have you money to buy a few thousand
pounds of lead? If so, do so. If you can, make it into shot in the
course of two weeks, No. 1–2–3."[96] Later in the month he wrote,
"we have nearly 2000 pounds of shot almost finished which
would have been ere this, had the sifters answered but these
sifters having been made of too thin stuff, shrunk. We are now
waiting for another set."[97] In the middle of May, Wilt reported
"we are entirely out of lead except 10,000 to 12,000 pounds at
Herculaneum which I intend making into shot and sending to
Pittsburgh my first opportunity."[98] Almost a year later, in June,
1815, he observed to Honey, "you have at last got the shot tower
in operation and although we have no lead to manufacture, I am
rejoiced at it. Hope you will lose no time in finishing what you

93 Wilt to Honey, March 5, 1814.
94 Wilt to Andrew Wilt, March 19, 1814.
95 Wilt to Andrew Wilt, April 3, 1815.
96 Wilt to Honey, April 3, 1815.
97 Wilt to Hertzog, April 24, 1815.
98 Wilt to Hertzog, May 15, 1815.

have of lead on hand. Hire hands for a short time unless you have expectation of getting lead or the manufacturing of it for others."[99]

In June, 1815, after two years of delay, disappointment, and frustration, the shot tower was ready for operation. On July 3, 1815, Wilt forwarded to Pittsburgh by John Evans, 14 boxes of shot weighing 4088 pounds,[100] and a little later another consignment of 4000 pounds by the *Speedy Return*.[101] The quality of the cargoes compared favorably with an equal amount of English patent shot, and this Wilt hoped would assure ready cash sales in the eastern market, as he was straitened for money to buy lead for both factories. Late in August, Wilt was able to send Honey $240 in bank notes and $260 in specie to purchase lead. At this time prospects for the opening of the Mississippi mines again brightened, but Wilt "preferred to see the United States drub the Sacs handsomely and then have the mines worked by white men." This he felt would make lead abundant.

On August 9, 1815, Wilt contracted with Keen and Levy to manufacture 10,000 pounds of shot at $2\frac{1}{4}$ cents a pound. They were to deliver the lead at Herculaneum and, according to the agreement, Wilt was to haul it to New Hartford at his own expense. The shot when finished was to be put into bags but not boxed. If Keen could procure lead he wanted an additional 10,000 pounds manufactured. Saint Amand began the manufacture of the lead,[102] and Honey moved from Herculaneum to New Hartford to direct the work. To indemnify Honey for the depreciation of his property in Herculaneum, that he would experience in promoting the town of New Hartford, Wilt allowed him $400. His wages were to be $900 a year, which at that time was a high salary, "but I believe him better worth that," wrote Wilt, "than most persons are worth half the

99 Wilt to Honey, June 12, 1815.
100 Wilt to Andrew Wilt, July 3, 1815.
101 Wilt to Andrew Wilt, August 7, 1815.
102 Wilt to Honey, August 9, 1815.

amount. He is attentive to business and ingenious in the shot tower."

The shot business, with all its disappointments and worries, was a safer and a more profitable undertaking than even merchandising at the prevailing cost of goods. The high price brought by lead stimulated the miners who were anxious to benefit by the advance and who, at different times, collected and placed upon the market large quantities of the metal. The only shipping points on the upper Mississippi were at Herculaneum and Ste. Genevieve, and within less than three years after the close of the war, more than 1,034,990 pounds of pig and bar lead, in addition to 1,356,700 pounds of patent shot, were exported from Herculaneum alone.[103] Moses Austin, had erected a shot tower at Herculaneum and here he brought his lead from Mine á Breton, a distance of thirty-six miles at a cost of seventy cents a hundred weight.[104] During six months, from February 20, to September 20, 1817, 23,531 pounds of crude ore were brought to the tower, where it was manufactured into shot and either exported or sold to local buyers. When Macklot, who was the first to erect a shot tower in the Louisiana territory, discontinued his business, he left Austin as Wilt's sole competitor. Wilt's tower at New Hartford was completed in January, 1815, and from December, 1816 to June, 1818, a period of eighteen months, Wilt and Elias Bates, a nephew of Moses Austin and owner of a warehouse at Herculaneum, exported 668,350 pounds of patent shot valued at $46,784.50.[105] Thus in spite of Austin's competition, when lead became cheaper and more plentiful after the war, the shot factory continued to be a profitable venture.

103 Schoolcraft, *op. cit.,* p. 125.
104 *Austin Papers,* I, 322.
105 *Louisiana Gazette,* June 26, 1818.

CHAPTER VI
PROBLEMS IN TRANSPORTATION

AFTER nearly a year and a half spent in preparation, the Saint Louis red lead was ready to be shipped from the West to compete in eastern markets with the imported product of the English factories. To manufacture lead was one thing; to transport it to the eastern markets was quite another, for in the days of flat and keel boats, sending heavy freight by water was a perilous undertaking. To carry a cargo up the Ohio, in spite of the difficulties and dangers attendant upon that route, seemed safer than to ship it to New Orleans where, during the war, it might lie for months awaiting a vessel to carry it around to Philadelphia. Moreover, should any American boat attempt to proceed along the coast to Philadelphia it would run the risk of being captured by British frigates on the high seas.[1]

In early March, 1813, Wilt engaged Burk, a boatman, to carry up the Ohio at three cents a pound, the first cargo of red lead made in Saint Louis, and the first manufactured west of the Mississippi. David Keely of Florissant, "a trusty person although in needy circumstances", was to go as a passenger on Burk's boat. Wilt commissioned him to sell a small quantity of the red lead along the Ohio at 15 cents a pound, knowing that the "potters would be glad to purchase at that price."[2] When Keely reached Pittsburgh he was instructed to give an account of the proceeds of his sales to Andrew Wilt, to whom the cargo was consigned. Before Burk's boat left Saint Louis, March 13, 1813, with its seventy-two kegs of red lead weighing 14,248 pounds, Kerr, Scott, Lindell, and Captain Andrews had sent their boats to Pittsburgh loaded with pig lead. Wilt notified his brother Andrew to make arrangements for the sale of the red lead even before Keely reached his city—lest the potters, merchants, and glassmakers be induced to buy the cheaper pig lead, which was on its way to the East in such great quantities.

1 Wilt to Hertzog, August 23, 1812.
2 Wilt to David Keeley, March 13, 1813.

When the new red lead product reached Pittsburgh the manufacturers subjected it to a searching scrutiny. The glassmakers
found some small particles in the paste which they called metallic
lead. They insisted that this would spoil the quality of their glass,
and they objected[3] to the price, which they maintained was too
high. Bakewell,[4] who manufactured red lead on a small scale
for his glass factory, offered only 10 cents a pound, a price that
would allow, with the cost of the crude lead at 6 cents in Saint
Louis, and the freight at 3 cents, only one cent for manufacturing. The quality of the red lead, together with the expense
attendant on its manufacture and its transportation, warranted
12½ cents wholesale and 15 cents retail, and Wilt refused to
accept less. Although Bakewell declined to pay Wilt's price, the
red lead found ready purchasers among the other glassmakers
of the city.

Rather than buy at Wilt's price, Bakewell continued to make
his own red lead, and later in the year bargained with Rozier[5]
of Sainte Genevieve for crude lead at 9 cents. This was
a bad bargain; lead was selling for 4¾ to 5 cents and
freight was 3 cents (for Rozier's transportation costs were no
less than Wilt's).[6] The expense would more than exceed
the contract price and Rozier could not afford to continue such
an agreement. In November, when crude lead was so scarce it
was difficult to secure in any quantity, Bakewell offered Wilt
10½ cents for the red lead. Wilt would not accept less than 14
cents, for should peace be established (and there were continued
rumors of peace) pig lead, owing to its scarcity, would be
worth 7 cents in Saint Louis.[7] To sell red lead in Pittsburgh at
10½ cents would be making worse than a bad bargain.

Just a month after Burk left Saint Louis another boatload
was ready for the East. On April 6, 1813, Wilt's own boat, the

3 Wilt to Andrew Wilt, August 14, 1813.
4 Bakewell, Benjamin, of the firm of Bakewell, Page & Bakewell.
5 Ferdinand Rozier, merchant of Sainte Genevieve.
6 Wilt to Andrew Wilt, September 20, 1813.
7 Wilt to Andrew Wilt, November 20, 1813.

Dolphin, started down the Mississippi with a cargo of 139 kegs of red lead weighing 27,067 pounds, 22 otterskins, and 700 pounds of bar lead.[8] The patroon was John A. Cameron, one-time Indian interpreter, "a pushing fellow and of some address". With him went young Papin, a member of one of the old French families of Saint Louis.[9] Cameron's instructions were to barter the bar lead along the way for provisions; the furs were destined for Philadelphia, but the red lead was to be sold or bartered for country linens, cotton stripes, stoneware, and cordage. The cash value of the lead was 15 cents, and for barter the value was reckoned to be from 18 to 20 cents, while the kegs were to be sold at 62½ cents apiece.[10] Cameron was appointed to keep an account of the sales of the bar and of the red lead, of the provisions purchased or bartered, of the disbursements for the boat, and of the advances of cash made to the crew,[11] the members of which had been hired by the month.

Cameron hoped to make the trip in three months. When he started the Mississippi was very high. This might have prevented a rapid passage, but the winds were favorable and Berthold, who was returning with his spring goods, reported that he saw Cameron "mounting the river rapidly."[12] On April 14 the *Dolphin* reached the mouth of the Cumberland. As the boat went farther up the Ohio, the high waters allowed her to make only six to seven miles a day, but Cameron wrote that he had overtaken boats that had left Saint Louis long before he had started and that Burk was only four days ahead of him.[13] May 4th found Cameron at Yellow Banks, 150 miles below the Falls, which he hoped to reach before the 29th of the month. Forty-five days was considered a quick trip from Saint Louis to the Falls

8 Wilt to Hertzog, April 10, 1813; Wilt to Cameron, Apr. 6, 1813.

9 Son of Villais Papin, then one of the principal blacksmiths of Saint Louis. Chittenden, I, 9–10.

10 Wilt to John A. Cameron, April 6, 1813.

11 Wilt to Cameron, April 17, 1813.

12 Wilt to Cameron, April 13, 1813.

13 Wilt to Andrew Wilt, May 29, 1813; Wilt to Hertzog, May 29, 1813.

at a stage of high waters, but Cameron expected to make it in even less time. After passing Louisville, he reached Marietta, Ohio, on June 19 and came to his destination on the 27th of June.

Along the way Cameron had made numerous sales. At Charlestown, now Wellsburg, West Virginia, Thomas Bakewell, brother of Benjamin and later a member of the glass company of Pittsburgh, "had an extensive stoneware manufactory."[14] He offered Cameron $14 per cwt., for the red lead, but the invoice price was $15, and Cameron hesitated. Wilt advised him by letter: "Our object being to sell our lead, take $14 per cwt., . . . though I think by hard screwing (which quality you possess) you might obtain $15."[15]

Young Papin, who had taken passage with Cameron, had gone to Pittsburgh to purchase equipment for his new blacksmith shop. Wilt sent word to Andrew, in Pittsburgh, to get the tools from the blacksmith and pay for them in trade, which "was the strength of the Pittsburgh merchants", and to sell to Papin for cash. Andrew carried out his orders.

Since the hands on the boat had been hired by the month, it would not do to delay in Pittsburgh an hour longer than was necessary. The return cargo consisted of glassware, iron, porter, and 50 barrels of whiskey, that had been purchased for not more than 37½ cents a gallon.[16] Cameron found his load in readiness and without delay he turned his boat down the Ohio. At the mouth of the Cumberland he picked up several bales of Georgia cotton which James Baird of Nashville had purchased and sent up for Wilt.[17] His journey, which at the beginning promised a quick return, was delayed because of the high waters, and he brought the *Dolphin* into port at the foot of Market Street on the evening of August 5—four, not three, months after leaving Saint Louis.

14 Cramers, Vadox, *Navigator* (Pittsburgh, 1821), p. 70.
15 Wilt to Cameron, April 17, 1813.
16 Wilt to Andrew Wilt, March 20, 1813; Wilt to Andrew Wilt, March 27, 1813.
17 Wilt to James Baird, July 10, 1813.

The porter that formed part of the return load was unsatisfactory—"only muddy grounds" according to Wilt, and so badly corked that few bottles could be used. Price and Hempstead bought three barrels of the porter and assured Wilt that it was of an inferior grade. "If you order any more porter from the same man you got the last from", wrote Wilt to Andrew, direct him "to cork the bottles better and give you better porter."[18] "Keep a sharp lookout", he cautioned, "on those Pittsburgh Rookies."[19]

In the meantime, Edward Hempstead[20] who had come back from Washington by way of Pittsburgh, brought a letter from Andrew who assured Wilt that he could easily sell a load of red lead. Wilt was anxious to get as much of his product on the eastern market as possible and on April 18, only two weeks after Cameron started down the Mississippi, he sent by freight 56 kegs weighing 10,011 pounds. He contracted with Campbell[21] to take the cargo at 3 cents per pound, but Clemson,[22] the principal owner of the boat, refused to take the load for less than 3½ cents. This was at an advance of one-half cent per pound, but Wilt accepted because it was as low or lower than he could freight it himself, and Clemson, rather than take the cargo for less than 3½ cents, would have purchased pig lead. Had he done this he would have injured Wilt's sale at Pittsburgh by overstocking the market.

Sending cargoes on heavily loaded keelboats up the Ohio was a problem not only of expense but of expediency. To get to Pittsburgh so as to dispose of the red lead to the glassmakers and potters before the vendors of pig lead reached the city, and to return with all possible speed with goods and whiskey for the Saint Louis store, was the aim Wilt set before every patroon as he pushed his boat away from the wharf at Saint Louis. The

18 Wilt to Andrew Wilt, August 21, 1813.
19 Wilt to Andrew Wilt, September 4, 1813.
20 Edward Hempstead of Saint Louis.
21 John Campbell of Saint Louis, later Lieutenant of U. S. Infantry.
22 Captain E. B. Clemson, U. S. Infantry, headquarters at Bellefountaine.

ordinary keel carried twenty or thirty thousand pounds and needed eight or ten men to propel it, but Wilt proposed to build his own boats and build them lower to the water line than the ordinary keel and large enough to carry fifty or sixty thousand pounds. These, he felt, could be managed by ten hands and each hand at $65 a trip, would reduce the cost of the voyage and at the same time make "rounding up" a crew a simple matter. The cost of a keel trip, to and from Pittsburgh, with its cordelle, poles, laborers, and provisions, was usually $1000.

When Cameron returned home August 5, 1813, and brought word that a steamboat of eighteen tons could be purchased for less than a thousand dollars, Wilt felt that the firm should invest in one at once; not in a small boat but in one of forty tons, which would probably cost six or seven thousand dollars, but it would pay for itself in five or six trips. To his brother he wrote:

I have premeditated a great profit indeed from the acquisition of one [steamboat]. I think at the immoderate price of $4000–$5000 for a large one it would pay for itself by running from here to Louisville, and from here to New Orleans, which must some day be a great depot for us unless we be diverted from our present plans of business.[23]

Instead of buying a steamboat, which he found upon investigation would be too costly, Wilt arranged for the building of a 30 ton barge to carry his lead to Pittsburgh. He hoped to pay for it partly in goods at the rate of $22 a ton.

It is to be regretted, at least from a commercial standpoint, that when on October 10, 1810, Robert Fulton and Robert R. Livingston addressed to the legislators of Upper Louisiana, who were holding session in Saint Louis, a memorial asking the exclusive right "to navigate the waters of your state or territory with boats moved by steam or fire", the request was not granted. Instead, after some consideration, the petition "was ordered to lie on the table." This decision delayed for several years the coming of the steamboat, for it was not until 1817 that the *Pike*, the first steamer on the upper Mississippi, reached Saint Louis.

23 Wilt to Andrew Wilt, September 25, 1813.

In June, 1813, hostilities raged all along the frontier. Nevertheless, another convoy of boats went down the Mississippi headed for the East. Thousands of pounds of crude lead made up the cargo. Among the shippers were Von Phul, Cabanné, Berthold & Co., and Smith. The latter took with him the pelts and furs which the Missouri Company had secured in the winter catch.[24] Prices on both lead and fur were high, and prospects of peace were still in the distant future.

On the morning of July 10 the *Betty,* Wilt's boat, left dock at Saint Louis with as much fuss and excitement, he said, as might be attendant on a ship leaving an eastern port. The *Betty* was the boat Massey brought back from Pittsburgh. She was small, and in consequence the expense was proportionately greater than that of sending a larger boat. Michael Ely, "who was much of a gentleman, a good accountant, and later clerk in the store at Saint Louis", acted as supercargo, with Liguest Chouteau as patroon. Each of the officers received $100 as remuneration,[25] while the men were hired for the trip at $65 "which was low enough." The boat carried a full cargo, consisting of 24,601 pounds of red lead, six packs of beaver weighing 608 pounds, 9 packs of bearskins containing 137 skins at a dollar apiece, 3 packs of buffalo robes, 1000 pounds of bar lead at $6.50 per cwt., 1000 pounds of shot at $7.50–$8 per cwt.

Ely was instructed to make the trip with all possible speed and to sell along the river. The red lead was invoiced at 15 cents a pound; buffalo robes (plain white) at $4 apiece, painted ones at from $5–$6. According to Ely's instructions, the red lead and buffalo robes might be traded for country linens at 50 cents a yard, tow linens at 25 cents, a good quality of chewing tobacco (10 or 15 kegs) for 10–12 cents, bed cords at $4 a dozen, or it might be bartered for any other products of the Valley that might have ready sale in Saint Louis. The bar lead was to sell at from 12½ to 15 cents a pound and would bring sufficient to purchase provisions at Cincinnati, which was the best place to

---

24 Wilt to Hertzog, June 26, 1813.
25 Wilt to Hertzog, July 10, 1813; Wilt to Andrew, July 3, 1813.

buy.[26] Money was scarce on the frontier, and since the owner of a boat must provide for the crew, a part of every cargo was set aside to be bartered for provisions along the way. The beaver and bearskins were to be delivered at Pittsburgh to Andrew Wilt, who had orders to dispatch them at once to Hertzog in Philadelphia. The beaver were from the upper waters of the Mississippi and "were mostly of the best quality." There had been sharp bidding when they were offered at auction. Kerr offered $2.25 per pound for the whole parcel, Smith and Von Phul bid $2.50, while Wilt paid $1 a pound for 125 pounds and $2.50 per pound for the balance, making the total cost of the 6 packs $1213.75[27] The Philadelphia hatters, who were the largest purchasers of furs, were willing to pay from $3 to $3.50 a pound for good beaver; for bearskins, unless the market was over-stocked, from $2 to $6 a pound.

On his way back to Saint Louis late in July Cameron met the *Betty* about 300 miles below the Falls. On August 5, the day Cameron reached Saint Louis, the *Betty* was at Louisville where Ely sold 30 buffalo robes; on the 16th of the month she had reached Cincinnati; at Marietta she passed Berthold, who was on his way back to Saint Louis, and late in September she docked at Pittsburgh. When the *Betty* reached Pittsburgh she was not only leaking badly, but needed caulking and a thorough over-hauling before beginning her homeward journey.

Could Andrew Wilt have exchanged her for a shorter and larger boat, one that could carry 40,000 pounds, much valuable time might have been saved. It took several weeks to make her seaworthy, and she did not leave the East until mid-October. Wilt expected her to bring his fall supply of dry goods, blankets, shoes, and coffee from Philadelphia and Pittsburgh. He wanted a large quantity of butcher, pen, and pocket knives, 50 dozen tin cups, some camp kettles, looking glasses, pudding pans, candle molds, writing paper, a few books of gold leaf, 6 boxes of pipes, kegs of nails, tar, and a ton of iron. Along the river Ely was

26 Wilt to Ely, July 9, 1813.
27 Wilt to Hertzog, July 10, 1813.

advised to pick up quantities of tow linen and flax. As flour was selling in Saint Louis at $18 a barrel, Ely determined, if the Pittsburgh price was high, to purchase flour, too, along the river. Whiskey was selling in Pittsburgh at 37½ cents, while in Saint Louis, Pennsylvania whiskey was worth ten cents more than Kentucky rye, so that a better investment could be made by buying liquors in the Pennsylvania town. The *Betty* reached Saint Louis about the 17th of November, loaded not only with Pittsburgh articles, whiskey, and tobacco, but with goods for Philipson and for Smith & Company, Wilt's strongest competitors. Ely's delay in Pittsburgh was an expensive one, for had he reached home in early October, at the same time as Lindell or Berthold, Wilt would have shared in equipping the Illinois Rangers to the possible amount of $2000 cash.

Cameron came into the home port with the *Dolphin* on August 5, and on September 15 with the *Red Bird* he started back to Pittsburgh with ten hands. This time he went as supercargo, and Joseph Morin was patroon. The cargo consisted of 113 kegs of red lead weighing 23,907 pounds; 300 buffalo robes; 122 bearskins bought at $1; 851 deerskins at $1.23; 2416 pounds of beaver at $52.06¼ per cwt.; 600 pounds of shot and about 3000 pounds of pig lead.[28] Cameron was told to sell or barter along the river at the following prices:[29]

Red lead	at 12½ cents
Buffalo robes	" $4–$5
Bearskins	" $2–$2.50
Deerskins	" 25¢–30¢
Shot	the more it brings the better
Beaver	at not less than $3

On September 20, Wilt wrote Cameron:

By the opportunity of McClurg leaving the place, I think it worthwhile dropping you an opinion of buffalo robes. Clark[30] now asks $3.50 for his, and I think you may obtain $5 for those you have, if you ask it, though they are invoiced at $4. Ely got $4 for the plain

28 Wilt to Hertzog, September 18, 1813.
29 Wilt to Cameron, September 15, 1813.

ones which were of a common quality, and $5 for painted ones that were not equal to your plain ones. Expect these must be good in Pittsburgh by the time you get there; therefore, the quicker you are in your voyage the better, Beat Manuel, 'tis your first object and I doubt not your success.[31]

On October first Cameron was at Yellow Banks and had sold robes at $4 apiece. His boat was leaking; the water had come in through the cracks in the floor and had damaged some of the robes. He contemplated exchanging boats with Ely on the river, but Wilt hoped his better judgment would prevent this as the *Betty's* cargo was more valuable and more liable to damage than that of the *Red Bird*. Three of his hands were sick, but he expected to be in Louisville by October 7 and in Pittsburgh by November 17.[32]

The lead in the *Red Bird* cargo was made in the furnaces that had been rebuilt during the summer months, and was superior to any that Henderson or Sparke had manufactured. It was of a good color and was free from those shining particles to which Bakewell and the other glassmakers had objected. These lumps, it was found, were due to subjecting the lead to too great heat, or permitting it to come in contact with the hot plate.[33] The new furnace eliminated this defect, producing an article that compared favorably with any imported from England.

The season was late so Cameron returned as soon as possible, for ice on the Mississippi might hinder his way up the river. His homeward cargo consisted of cordage, tobacco, linens, glassware, and 20 barrels of whiskey which was now selling in Saint Louis at 87⅓ cents to a dollar a gallon.[34] "Whiskey is 62½ cents in Kentucky", Wilt wrote to Andrew. "Hope you have sent the *Red Bird* back with a load of whiskey that costs 56 cents and when sold here will bring 87½ cents. I have not a drop. Iron I

30 General William Clark, U. S. Indian Agent.

31 Wilt to Cameron, September 20, 1813.

32 Wilt to Andrew Wilt, October 9, 1813.

33 Wilt to Hertzog, October 23, 1813.

34 Wilt to Hertzog, September 11, 1813; Wilt to Andrew, Nov. 20, 1813.

want. I now get 15 cents for it." At Cape Girardeau, Cameron stopped to get a quantity of pork which Daniel Steinbeck, a merchant of that little town, had purchased for Wilt.

Cameron brought the *Red Bird* to Saint Louis on the second of February, 1814, after a quick passage of 25 days from Pittsburgh. Fortune had favored him by keeping the river free from ice, a thing rather uncommon at that season of the year.[35] The *Red Bird* was too worn to weather the high waters of the Mississippi and Ohio Rivers again, but Wilt used her in bringing wood across the river from his lands on the L'Abbe Creek, where the only supply of wood for the red lead furnace could be secured.

On Tuesday, October 5, 1813, Wilt loaded another boat, the *Enterprise*. The patroon in this instance was Captain James Rankin who with his little family, lived in Saint Louis, where he enjoyed the respect of everyone. A. Septime, Louis Gregouri, Joseph Chenin, Ronore Dame, Louis Tobie, Joseph Mallet, Antonie Cabassier, and Alexander Page, all experienced boatmen, formed the crew.[36] They left Herculaneum with 23,155 pounds of pig lead, French weight, and 21 kegs of red lead amounting to 4731 pounds English weight.[37] The *Enterprise* was weak but she floated proudly down the river, as if promising to carry her cargo safe to port. It was late in the year, and the boat would scarcely have time to reach Pittsburgh before ice formed. Rankin's instructions to sell the red lead at 12 to 15 cents at Cincinnati, or leave it there on sale, were given him in the following letter:

Suppose by the time this letter reaches its destination you will be at or near Cincinnati and believing that a small quantity of red lead might be sold at that place—I have written Andrew Dunsett to receive from you two thousand pounds, for which you will please take his receipt. I think we will find an advantage from its lightening the boat for going through the Rapids. Should he however, give you no

35 Wilt to Hertzog, January 8, 1814.

36 Wilt to Andrew Wilt, October 9, 1813.

37 Wilt to Andrew Wilt, October 9, 1813; Wilt to Hertzog, October 16, 1813.

encouragement respecting the sale of it, you may continue on with it—I leave you to judge.[38]

Rankin was counseled to barter for tobacco at Louisville, at other places higher up the river, and to send the cargo back to Saint Louis by the first boat that would take it.

Since Wilt needed a representative at Cincinnati who would sell or barter his red lead for him, he ventured to send a message to Dunsett, who had formerly acted as agent for the firm but who had become estranged since the Mussina affair. He wrote as follows:

Being desirous of forming a correspondence with some respectable person in your place and knowing that you have formerly done business with my Uncle, Joseph Hertzog of Philadelphia, though estranged in some manner thru ill devising tricks of Z. Mussina, believing however that you can have no objection to reassume a business that may in the long run be advantageous to yourself and me, I have thought proper to write this day to Capt. Rankin on board my boat, the *Enterprise,* to leave two thousand pounds of red lead with you, do you give him any encouragement to suppose it can be sold with you—which I do not doubt since it is an article made great use of by painters and potters. You will please sell the red lead at 12½ cents the pound, and if you can have pay for the kegs besides, it would be desirable. The proceeds you can lay out in cordelles of a good quality—one-half inch thick and tarred; a few good cables, two or three dozen camp kettles, three or four dozen pudding pans assorted sizes, and a few barrels country "Sugar" if it can be had at 10 cents—or whiskey at a reasonable rate. Tobacco of a good quality would also answer and if any person should call for those articles with an order from myself or brother at Pittsburgh, you will please deliver them.[39]

Dussett must have accepted this offer, for on February 12, 1814, there was a large consignment of the red lead at his ware house in Cincinnati awaiting sale.

38 Wilt to Captain James Rankin, October 9, 1813.
39 Wilt to Andrew Dunsett, October 9, 1813.

Wilt was spared none of the many difficulties attendant upon business ventures. When Captain Rankin reached Marietta, Ohio, a Nathaniel Clark attached the cargo of the *Enterprise*, evidently for some debt of Rankin. Andrew went down from Pittsburgh, instituted a suit to regain the goods, and notified his brother, who sent the following communication:

Yours dated Marietta, Feb. 9, is to hand, I am not a little surprised at the information received by it—the whole proceeding, I consider most outrageous and the perpetrator (Clark) should be well handled for such infamous conduct. Knowing as I do that his proof to prove the property Rankin's could not authorize the like act, indeed in my humble opinion the honorable court in granting a continuance is hardly justifiable as it must thereby prevent the boat from reaching Pittsburgh, which may occasion a serious loss, in case of peace, or a diminution in the price of lead at Pittsburgh, besides the laying out of the funds therein invested. True this Clark (who cannot be a gentleman) may be sued for damages but may by that time prove insolvent—if this Clark should by means of foul play make the property Rankin's (which from the little dependence in courts and juries in this Western country might be the case) you can continue the suit as well as he has done, and which the court I hope will not pretend to refuse, until I can send depositions from here to knock down all opposition, believe I shall send on next mail Honey's deposition at any rate. I do not see why you could not replevy. When a person seizes things not his own, by giving security you can always replevy back which is all he could wish. By your giving security, take care you rate the damages sufficiently high. The invoice and every other paper in Rankin's possession will show to whom the property belongs. I have received no communication from J. L. Laidley, Esq. Rankin's actions are most likely caused by fear absurd as they are. You might I think replevy the property as mine, the replevin Law being for the purpose of recovering a man's property, no matter what may have been the pretext for seizing. A. Septlivres got at Herculaneum one buffalo robe $4 and Antoine Cabassier at same place sundries for $4.25. I have Honey's statement of advances to hand and repairs of boat with the pig lead. The only charge to Rankin is for provisions and boat furniture $261.94 which provisions he charges to me again and such expenses as he may make for the boat's use on the route as well as the balance due the hands, he crediting me with the amount of sales made on the route and such moneys as he receives for my account. In the $261.94 is included $100 cash advanced by Honey for purchasing provisions on the route. The boat was bought by Honey who you know is doing business for me at Herculaneum, of a Mr. Bates by his draft on Moses Austin in favor of James Bryant for $175 which with repairs makes her cost $225.62½

C. Wilt[40]

It was necessary to acquaint Hertzog with the unfortunate altercation between Clark and Andrew. This Wilt did in the following letter:

I received by this mail a letter from Andrew dated Marietta, Feb. 9. He has no doubt advised you of the contents relating to the attachmen laid on the boat *Enterprise* and cargo by one Nathaniel Clark, which appears to me one of the most scandalous things I ever heard. I hope that Clark is a man of property, that we may be able to recover damages from him since I am satisfied he can have no proof whatever to support his actions. I wonder in fact at the Court permitting him to continue his suit as Andrew has sufficient documents to show the owner of the property. I could next week send Honey's depositions of his having shipped it also for my acct., but A. writes me it can not reach the trial in time and that he has sufficient proof without, in the opinion of his attorney. A. writes me that Rankin has absconded, most probably through fear. We are certainly unfortunate in this country in regard to replevins and attachments. I felt somewhat uneasy on the receipt of his letter but when I consider the absurdity of the measure, the danger appears much less terrible than it at first did, as a court and jury can give but one verdict, which must be in our favor.[41]

The case did not come before a jury, as Andrew and Clark effected a compromise. This proceeding evidently satisfied Wilt, although doubts of Clark's honesty persisted. He wrote: "Your No. 30 is at hand, with the pleasing intelligence of Clark's hav-

40 Wilt to Andrew Wilt, March 12, 1814.
41 Wilt to Hertzog, March 12, 1814.

ing compromised . . . hope you may make him sweat for his temerity and that he has not played a trick by releasing his security which I understand to be the case and himself clears out in the meantime."[42] After the settlement at Marietta, Ohio, Andrew took the boat to Pittsburgh where Wilt hoped "her cargo may bring a good price."

Rankin fled from the scene of the trouble, but later returned to Saint Louis where Wilt attempted to settle with him. Andrew, however, had neglected to send a statement of the loading which he had received from Rankin. Wilt explained to Hertzog: "I am not able to settle with him and have said nothing to him about it. Honey tells me the house I thought he owned belongs to his son so that I do not expect to get much from him."[43] Since nothing further is found in Wilt's letters we may conclude that the entire affair was settled by the compromise between Clark and Andrew Wilt.

Wilt's boats plied between Saint Louis, Pittsburgh, and New Orleans until the close of the summer of 1815 when the "barging business" was discontinued. This was caused by readjustments which became necessary after the close of the War.[44]

42 Wilt to Andrew Wilt, April 16, 1814.
43 Wilt to Hertzog, June 11, 1814.
44 Wilt to Hertzog, July 31, 1815.

CHAPTER VII

VENTURES IN TRADE DURING THE WAR

THE outbreak of the War of 1812 was the signal for the merchants of St. Louis to raise the prices of their goods, for not only would the danger of Indian raids along the Ohio make transportation doubly hazardous, and communication with the East by way of New Orleans uncertain, but the supply of foreign goods so necessary to the Indian trade would become even more limited. Months before the declaration of hostilities the Non-Intercourse Act of 1811 and the activity of the French squadron on the high seas, and English cruisers along our coast, made it exceedingly difficult for any vessel except the English to enter our ports; yet some American merchantmen and a few Spanish and Portuguese bottoms brought in their cargoes,[1] the value of which had, through war insurance, freight, and war risk, been increased sometimes a hundred-fold.

Amelia Island and St. Mary's River became the scene of a great trade. American cotton and other products lined the shores waiting for foreign ships, and British vessels were discharging merchandise to be smuggled into the United States or taking on cotton or naval stores. This caused a two-fold loss to the United States. The American shipowner lost freight on American merchandise, and the United States government collected no duties on goods smuggled from Amelia Island, Bermuda, and Halifax. French and British goods were sold everywhere in disregard of the Non-Intercourse Act, which prohibited commerce between the United States and France and England.[2]

During the early spring months of 1812, when smuggling was rife, several ships loaded with dry goods, blankets, and crockery, found their way to Amelia Island under the pretense that the island belonged to East Florida and in consequence was Spanish

1 Hertzog to Wilt, June 6, 1812.

2 Adams, *op. cit.*, V, 165.

territory.[3] These goods, shipped directly across the intervening channel, a narrow passage of from two to four miles in length, were landed in the United States where they sold at an advance of 350 per cent.[4]

The United States government, according to Hertzog, bought the blankets and coarse cloth for use in the army, while the remaining goods "vanished quickly." Another consignment of British goods, which had run the gauntlet of the blockade, was sold in Philadelphia during the first week of June at the enormous increase of 400 per cent.[5] The price of coffee had risen 10 cents a pound, tea 50 cents, sugar $4 per cwt.,[6] Hyson tea 90 cents, while a consignment of 30,000 pounds of pepper was sold at 35 cents a pound.[7] Prices on all other imported articles advanced in the same proportion. In view of these advances in the eastern market Hertzog advised Wilt to raise the price on his goods in Saint Louis:

When you consider war freight, war insurance, absolute scarcity of goods, and the great spirit of speculation that prevails, you will not be extravagant to expect an addition of 100 per cent profit, and if you do not raise your prices high enough at once, depend upon it you will be tricked out of your goods . . . and be forced to do without supplies, for it will be impossible to send you any.[8]

Although Wilt was willing to earn a large income from his invested capital, he was wary lest excessive prices drive his customers away, for he knew that "people grumble a good deal at high prices."

On the North, too, the Canadian border with its forests, lakes, and rivers afforded many open doorways between British territory and the United States through which foreign goods might be brought into the western country. To guard this line of

3 Hertzog to Christian and Andrew Wilt, May 19, 1812.

4 *Ibid.*

5 Hertzog to Wilt, June 6, 1812.

6 Hertzog to Wilt, June 27; Ming's *Price Current* for June 27, 1812 (New York, 1812), confirms the rise in prices.

7 Hertzog to Sutton & McNickle, July 11, 1812.

8 Hertzog to Wilt, June 27, 1812.

wilderness, the government stationed troops at strategic points, and the state of New York called 1600 militia to patrol her frontier.[9] But in spite of these precautions Indian goods found their way into the trading posts, some being brought down from Montreal to Mackinac thence to Saint Louis by way of the Great Lakes and the Mississippi.[10]

In a complaining letter to Hertzog, Wilt wrote that Cabanné and Chenié, Saint Louis merchants, with Joseph Philipson as a silent partner, made two attempts to evade the Non-Intercourse Act along this northern route. The first was successful; the second, nearly disastrous. On the second occasion about eleven o'clock on the night of September 12, 1812, two boats, loaded with smuggled goods and patrooned by these men, dropped silently down the river and entered the port of Saint Louis. Scarcely had the boats touched the wharf when they were seized by a posse of citizens led by Captain Hempstead[11] who had his orders from Governor Howard. The two leaders and the entire crew were arrested. Governor Howard placed a guard on the boats and stored the confiscated goods in one of the taverns of the town.[12] The boats and their crews had hardly been taken into custody when another keel was brought to shore under guard. Thus there were three prizes in the port of Saint Louis at one time, evidence that unlawful trade was being carried on.[13] The following morning there was great consternation in the village when the identity of the prisoners became generally known, for both Chenié and Cabanné were successful business men and were highly esteemed by their fellow citizens.

Cabanné offered Governor Howard double the value of the goods as security if he would return them, and he promised to

9 Adams, *op. cit.*, VI, 344.

10 Wilt to Hertzog, September 13, 1812.

11 Captain Stephen Hempstead, Sr., father of Edward and Charles Hempstead.

12 Charles Gratiot to John J. Astor, September 27, 1812, Gratiot Letterbook, Missouri Historical Society Collections, St. Louis.

13 Wilt to Hertzog, September 13, 1812.

await the decision of the court as to the final disposition. The Governor refused not only the return of the goods but Cabanné's papers as well. Thereupon Cabanné petitioned the Secretary of the Treasury, Gallatin.

In October, at the last session of the General Court at Ste. Genevieve, a grand jury was selected to determine whether Cabanné had been at St. Joseph, Michigan, and whether Mackinac was in the possession of Great Britain at the time that the two men left the town with their merchandise. A true bill was brought in against them and they were compelled to give $30,000 as a pledge of their appearance at the May, 1813, term of court.[14] Charles Gratiot explained Cabanné's predicament in a letter to John Jacob Astor:

This excessive bail prevented Cabanné from attempting to obtain the necessary proofs of his innocence. The papers which could justify him were withheld from him by the Governor. Cabanné had a clearance when he went to Saint Joseph, Michigan, which would prove that the goods he purchased at Mr. David's store, were goods on which duty had been paid in Boston, and from thence had been sent to Mackinac.[15]

The people of Saint Louis sympathized with the families of the two men, yet there was a strong sentiment that an example should be made of the offenders and that dire punishment should be meted out to them in order that others might be deterred from engaging in this illicit trade.

Among the parcels of confiscated goods were 602 packs of skins. Some of these belonged to the Southwest Fur Company in which John Jacob Astor was interested. In order that Astor might not lose his furs, he interested himself in favor of Cabanné and Chenié, and in the following spring, partly through the efforts of the New York fur merchant, the two were acquitted[16] "by a jury of twelve lawful men".[17]

14 Gratiot to John J. Astor, October 8, 1812.
15 *Ibid.*
16 Porter, *op. cit.,* I, 275.
17 Charles Gratiot to J. J. Astor, May 13, 1813.

On September 13, 1812, the day following the seizure of the boats, word came that the English and their savage allies had taken Mackinac, "which was not a thing impossible as there were only about twenty-four cast-off Canadian boatmen stationed there."[18] The news aroused the fears of the Saint Louis merchants, lest the British traders use this strategic point to smuggle their goods into the United States and then, "adieu to all our prospects in the rise in goods and our expectation of gain. If the goods from Mackinac are brought here, the prices will fall immediately and we be left with all our goods on hand."[19] But the Chenié-Cabanné goods—the only smuggled articles seized in Saint Louis—were sold before December at "pretty high prices." The merchants did not expect any further supplies from the northern border because of the difficulty in passing the Indians and the certainty that the goods would be confiscated should they reach Saint Louis.

Late in the autumn, after the war had actually begun, English merchants and manufacturers under United States licenses, imported great quantities of their wares, and as the British products became plentiful, prices fell, although imports still sold at from 20 to 50 per cent advance in sterling. "I had bought none", wrote Hertzog, "first, for want of funds, second, it is too late to send them [to St. Louis]; third for fear of smuggling among you from Canada and lastly, I think they will be down. So that you may buy smuggled goods cheap if there are any [in your vicinity]."[20]

In Saint Louis during August, September, and October, 1812, business was so dull that Wilt's sales amounted to only $20 to $30 a day. "All kinds of business are stopped since the war," he wrote, "and money is unaccountably scarce. But", he added,

18 Wilt to Hertzog, August 23, 1812.

19 Wilt to Hertzog, September 13, 1812.

20 Hertzog to Wilt, October 6, 1812.

"Immediately upon the repeal, in June, of the British Order in Council, ships were loaded and sent to America. All summer the effect of the arrival and release of these goods was felt in stagnation of prices of imported articles." Benzanson, *op cit.*, p. 152.

"this may be owing to the farmers being out in volunteer corps."
Later, in October, when prospects brightened, he wrote, "Business has been dull here for some time but hope it will revive as
$17,000 to $18,000 are due to be paid to the troops this week,
of which I hope to take a little." Election day,[21] too, offered an
opportunity to net some two or three hundred dollars, in spite
of the fact that he anticipated carousing, drinking, and broken
heads during the course of the day.[22]

In compliance with instructions from Hertzog, Wilt sent on
the list of articles he would need during the fall and winter,
and suggested that if the prices were too high the list should
not be completed,[23] for in case of peace he did not want a
quantity of expensive goods on hand. This list of articles was
purchased at the reduced prices then prevailing in the East,
and the first invoice was sent down the Ohio in a public boat
which, unfortunately, was detained in Louisville, where a cargo
of clothing it was scheduled to pick up was not quite ready for
shipment.[24] Kerr, a rival merchant, who had been in Pittsburgh
during the time of reduced prices, purchased his stock and
started homeward several days after Wilt's goods left the East.
He reached Saint Louis the last of November and had disposed
of a large share of his merchandise before Wilt's invoice arrived.

About the time this consignment of goods reached Saint
Louis, Anshutz, from Pittsburgh, shipped what Wilt called Invoice No. 7. The consignment, exclusive of freight, amounted
to $1365.94 worth of Philadelphia goods and $410.28 of Pitts-

21 November 4, 1812.

22 In 1812, Missouri was organized into a separate territory and was
accordingly entitled to a legislative body and to a delegate in Congress. On
November 4, the voters would elect a representative to be sent to the National Capitol and also the members of the territorial legislature. The candidates for Congress, according to Frederick Bates were "Hempstead, the
heir apparent, Gratiot, the indefatigable, Easton (I want epithets), and
Provonchere, the forlorn hope." Edward Hempstead, true to Bates' supposition was elected first representative to Congress from Missouri.
Frederick Bates to William Carr, July 31, 1812. Bates Papers, Missouri Historical Society Collections.

23 Wilt to Hertzog, August 2, 1812.

24 Wilt to Hertzog, November 29, 1812.

burgh articles. When McClurg, the patroon, reached the Mississippi, it was frozen over and the weather was so cold that the boat was held fast in the ice in the eddies of Cinques Hommes, at a point a few miles south of Sainte Genevieve. McKnight and Brady, who also had goods aboard, sent an express down for the merchandise, but Wilt waited for his consignment until McClurg brought the boat up the river.[25] This he did on January 1, 1813. Business had reached one of the lowest levels ever experienced by Saint Louis merchants, the result, in some measure, of the severe weather, which prevented boats with their cargoes from coming up the river, and buyers from crossing to Saint Louis from the Illinois side.[26]

Throughout the fall and winter the Saint Louisans were fearful of an invasion by the Indians and British from Prairie du Chien. On Monday, February 15, 1813, a large number of the principal inhabitants met "to consult on the situation of the country in consequence of the war." They appointed Colonel A. Chouteau, C. B. Penrose, William Christy, Bernard Pratte, and Dr. B. G. Farrar as a committee. On the following Wednesday this committee submitted a report recommending that trenches be dug all around the town; that the four old Spanish blockhouses be put in repair; and that the town be picketed or fortified.[27] The expense of securing and placing the pickets was to be apportioned among the citizens according to the property or wealth of each person. The quota assigned to Wilt, who was considered one of the leading men of Saint Louis, was "276 feet to be enclosed by pickets not less than 10 feet long and 6 inches in diameter." The cost of this approximated $150. While these war-like preparations were being made, Saint Louisans heard "the unpleasant news of Harrison's having received orders from the Secretary of War to fortify his army in; that the Kentucky Militia whose time was expired are returning home." Wilt wrote:

25 Wilt to Hertzog, December 27, 1812.
26 Wilt to Hertzog, January 7, 1813.
27 Wilt to Andrew Wilt, February 20, 1813.

I cannot account for the Secretary of War's orders. It would seem as if our Cabinet wishes to protract the war and make the Ohio a frontier. Instead of sending sufficiently respectable bodies that would *look down all opposition,* they send out small detachments and before these arrive at headquarters and become a little disciplined, their time expires and they return home. It is rumored that a peace is expected, from what source I know not. Shame on the United States if they submit to a shameful one—nothing less than the Canadas, I say.[28]

A great sigh of relief went up when word reached Saint Louis on April 3, 1813, that no British troops were at Prairie du Chien. General Howard, who had gone up to meet the enemy, had returned to the city. "The picketing [of the town] falls through," wrote Wilt. "I was lucky in being disappointed on a contract I made for pickets."[29]

In the spring of 1813, when Hertzog began his purchases for the western store, prices again soared. In March, 800 parcels of dry goods were sold at 220 per cent to 334 per cent advance,[30] and the crockery bought in April at 300 per cent advance in sterling, was low compared with the 700 per cent[31] advance asked for the same article just three weeks earlier. In so high a market and with a possible peace in the offing, (for at the moment, rumors persisted that through Russian mediation hostilities would cease)[32] Hertzog thought it wiser to buy in small quantities and then only such articles as would suffer no great decline in price should peace be made.

Since there was little danger of smuggled goods coming down the river, and since all goods were selling at so enormous an advance, it was necessary that greater dispatch be used in bringing consignments down the Ohio to Saint Louis, if a "handsome profit" was to be realized before peace was concluded. That use-

28 Wilt to Hertzog, March 6, 1813.
29 Wilt to Hertzog, April 3, 1813.
30 Hertzog to Wilt, March 15, 1813.
31 Hertzog to Andrew Wilt, April 10, 1813.
32 Hertzog to Wilt, March 15, 1813.

less and expensive delays in loading and dispatching boats from Pittsburgh might be eliminated, Hertzog determined to open a branch store in that city with Andrew Wilt in charge.

Andrew, the younger brother of Christian, was then nineteen years old. He had gone to Saint Louis in June, 1812, just before the outbreak of the war, and was there when the boats with the smuggled goods from the Canadian border were seized. He was expected to learn the details of the western trade and to replace Mussina as the firm's agent along the Ohio, but he had been ill the greater part of his eight months' stay in the West. On November 1, 1812, he was stricken with a kind of bilious fever,[33] and on November 15 "his malady continued violently."[34] Doctor Farrar considered him dangerously ill. "His blood was very much inflamed as well as some taken from him last night. The bleeding on Thursday was of infinite use to him. I hope he may get better but he is yet very low", wrote Wilt to his family. Nevertheless, Andrew recovered before the winter was far spent and familiarized himself with the needs of the country, with the conduct of business in the Middle West, and with the wants and prospects of the lead, candle and soap factories in Saint Louis belonging to the firm. At the same time he met the Indian traders and the trappers, the merchants and the lawyers, and made many friends among the young people in the little city. He left Saint Louis for his new home in Pittsburgh on the afternoon of February 16, 1813, with William Massey as his only companion.[35] Massey had been employed as a clerk in the store and went to bring back the spring invoice of goods. The two young men traveled across the country on horseback, and Christian was not without some apprehension for their safety, as news had come since their departure of the "murder of two families on Cash River near the Ohio, about forty to fifty miles from the Mouth, by a party of the Mascau Nation of Indians."[36] However, the two travelers met no war parties

33 Wilt to Hertzog, November 1, 1812.
34 Wilt to Hertzog, November 15, 1812.
35 Wilt to Hertzog, February 20, 1813.
36 *Ibid.*

and reached Pittsburgh about the middle of March. The last of
April found Andrew occupying the "finest stand in town." It
was situated on the northeast corner of Market and Fourth
Streets, where it commanded the country trade and the boat
business. He had an "extensive assortment of dry goods, groceries, ironmongery, crockery, and shoes of almost every description," which he promised "to sell at the lowest prices for money,
or take in payment whiskey, flour, flax, bacon,"[37] and other
products of the Valley.

His duties were two-fold. Hertzog instructed him, as storekeeper, to attract all the Saint Louis buyers to his place of business and to look out for the Ohio and Kentucky traders and sell
to them at moderate advances over the Philadelphia price.

You can exchange your goods for saltpeter, powder, paper of all
kinds, ropes, hemp, linens, thread, linsey, furs, rags, whiskey, pork,
bacon, vinegar, flour, nails, glass and a great list of articles besides,
which will be brought to your market, many of which will bear
wagoning to Philadelphia, many you can sell on the spot, and many
will answer for Christian in Saint Louis.[38]

As agent of the Hertzog-Wilt interests, Andrew received the
firm's supplies coming from Philadelphia; purchased in Pittsburgh whatever articles were needed; directed the hiring of both
patroons and crews of the firm's boats, and shipped all goods
going to the Saint Louis store.

Christian Wilt, at this time, had undertaken to supply not
only home trade but also the militia camps through his sutling
ventures. He planned to keep his stores at the lead mines well
stocked, and to equip the expedition which he expected to send
into the Southwest under Luttig. Consequently it was imperative, not only that his general assortment be large, but also that
it contain articles appropriate for all these speculations. Before
Massey and Andrew left Saint Louis, he had sent a list of needed

37 Hertzog to Andrew Wilt, April 27, 1813, (Advertisement for Pittsburgh paper).

38 Hertzog to Andrew Wilt, April 12, 1813.

articles to Philadelphia and he expected these would be in readiness by the time that the young men reached Pittsburgh so that Massey could return with the goods immediately. From Philadelphia, with the ordinary assortment of dry goods, he ordered black and pink canton crepe that would sell at $1.50 a yard and pieces of "low priced cloth" to sell at $3 a yard, bolts of various kinds of New England cottons, shoes of all sorts and sizes, groceries, Imperial and Hyson tea, coffee, and sugar.

Sugar, Hertzog advised, was selling in Philadelphia at $17 to $18 per cwt.,[39] and the only kind available was maple or lump sugar which sold at 24 to 30 cents a pound. Hertzog suggested that sugar and molasses could be obtained more cheaply from New Orleans. Wilt did not include hats in his inventory, for a supply could always be procured from the Saint Louis hatters who were usually deeply in his debt.

From Pittsburgh Wilt wanted for general sale: 50 barrels of whiskey at 30 cents a gallon, which would retail in Saint Louis for $.87½–$1 a gallon; a quantity of wire to sell at 15–16 2/3 cents; 400 iron hoops for barrels and the same quantity for half barrels; 500 quarter of screw augers, No. ½ inch; a quantity of ¾ sickles, good ones, to sell at $1.75 apiece; a quantity of ½ pint tumblers and pint flasks; three boxes of 7 × 9 window glass, good axes, brass sifters, iron sifters, fire fenders, and nails, keg of 4, 6, 8, 10, 12, 20, 24 cut. Wrought nails sold better than cut ones, and if Andrew could procure a quantity, they could be sold cheaper than when purchased in small lots. For the camps he needed: saddles, bridles, snapples, 3 point blankets, which in Saint Louis were selling at $6.50, 12 dozen stone jars assorted ½–3 gallon, some 3 gallon jugs, 50 dozen tin cups, and camp kettles.

For the Indian trade he ordered 18 pieces of blue cloth; 14 brass butcher knives; 387 pounds assorted beads; 4 dozen fire steels; 1 dozen tinder boxes with flint and steels; 11 dozen looking-glasses; strouding, blankets and shawls. From places along the Ohio, Massey could pick up tow linens, flax, to-

39 Hertzog to Andrew Wilt, March 24, 1813.

bacco, cordage, ropes, and plenty of country linens. Cotton could be obtained from Baird in Nashville.

On his arrival in Pittsburgh Massey purchased a new keel and waited to take the goods back to Saint Louis. It was not, however, until the 6th of April, nearly a month later, that the first wagon-load of merchandise left Philadelphia for Pittsburgh, because, until that date, no wagons for general use between the two cities were available.

Owing to the demands for teams to carry government stores to the West, the carriage rate from Philadelphia to Pittsburgh rose from $4 a load to $8–$9–$9.50.[40] Hertzog employed his own regular "wagoners" but many of his men, induced by the higher freight rates offered by the federal government, left him to carry army goods. To "wagon" his purchases to Pittsburgh, Hertzog was obliged to call on the "White Horse", a Philadelphia stable owned by a Mr. Kennedy who had wagons that were regularly engaged in western hauling.[41]

When the teamsters finally brought their loads into Pittsburgh, Massey with Andrew's assistance filled the waiting boat and took it to Saint Louis. The lot included a few pieces of bombazine, black crepe, silk gloves, fine cotton hose, white jean, cotton stripes, India calico, and three casks of ironmongery. The first cask of iron was bought at 170 per cent advance. In the assortment were table and tea spoons from Stuttgart, steel hammers, shoe nippers, carpenters' pincers, compasses, box locks, sharp bits, stirrups, iron spurs, plated stirrups, snaps, tobacco boxes, curry combs, amounting in all, to $1600. There was also a complete assortment of butt hinges, up to that time not made in this country, which had been purchased at 385 per cent advance on the pre-war prices.[42]

"The assortment I send you," Hertzog wrote to Wilt, "contains a good variety and the missing articles are such as are so dangerously high, you could not sell them at cost and carriage.

40 Hertzog to Wilt, March 15, 1813.

41 Hertzog to Simon Philipson, March 24, 1813.

42 Hertzog to Andrew Wilt, May 1, 1813.

They make about 90 cwt., and if they reach you in safety, no doubt will make a good profit."

Prices were unquestionably fluctuating at a high level but, because of the irregularity of the mails between the East and the West, it was difficult for the frontier merchant to take advantage of them. It took a week for a letter bound westward from Philadelphia to Pittsburgh to reach its destination; from Pittsburgh to Saint Louis required about four weeks if there was no accident or delay; and from New England to Saint Louis a letter might be months on the way. To carry mail from Saint Louis to Philadelphia took not less than thirty-five days. The expense of letter-writing was also considerable. For every letter, composed of a single sheet of paper destined for a place not exceeding forty miles distant, the fee or postage was 8 cents; for 500 miles, 25 cents, and in like proportion, as the distance increased. For double letters, or letters of two sheets, the postage was double; for triple sheets, triple fees were charged,[43] and so on, as the distance and bulk of letters increased, so, too, the postage. Stamps did not come into use until 1847[44] and up to that time postage was usually not prepaid, though sometimes this was done.[45]

The mail was scheduled to arrive at western post towns once every week, but the regulation was more honored in the breach than in the observance. The post towns were: Saint Louis, Sainte Genevieve, Fort Massac, Vincennes, Louisville, Cincinnati, Marietta, and Pittsburgh. The mails left the Saint Louis post office, which was located on Third Street at the foot of Court Hill, once every Friday, except in the winter. All letters had to be in the post office before sunset on Thursday or they "would not be forwarded until the subsequent mail day."[46] The

43 *Louisiana Gazette,* August 23, 1810.

44 Lionberger, I. H., *The Annals of St. Louis, 1764-1928* (St. Louis, 1929), p. 39.

45 Rich, Wesley E., *The History of the United States Post Office to the year 1829* (Cambridge, 1924), p. 69.

46 *Louisiana Gazette,* August 23, 1810.

posts of Herculaneum, Mine á Breton, and Sainte Genevieve were sent out every fortnight on Wednesday. All mails were carried by post-riders under contract. Postmaster General Granger directed an agent of the Post Office in the Indian country to choose for post-riders "persons of integrity, sound health, firmness, perseverance, high ambition, and pride of character. Among these a preference is due to young men, the less the size the better."[47] These riders rode on horseback through trackless and savage-infested forests, but those going from New Orleans via Natchez encountered added difficulties in the hot, flat, and swampy country through which they had to pass. There is little wonder, then, that the delivery was uncertain and often irregular. Nevertheless, when the mail failed to arrive on time, the complaints were loud and wrathful. During the week of February 7, 1811,[48] no mail from the East reached Saint Louis. This occurred again during the first week of April[49] and, when by the last of the month none had arrived, the *Gazette* complained in disgust: "We are tired of recording failures of this kind." Reports reached Saint Louis that a post-rider had run away with the mail, and Charless, editor of the *Louisiana Gazette,* commented: "Would to heaven that the contractors and these postmasters who are in the habit of robbing the portmanteau of our Atlantic newspapers would take the same road, so that something like integrity and punctuality might grow out of the incident." A few weeks later he wrote ironically:[50] "No mail for the last two weeks. A gentleman from Vincennes reports that the flies have descended the different water routes in such numbers as to create fears for the safety of the mail bags." On Saturday, February 15, 1812, the *Gazette* once more lamented: "No eastern or southern mail had arrived when this paper was put to press. It is now six weeks since we have had a mail and then a broken one. . . . Our last Washington date is December 17."

47 Rich, *op. cit.,* p. 83.
48 *Louisiana Gazette,* February 7, 1811.
49 *Ibid.,* April 4, 1811.
50 *Ibid.,* April 26, 1811.

Wilt wished "the devil had some of the postmasters and post-riders if it would make them act with more promptitude."

Since mails were so irregular and not to be relied upon, it is little wonder that Wilt, like other Saint Louisans, entrusted his letters, business and social, to travelers who would deliver them safely and speedily. Hempstead, on his way to Washington, never failed to take Wilt's messages to Andrew in Pittsburgh and to Hertzog in Philadelphia. General Clark, who with a group of gentlemen, including Cameron, left Saint Louis on December 14, 1812,[51] took Wilt's letters with him as far as Pittsburgh, and Benjamin O'Fallon, General Clark's nephew, who was one of the party and a close friend to Wilt, promised to carry them on to their destination in Philadelphia.

Later, on May 15, 1813, when Major Robert Lucas in company with Robert Steward and Joseph Miller, two of Astor's "Overlanders," left Saint Louis for Canada, each carried important letters from Wilt; some were addressed to Andrew in Pittsburgh, some to the home folks in Philadelphia. The following month, Ramsey Crooks, whom Wilt called, "an intimate acquaintance of mine and one of the persons who accompanied Hunt to the Pacific Ocean," went to Philadelphia and on to New York in order to report to Astor the fate of his western expedition.[52] This afforded Wilt another opportunity to send messages to his relatives in the East. Penrose, Shreve, and Charles Gratiot also carried to the eastern cities for the young Saint Louis merchant correspondence relative to his mercantile, shot, soap and candle ventures.

In spite of disappointments in the delivery of mails from the South and East, and worries over his money problem, Wilt watched with great satisfaction the progress of the new brick store which he had begun in the spring of 1812 and which the workmen were now fast bringing to completion. "Three other brick houses are building which I am glad to see," he wrote,

51 Wilt to Hertzog, December 14, 1812.
52 Wilt to Hertzog, June 26, 1813.

"as it will make the lots rise."[53] At this time Wilt owned large parcels of real estate both within and about the town of Saint Louis, and he was interested in anything that might enhance their value. The "three other brick houses" were those of Bartholomew Berthold, William Smith, and Manuel Lisa. Late in 1812 Berthold moved into his new brick residence and store, in Block 8 on Main Street between Market and Chestnut. William Smith, Sr., at No. 7 North Main Street, had the second brick building, which he used both as a store and dwelling.[54] In spite of hard times, war, and the scarcity of workmen, Wilt's brick store was completed just a year after war had been declared. This, according to Billon, was the third brick building in Saint Louis.[55] Manuel Lisa, in the same block with Berthold and Smith, erected the fourth two-story brick dwelling and store in the metropolis of upper Louisiana, while McKnight and Brady, who had the honor of building the fifth,[56] erected their house in the block above and on the opposite side of the street, between Chestnut and Pine.

The bricks of the first houses were probably supplied by Samuel Bridge, who, in the fall of 1811, had a quantity of brick which he priced "at $3 per thousand as they come, and $6 if picked." For the convenience of the townsfolk Charless, at the *Gazette* office, was authorized to sell brick for Bridge, as the brick yard was at the margin of the creek[57] near the south end of the town. That some brick had been filched from the yard is evident, for Bridge[58] through the columns of the *Gazette,* re-

53 Wilt to Hertzog, August 16, 1812.

54 Billon, *op. cit.,* p. 247.

55 *Ibid.,* p. 261.

56 Scharf, *op. cit.,* p. 150.

57 Mill Creek.

58 Bridge was a cooper by trade. He came from Massachusetts in 1799 and settled in New Bourbon, where he worked at his trade. Before 1811 he came to Saint Louis where he saw the possibilities of brick making, built a kiln in the southern part of the town and supplied the builders with the brick they needed for their new stores. In making brick, bundles of straw, cut in six inch lengths, were added to enough clay to make one

quested those who had taken away bricks to call upon him and settle for them.

In May, 1813, although Wilt's building was almost ready for occupancy, the goods that Massey was bringing to stock the new store had not yet arrived. The paymaster, early in the month, distributed $40,000 to the Illinois rangers, but since his spring goods had not come, Wilt complained that he was "obliged to let considerable cash pass through my fingers which I am obliged to see paid to my neighbors."[59] Brady had arrived on the 17th of April, nearly a month before, with groceries, dry goods, and blankets which he offered at "reasonable prices." Von Phul brought back a large cargo, part of which he sold in Lexington and the remaining articles Smith, his partner, sold to Philipson, who had "wagoned" his goods up from Sainte Genevieve to a place opposite Saint Louis and then ferried them across the river. He displayed his assortment at Wilt's old stand and proved, as before, a formidable competitor. Wilt comforted himself with the thought that when Douglas, the paymaster for the Missouri troops came, not only would he have a complete assortment, but he would also have the added advantage of displaying his goods in his new store, and goods well displayed are half sold. It was at this time, too, that the additional companies for which Congress had provided, were being organized in and around Saint Louis, and the summer promised a rich harvest in trade. To members of these companies Wilt offered generous credit and for the collections he depended upon John Honey. In a letter of February 5, 1813, he wrote: "Enclose you the accounts of the volunteers. The certificate of Clayburn Thomas I have already received. I send you also the account of two or three of the Buckskin Company. Perhaps you can obtain their certificates for me." The pay of the privates was

hundred bricks. The moulding was done by hand and the surplus clay was struck off with a strip of iron. Moulds, a foot long, six inches wide and four inches deep, were prepared. Planks were used in this construction. The moulds were not built airtight lest the sun-drying process might be hindered and the work delayed.

59 Wilt to Andrew Wilt, May 29, 1813.

ten dollars a month and on discharge each one received a bounty of one hundred and twenty-four dollars, together with a certificate for three hundred and twenty acres of land, which made credit to volunteers a safe investment.[60]

On Tuesday morning, June 13, 1813, Wilt moved into his new store opposite Yosti's tavern, where the courts of the territory sat from December, 1804, to December, 1806. Massey's boat with young O'Fallon on board had arrived in port the Sunday previous, after a "long passage of twenty-two days from the mouth of the Ohio."[61] It brought a supply of manufactured and imported goods from Pittsburgh, and domestic produce which had been procured in the settlements along the river by bartering lead and buffalo robes in exchange for tobacco, country linens, cordage, and stoneware. This fresh supply of merchandise went directly to the new store at the corner near the junction of Main and Locust. Wilt rejoiced that "we are now free of rent, and as soon as people know I am removed we shall sell as much as other stores." On June 26 he reported "our sales now average $50 per day cash."[62] This amount, with his credit and barter transactions, made good business. He missed, however, one valuable line of merchandise which he had ordered, but which had not been delivered. Had blankets, butcher knives, beads, strouding, and vermilion which the Indians wanted been included in Massey's cargo, Wilt "could have made more good sales to the Indian traders."[63]

To the people of Saint Louis there were constant reminders at this time that a bloody war was being waged along the rivers of the West. During the early summer a party of Winnebago Indians plundered one of the settlements in the Saint Charles district, and when a company of Rangers sent to check their ravages met the Indians near Fort Madison on the Mississippi,

60 *Annals of Congress,* 1813–1814, p. 940.

61 Wilt to Hertzog, June 19, 1813.

62 Wilt to Hertzog, June 26, 1813.

63 Wilt to Hertzog, July 24, 1813.

four soldiers were severely wounded in the encounter that followed.

We are all in movement here again. It is said that 2000 Indians have crossed the Mississippi at Cap au Gré where we have a small fort which is about forty miles from here. General Howard has sent orders for all the militia and volunteers to march immediately. Some companies were ordered to march from their muster grounds. Henderson commands a piece of flying artillery.[64]

Early in the morning of August 7 a notice was posted requiring the Saint Louis Volunteer Artillerists to "meet at the Court House in the town at three o'clock this day completely equipped with six days' provisions if possible." According to the Territorial Laws a citizen soldier had to provide himself with a good musket, with a bayonet and belt, or fusil, two spare flints, and a knapsack and pouch, containing not less than twenty-four cartridges; or a good rifle, knapsack, powder horn, and powder, with twenty balls and one-quarter pound of powder.

Henderson, who was a member of the volunteers, commanded, as previously stated, a piece of "flying artillery"; Charles Lucas was captain, and Charles Hempstead, first sergeant of the company. Wilt followed the next morning as a member of one of the militia companies, for he wanted "to get a fair shot at an Indian."[65] Great excitement must have prevailed throughout the town, for citizens turned out with alacrity. "It is supposed, embodied, they would amount to 1220 from this territory alone, a force sufficient to expel all the savages on the Mississippi." On August 22 the *Gazette* reported that "Saint Louis now boasts one troop of horse on the frontier, one company of riflemen on board a galley at the mouth of the Illinois, one of artillery, and a veteran company of men now over forty-five years of age, five companies comprising almost every man in the place."[66]

64 Wilt to Andrew Wilt, August 7, 1813; Wilt to Hertzog, August 7, 1813.
65 Wilt to Andrew Wilt, August 7, 1813.
66 *Missouri Gazette*, August 22, 1813.

Although the danger on this occasion did not prove so great as was anticipated, and the soldiers soon returned to their work, troops regularly left Saint Louis every spring and .fall, going up the river to relieve those whose terms had expired. At other times, when danger from Indian attacks became acute, companies were formed and equipped, and in each instance the Saint Louis merchants disposed of large quantities of clothing and provisions at greatly advanced prices. To supply these companies with provisions alone would have been a profitable undertaking. The Indian department at Portage des Sioux consumed 200 pounds of pork, 296 pounds of flour, 112 pounds of beef, 270 pounds of salt, and 3 gallons of whiskey in 27 days, while one detachment of militia, according to the abstract of provisions signed by Frederick Bates,[67] used 1935 complete rations and 409 gills of whiskey in 27 days.

Congress, because of the influence of Edward Hempstead, Missouri's delegate at Washington, provided for the organization of three additional companies. In May, 1813, when these new troops and the Missouri and Illinois companies prepared to move, Wilt had a large share in furnishing their blankets, shoes, ammunition, and provisions, which he exultantly said, "will throw some money into our hands."[68]

Soap was among the articles in constant demand both by the army and by the local trade and since it could be easily manufactured on his premises, Wilt opened another shop for this branch of his business. He built on his lot at Locust and Main an 18 × 18 soap house where he installed a thirty gallon kettle. Adjoining this he added a shed for soap tubs and for two ash tubs with a capacity of forty bushels each. Henderson, an experienced soap-boiler as well as candle-maker, was placed in charge of the business. Ashes were the first requisite in soap-making and to get sufficient quantity was not an easy task, for eighty bushels at least were needed for each week's output of

67 Frederick Bates, Secretary of Missouri Territory, May 1 to May 22, 1813.

68 Wilt to Andrew Wilt, May 29, 1813.

soap. After the business had become well established, and the demand for ashes became greater, the firm was obliged to pay 25 cents cash for a bushel.

For the other ingredients Wilt sent to the eastern markets and suffered, as he had many times before, long delays and disappointments before he received the articles needed. His first order included: 2 gallons of spirits of wine; 100 pounds caraway seed, which Henderson proposed to use instead of sassafras for scenting the soap; 3 pounds of essential oil; a soap pan (to be made in Pittsburgh), the dimensions of which Henderson had given Andrew Wilt before he left Saint Louis for the East; 10 pounds resin, one pound of which would make 1½ kettles of brown soap; and a small quantity of oil of roses. The oil of roses was an expensive item, but a cake of the "rose soap" sold in Philadelphia at 50 cents, and the price in Saint Louis would make the manufacture of this variety very worth while. Last, but not least, he ordered a stamp for the Windsor soap that he intended to manufacture.[69] The only purchasable stamp in Philadelphia or New York for this soap was one with a king's crown with "London" printed beneath. A stamp of this kind was bought and sent to Wilt.

In January, 1813, Major George Wilson, a member of the Public Safety Committee of Saint Louis and agent of John White Company on the Mississippi for the Sacs, Renards, and Sioux, made a contract to take from Wilt all the Windsor soap he could manufacture. In keeping with the terms of the contract, Major Wilson sold his lard in the rough to Wilt at six cents a pound and paid sixteen cents a pound for the finished product. In early March, 1813, when Henderson's first batch of Windsor soap for Major Wilson was finished and a small quantity, stamped of course with the "Crown" and "London", was put on sale at Wilt's store, a great hue and cry went up. The people strenuously objected to having an enemy's name on the American product and demanded that an "Eagle" instead of

69 Wilt to Hertzog, February, 1814.

a "Crown", and "Saint Louis" instead of "London" be stamped on the new cleansing product.[70]

A stamp so made and marked had to be procured before the people of the western town would use the soap. The quality of Henderson's soap was "good white" and with the changed stamp sold readily, not only in Saint Louis, but also in the towns along the Ohio. In April, 1813, Henderson had nearly 2000 pounds additional of the soap finished. This was the complement of Major Wilson's first order.[71] In the meantime Wilt collected "stuff enough to make 15,000 pounds of soap"[72] which was to be converted into shaving and brown soap, and later, when more raw materials could be gathered, marble soap would be added to this already long list of cleansing compounds.

The shaving soap was not a success, for although "clear and handsome" when first made, it became yellow with age. The people complained that it was ropy, which they attributed to the sassafras, but it was more likely due to the "sticky nature" of the lard which was used in its composition.[73] Henderson, after having made several attempts to remedy the defects, discontinued its manufacture.[74]

The French people preferred the brown soap, which was colored with resin, to the white,[75] and called it "Savon de France" in keeping with their practice of giving French names to many things they used. The cost of manufacturing either brand of soap was 16 cents a pound. The selling price for the white was 30 cents a pound, and 25 cents for the brown, giving ample margin for profit.

Soap and candle-making went hand in hand in the early days. In this way Henderson began the manufacture of dipped and mould candles at the same time that he began making soap.

70 Wilt to Hertzog, April 23, 1814.
71 Wilt to Hertzog, April 17, 1813.
72 Wilt to Hertzog, March 20, 1813.
73 Wilt to Hertzog, June 11, 1814.
74 Wilt to Hertzog, September–December, 1814.
75 Wilt to Hertzog, July 3, 1813.

Before kerosene lamps, gas jets, and electric bulbs came into use, candles were the only means of lighting. These candles were made from deer or buffalo tallow, but because deer tallow was harder, Henderson preferred it to that of the buffalo. The hunters and traders brought only small quantities of the tallow to Saint Louis, for it had not as profitable a sale as the fur of the beaver and other animals. The only dependable place to procure large amounts of the tallow was at the United States factories, which the government established along the Mississippi and Missouri Rivers, or at the sutling stations to which the Indians and hunters brought their catch. During the war, whenever the Indians were peaceable, Wilt got his stock at the sutling stations located at Cap au Gris and Loutre Island. When these sources failed him, he bought tallow wherever he could get it, often paying as high as 13 cents a pound. One of the chief objects in sending Luttig into the Southwest in July, 1813, had been to obtain a larger and cheaper supply of tallow in order to keep the factory running.

In March, 1813, while Henderson was making his first batch of soap, he worked up 4000 pounds of tallow into candles. The tallow had been supplied by Major Wilson, who paid 8 cents a pound for the making of the candles. Wilt delivered a pound of candles for every pound of tallow supplied. All through the war Major Wilson paid from 3 to 4 cents for the manufacture of his dipped candles, which even the Philadelphia candle-makers considered good pay. Mould candles made in the form of 4's and 6's were much sought after and brought, at retail, 25 cents a pound; at wholesale, 18 cents.[76] But Wilt had no moulds and there was no way of getting a supply except by ordering from Pittsburgh or Philadelphia, where they would probably have to be made after the orders reached the eastern cities. Early in the spring Wilt wrote for moulds and supplies for the manufacture of candles and soap. In our day of mass production, telegraph, telephone, and air mail it is difficult to realize the length of time that intervened, in the days of post-riders, between the dispatch

76 Wilt to Hertzog, December 3, 1814.

of an order and the receipt of the needed articles. Nor can we appreciate fully the inconvenience arising from the irregularity and uncertainty of the posts.

Wilt wrote to New Orleans on July 31 inquiring about the prices of candles and soap. Two months later he received a reply. Morgan, his New Orleans representative, warned him that dipped candles were not saleable but he quoted mould candles 5's (18) and 6's (15) at 30–35 cents; brown soap, in boxes of 40 pounds, net at 25 to 28 cents. He advised Wilt, however, not to send either should peace be declared.[77] He assured him that both these articles could then be procured at much lower prices from the ports of the Atlantic coast. Wilt, who felt that the war would be prolonged, prepared late that year to send down a cargo of candles and soap to be exchanged for a badly needed supply of sugar and coffee. The rumor that 3000 Indians were on the warpath disrupted his plans for the moment, because Joseph Henderson had been ordered out on the military expedition; but the rumor was without foundation and in the latter part of October Henderson was back at his job of candle and soap-making. On December 4, when John Macklot started down the Mississippi to New Orleans, he had 1586½ pounds of mould candles, which were "of an elegant quality" ready to send. Wilt expected they would command a quick sale in New Orleans at 35 to 37½ cents a pound.[78]

Henderson was a real soldier. He had been appointed second lieutenant in the militia and was always ready when recruits were wanted, yet before the organization of the spring expedition, which left Saint Louis about the 26th of April, 1814, he had 400 dozen Windsor soap ready for shipment. Lindell's boat, which left Sainte Genevieve on May 25 for Pittsburgh took 11 boxes containing 40 dozen.[79] Wilt advised Andrew, to whom they were consigned, to sell these by the dozen (12 cakes to the pound) for at least a dollar a dozen. While Henderson was with

77 Wilt to Hertzog, October 9, 1813.
78 Wilt to Hertzog, December 4, 1813.
79 Wilt to Hertzog, May 28, 1814.

the militia, the soap and candle business was at a standstill. By July the candle supply was almost exhausted, and Wilt was unable to meet the demand of his Saint Louis customers. In September, Henderson returned, but he had been wounded in the shoulder and did not resume work until January, 1815, and then he was able to work with only one hand. Even with this handicap, however, he kept the factory running at its full capacity.

The soap and candle enterprise was now on a paying basis, and Henderson wanted a half share in the profits, instead of one third as originally agreed. He also demanded the right to make soap and candles for himself when not employed in the joint concern.[80] As this request was refused, he decided to manufacture soap and candles on his own account.[81] He got the rough tallow from a local butcher at 10 cents a pound and invested in 3 barrels of resin which he used in coloring the brown soap, so much sought after by the French inhabitants of the town. He offered to contract with Wilt to make soap at 16 cents a pound and candles at 4 cents. When Wilt refused, Henderson lowered his price on dipped candles to 18¾ cents to undersell Wilt's 25 cent mould candles.[82] But in spite of the competition, Wilt hoped that his business would not decline, since he had gone to the expense of building a soap factory and installing fixtures for the manufacture of both soap and candles. "Besides", he wrote, "a steady man would make money in this country, which Henderson has not been."[83] In July, 1815, a Mr. Lycette, whom Wilt described as "a very decent young man",[84] came from Philadelphia to replace Henderson. He rendered 600 pounds of rough tallow, which had been bought from a butcher at 10 cents, the same price that Henderson paid; he cut a quantity of wick and before the end of the first month he had 300

80 Wilt to Hertzog, January 7, 1815.

81 Wilt to Hertzog, February 6, 1815.

82 Wilt to Hertzog, June 5, 1815.

83 Wilt to Hertzog, February 20, 1815.

84 Wilt to Hertzog, July 10, 1815.

pounds of the candles ready for the market. This was quick work, considering that he had lost a week on account of illness during his first days in Saint Louis. Lycette warned Wilt that it would be necessary to have large and efficient equipment, if he wished to take off 8000 to 10,000 pounds of soap at one boiling, and the same would hold good in the preparation of candles.[85] He advised that a 90 gallon kettle be placed, that a large crib be set up, and a sufficiently large ash tub be constructed. In order to meet these demands Wilt ordered two 90 gallon kettles installed and prepared to build a large crib.

Lard would be plentiful as soon as the war was over, and the farmers returned to their fields and stock. But lard alone would not answer the purpose, for in making soap Lycette used also a quantity of tallow. The Indians would bring several thousand pounds of tallow down the Missouri in the spring, and Wilt contracted at Cap au Gris for whatever quantity might be received. To get sufficient ashes for the larger quantities of soap was another problem. Henderson had been able to collect only 50 bushels per week at 12½ cents per bushel, and Lycette, with the added equipment, would need at least 200 bushels per week. Nothing daunted, Wilt engaged men at Cahokia, and at other places near by, to collect ashes and bring them to Saint Louis.[86] Since wood was the only fuel used in the houses of Missouri and Illinois, both for cooking and heating, he managed to gather a sufficient quantity of ashes during the winter.

To complete the improvements suggested by Lycette took some time. It was difficult to get planks suitable for making the crib; in addition the expense of construction was no small item, and carpenters and mechanics, although they demanded high wages, were not always dependable. Wilt complained:

I have lately paid fifty cents per keg for lead kegs which are of inferior quality. The rough staves cost here $4 per 1000 and hoops $1 per 100. . . . Pork barrels will bring $1.25 by the quantity, and all small work sells very high. Well-made 3 and 4 gallon kegs are

85 Wilt to Hertzog, August 14, 1815.
86 Wilt to Hertzog, July 31, 1815.

$1 ; 6¼ cents is charged for setting a keg hoop; 12½ cents for setting a barrel hoop. Boxes for shot can be made under contract for 10 cents apiece, and all other work is charged in like proportion. . . . Owing in great measure to the high prices the men get for work, this is a dangerous country for young men as it is easy for them to get into bad habits, especially mechanics who are for the most part gamblers, drunkards, and indolent to the highest degree.[87]

The conclusion may be drawn that with these prices and under these conditions the cost of the soap tubs and the other improvements made at the factory on Locust Street meant a heavy outlay.

In spite of many difficulties that beset Wilt in the prosecution of his various projects, he was in a large measure successful in the conduct of his business. Although his exact financial standing cannot be ascertained, because no complete records of his business transactions are extant, one may however, from his letters, get some idea of the volume of his business by taking as a criterion the income from *two* of his projects: furnishing supplies and equipment for the War Department and operating his red lead factory during the first months of hostilities. The amount of his drafts on the War Department from December 20, 1812, to March 13, 1813, totaled $3141.13; the 80,000 pounds of red lead at $13.50 per hundred, manufactured and shipped during the same period, amounted to $10,400, and this with the 30,000[88]

---

87 Wilt to Hertzog, June 5, 1815.

88 Wilt to Hertzog, March 13, 1813.

Drafts on the War Department in favor of Wilt or transferred to him:

1812 Dec. 20,	Draft	No.	28	Pierre Chouteau on W. Eustis	$524.18
Dec. 27,	"	"	29	N. Boilvin on W. Eustis	500.00
1813 Jan. 23,	"	"	30	N. Boilvin on W. Eustis, favor C. Wilt	466.95
Feb. 6,	"	"	31	N. Boilvin on W. Eustis, favor C. Wilt	450.00
" 13,	"	"	32	N. Boilvin on W. Eustis, favor Blondeau	100.00
" 13,	"	"	33	N. Boilvin on W. Eustis, favor Bertold and Chouteau	300.00
" 13,	"	"	34	Wm. Morrison on Wm. B. Bryan, favor Hempstead (30 days)	500.00
Mar. 13,	"	"	35	P. Chouteau on General Armstrong, Secretary of War, favor C. Wilt	300.00

pounds of pig lead valued at 6½ cents per pound, made a total
of $15,591.13. To transact business on so large a scale, banks
were needed; but up to this time Saint Louis had no financial
institution.

Just a year before the outbreak of the War, the charter of the
Bank of the United States expired, and from 1811 to 1816 there
was no national bank. The liquidation of the bank left the country not only without adequate banking facilities, but it caused
about seven million dollars of specie to be sent back to England in payment for stock owned in that country.[89] At the
same time the depleted funds in the Treasury of the United
States prevented, among other things, the regular payments to
the troops throughout the West, upon which the frontier merchant so largely depended.

In Missouri, fur peltries and lead were being exported in large
amounts and payments were made in lieu of specie in various
commodities. Paper money was used considerably, but bank
notes of the surrounding states were not always a safe medium
of exchange. On July 10, 1813, the *Gazette* printed the following
warning:

The public should be on their guard in taking Bank Notes of Kentucky, Tennessee, or Ohio, as we are informed that numerous coun-
terfeits are in circulation. Yesterday morning, a ten-dollar note of
the Lexington branch bank of Kentucky was pawned off on a citizen
of this place (Mr. L'Andreville). The note is shorter than the genuine notes and the names are badly executed, particularly John
Instone and Robert Alexander. The design in the corner of the
Plough, Buck and Copse of Woods is wretchedly executed. It is
numbered 396 and dated May 20th, (1808). The paper is white and
coarser than the genuine. The rascal who passed this note is known
and will be apprehended, if possible.[90]

While the state banks were using their questionable paper,
the sale of public lands had risen from 864,536 acres in 1814 to

89 Cable, John Ray, *The Bank of the State of Missouri* (New York,
Columbia University, 1923), p. 31.

90 *Missouri Gazette*, July 10, 1813.

5,475,648 acres in 1819, years of speculation during which Missouri Territory was without banking facilities.[91] It had by that time become evident to every business man in Saint Louis that economic organization had reached a stage where a local bank was badly needed. Leading merchants, therefore, planned to organize a bank and to induce the United States to deposit there the funds for the payment of the troops. This would assure a more regular payment, and the town and country would be benefited by the money thus put into circulation.

On August 12, 1813, application was made to the Territorial Legislature sitting at Saint Louis[92] for a charter to organize a bank of issue under the title, "Bank of Saint Louis."[93] The Legislature seems to have passed the bill with little or no opposition. The charter was granted with the stipulation that a branch without issue privilege be opened at Sainte Genevieve. The capital was $100,000, exclusive of any stock which might be taken by the territorial government.[94] The charter permitted the bank to begin operations when one-half of the capital, or $50,000 had been subscribed,[95] but this amount must be subscribed before December, 1817, under penalty of the forfeiture· of the charter. A meeting of the commissioners, Auguste Chouteau, J. B. C. Lucas, Clement B. Penrose, Moses Austin,[96] Bernard Pratte, Manuel Lisa, Thomas Brady, Bartholomew Berthold, Samuel Hammond, Thomas Riddick, Rufus Easton, Robert Simpson, Risdon Price, and Christian Wilt[97] was held each month. At these meetings Wilt acted as Secretary.[98] Books of subscription were opened on December 15 at Saint Louis, Saint Charles, Herculaneum, Mine á Breton, and Sainte Gene-

91 Cable, *op. cit.*, p. 33.

92 Wilt to Hertzog, July 24, 1813.

93 Geyer, H. S., *Digest of Laws of Missouri* (St. Louis, 1818), p. 86.

94 Charter, Bank of St. Louis.

95 Wilt to Hertzog, November 6, 1813; Charter of the Bank of St. Louis.

96 Cable, *op. cit.*, p. 53.

97 Billon, *op. cit.*, p. 85.

98 Wilt to Hertzog, November 6, 1813.

vieve in the Missouri territory, and at Kaskaskia and Cahokia in Illinois territory. The provision of the charter for opening subscription books in several places was the usual custom at this time, largely because of fear of domination by the moneyed classes; but in this instance, the reason seems to have been the need of attracting all available capital.[99]

Shares were sold at $100 each.[100] Payment for stock was due on demand of directors, but the charter contained no requirement that the stock should be paid for in specie. However, when the call for the final payment was made in September 1817, the directors required that it must be made in gold, silver, approved paper of the Banks of Cincinnati, Vincennes, Richmond, the State Bank of Tennessee, the Bank of Kentucky, and such other paper as was accepted by the United States government in payment for land and taxes.[101] Loans were to be secured by at least one indorser, but for some reason we find that by November only a little stock had been subscribed. Penrose, to whom Wilt owed his appointment as commissioner, suggested that the legislature at its next session alter the charter and permit the bank to open when the commissioners thought proper, and at the same time permit the officers to accept lead, furs, or peltries as collateral in place of endorsement, provided these commodities were actually deposited in the bank, or within a mile of it. Such collateral could be sold on ten days' notice to pay the debts of the borrower. Not all of the merchants considered this last proposition advantageous, but all agreed that it would furnish a means by which the prices on lead and peltries might be fixed.[102] The interest rate was limited to six per cent payable in advance. Wilt assisted in drawing up the new charter which was written by Easton under the direction of Judge Lucas.[103]

99 Cable, *op. cit.,* p. 48.

100 *Missouri Gazette,* January 21, 1815.

101 *Missouri Gazette,* September 28, 1816.

102 Wilt to Hertzog, November 6, 1813.

103 *Austin Papers,* I, 232.

In July, 1814, Wilt wrote, "the bank was considered to have fallen through," and "no installments have been demanded."[104] The bank, however, did open formally in 1816. This delay in opening was due to the scarcity of local capital. The bank occupied the rear part of the building that Riddick and Pilcher used as a store. Samuel Hammond was the first President and John B. N. Smith acted as cashier. Business must have been good, for in August, 1817, they purchased the old stone house on the east side of Main Street between Elm and Myrtle, and fixed it up for their first banking house. They tore down the stone front and erected a new brick one, thus making, at least in appearance, an entirely new building.[105] In spite of all these details of preparation, the life of the bank was ephemeral. In March, 1818, it suspended payment; it re-opened in March, 1819, and for a short time attempted to pay its indebtedness, but its final closing occurred on July 24, 1819.[106]

The Bank of Saint Louis had many difficulties in its short span of life. The people were wholly unacquainted with banking practices; business turnover was slow; and in the discharge of obligations there had been little education.[107] In the meantime the Bank of Missouri had been organized and so impressed was Wilt with the need of having a bank in Saint Louis that he invested in thirty shares of the second institution. Of his holdings he evidently, later, sold one share, for in the "list of stockholders of the Bank of Missouri on this 14th day of August, 1821, the day on which she stopp'd specie payments",[108] Christian Wilt, deceased, is shown as having twenty-nine shares. The Bank of Missouri had a larger capital and the custody of the public money for the land district of Missouri. Its history, however, was as short and inglorious as that of its sister-bank, the

---

104 Wilt to Major Climpson, July 2, 1814.

105 *Missouri Gazette,* August 7, 1817.

106 *Ibid.,* July 24, 1819.

107 Cable, *op. cit.,* p. 48.

108 Original document in the Julius S. Walsh Collections, Missouri Historical Society Collections, St. Louis.

Bank of Saint Louis.[109] After these failures the city was left
without banking facilities except for some private agencies
which issued notes of very uncertain value. For many years the
business man lost interest in local banks and preferred even to
revert to a state of barter.

During the fall of 1813, before the Bank of Saint Louis was
fully organized and when a find of precious metal was most
welcome, William Bates brought to Wilt a piece of ore that he
believed contained silver. McGirth, who found the ore, said that
there was a large quantity of it on the surface, but he would not
disclose the location of his find until he had been compensated
for the discovery. Sparke assayed the ore in a crucible in one of
the lead furnaces, but it was too hard to melt thoroughly. He
admitted there certainly was metal in the ore but he doubted that
it was silver. Bates suggested that, if in a further test silver was
found, Wilt should buy the right of discovery and apply to the
government for the use of the mine. No laws regarding silver
leases had been passed, but the United States government was
very liberal regarding lead mines, retaining as revenue only 10
per cent of the output. There was little doubt that Congress
would be equally liberal in leasing silver deposits,[110] but other
matters claimed Wilt's attention and the silver speculation was
dropped for the moment.

Prices were rather high and money was more plentiful than
it had been for a long time, when the United States government
paid the troops in the late summer of 1813. It was at this time
that Wilt prepared to venture into the wholesale trade; to organize sutling expeditions at the various camps and forts along the
river; and to send agents into the different sections of the country where merchandise could be sold or bartered. Wilt's first
experience in wholesale business, on a large scale, opened with
Thomas Hempstead, who conducted a store at the camp on the

109 It is said that Moses Austin's loss of his fortune because of his connection with this bank turned his thoughts to the colonization of Texas.
Missouri Historical Society, *Collections*, III, 372.

110 Wilt to Hertzog, October 2, 1813.

Missouri for his brother, Edward Hempstead. He proposed that Wilt furnish him with all his goods and take a percentage on the sales made at the post.[111] Wilt accepted what appeared to be a good bargain and the first sales item of $327 is recorded on June 19, 1813.

At the same time R. H. Price, who supplied three stores, one of which was at one of the camps, purchased of Wilt $383.70 worth of goods and proposed to take another lot worth $2000.[112] Wilt also had among his patrons Bernard Pratte, Sr., who bought all his goods from Saint Louis merchants and supplied the mounted volunteers of Illinois at an estimated annual profit of $10,000. In attracting the trade of these merchants, Wilt offered some articles, as merchants do today, at a lower price than the other stores were asking and at the same time endeavored to get as much specie as possible.

Wilt's account with the sutling firm of McNair and Kerr ran to $500. Alexander McNair,[113] while still a young man had served in the regular army as a lieutenant of infantry. He resigned his commission to engage in civil pursuits and amassed a small fortune. When McNair later gave up his share in Kerr's sutling venture, in the hope that he might be appointed Colonel of the Rangers,[114] and went with the fall expedition against the Indians, Wilt purchased the share for $800. This gave him an opportunity to supply the Rangers at Cape Girardeau, Loutre Island, and Cap au Gris. These goods usually sold at a 50 per cent advance, and in two months Wilt and Kerr had $4000 to their credit.

When Kerr, without consulting Wilt, sent a supply of goods to the Illinois Rangers on the other side of the river, Price, who sutled for the Illinois troops, retaliated by sending goods to Captain Ramsay's company at Cape Girardeau. This caused a

111 Wilt to Hertzog, May 29, 1813.

112 Wilt to Hertzog, June 19, 1813.

113 Alexander McNair, later the first Governor of the State of Missouri.

114 Frederick Bates to James Pleasant, Jr., March 8, 1812 (Bates Papers), Missouri Historical Society Collections, St. Louis.

disagreement between Wilt and Kerr and prevented the shipment of goods to the soldiers in the other camps. Captain Boone
at Loutre Island left without goods, arranged with a Doctor
Wellington to furnish supplies for his troops.[115] This was dis-
concerting, but not disheartened, Wilt on February 13 sent on
his own account an invoice of goods to Captain Boone's Rangers.[116] Later he also furnished Captain Musick's company at
Cap au Gris with needed supplies and equipment.

After these transactions Wilt's assortment was pretty well depleted, and he dispatched Massey to Pittsburgh for shoes, camp
kettles, tin cups, pint flasks, tow linens, tobacco, and other needed
articles. His supply particularly of rum, sugar, and coffee had
fallen so low as to cause him anxiety. On July 31, Benjamin
Morgan of New Orleans notified him that coffee was selling at
20 to 22 cents, brandy at $2.50 to $3 a gallon, and sugar at $9
to $10 a barrel.[117] In ordering his supply of sugar, Wilt limited
his purchase price to 8 cents a pound. This was too low as the
unharvested crop was being offered at 7 cents, and when later
speculation raised the price, Wilt ordered ten barrels and paid
the speculation price. For supplying the army and sutling posts
this quantity did not last long and in September he found himself "quite out of sugar and coffee."[118]

Since he was without cash and the country had no "hard
money", he proposed to send Cameron to New Orleans in the
spring with a keel of 30,000 pounds of lead. This, together with
soap and candles, could be sold or bartered for sugar, groceries,
coffee, rice, rum, brandy, copper, and crockery. With freight at
3 cents a pound, a boat could go and return for $1000.[119]
Groceries brought to Saint Louis from Philadelphia by way of
New Orleans would be cheaper than sending a boat up the Ohio

115 Wilt to Hertzog, January 15, 1814.

116 Wilt to Hertzog, February 12, 1814.

117 Wilt to Hertzog, July 31, 1813. (Quoted from B. Morgan's letter to
Wilt.)

118 Wilt to Hertzog, September 11, 1813.

119 Wilt to Hertzog, November 29, 1812.

to Pittsburgh. Sugar bought in New Orleans (French weight) at $8 to $9 a barrel, could be sold in Saint Louis (English weight) at $18 to $20.[120] In March, before Cameron's boat was ready, a Mr. Andrews from New Orleans brought up 70 barrels of sugar and a quantity of coffee. He sold the sugar to Saint Louis merchants at 17 cents per pound and the coffee, an inferior grade, he offered at 31¼ cents. Wilt purchased ten barrels of sugar but notified Massey to bring from Pittsburgh 20 barrels of good coffee.

Massey returned from Pittsburgh in June. Cameron, instead of going to New Orleans, went up the Ohio to Pittsburgh, leaving Saint Louis the first of April and returning August 6. McClurg coming about the same time brought some articles by freight. On unpacking the goods brought in by Massey, Cameron, and McClurg, Wilt was disappointed to discover that many necessary things were missing, that some were of inferior quality, and that others were unsuitable for the western country. He had built a large patronage among the Rangers, the Indian traders, farmers, and housewives, and to disappoint them would be to lose his hard-earned prestige. The purchase of large quantities of cheap articles because they were cheap, might do in Philadelphia, but the Saint Louis people would take only commodities that were good and serviceable.

Wilt voiced his dissatisfaction in his letters to Hertzog who, having made the purchases, was responsible for this situation:

Common shoes for this place should be large enough for soldiers whose feet are not immoderately small. Pointed and old fashioned kid and morocco shoes will never sell. I would be glad to obtain $1 a pair for them. I have still nearly a trunk of old black morocco which are both too large and small. Some of the 'aime fair' have monstrous feet and some of the Creoles *mighty* small ones. The men's morocco pumps . . . are mostly too narrow and low in the instep and are apt to rip.[121]

120 Eight pounds was the difference between French and English weight. Bulky merchandise was bought at French and sold at English weight. Wilt to Hertzog, January 15, 1814.

121 Wilt to Hertzog, October 16, 1813.

He wrote again:

German mill and cross-cut saws will not answer in this place because they are not large enough. I have sold only two or three at $4.50. My advice is that you sell at auction what you have on hand as I cannot use them here in Saint Louis. I have plenty of books, and though they are slow they sell at a good profit. Bates bought the Encyclopedia at $9 a volume. I have more *Love's Labor Lost* than I will sell in fifty years in this place. The urns will never sell. Latches and latch hooks are a poor article. Sockets and shovels ditto. Sickles, of the quality sent last, will not sell as they are not good and their teeth do not take hold. Tin tobacco boxes or snuff boxes are not liked by the French. Horse nets won't sell even if offered at cost. The last silk Chambry won't sell. Common breast pins won't sell. Cork tweezers are of same quality. Ammotto, people won't have. Spirits of camphor nor hive syrup don't sell. Sago won't sell at all. Twilled cotton tape in rolls sells slow. I sell mine at $1. The case of pins last sent are a cheap lot. The 5 pounds are as small as the 3½ pounds. In fact they are all alike and all small.

Your steel heads and throats are charged $1.80 per dozen, which must be an error. They are higher than plated ones and by far higher than I can sell them for. It must be per gross. India book muslin will never sell here. I believe the nicknacks are nearly all sold. Would I could say the same of gig whip-lashes and gridirons, though they sell occasionally. I have more than is necessary. . . . The fur bonnets won't sell because they are not the proper form.[122]

The tin cups from Philadelphia were cheaper than from Pittsburgh. The last cost $1.90 with soldered handles. "You have sent me no ginger, an article that bears a good profit. No Madras handkerchiefs, an article better than shawls."[123]

Because articles needed at the moment were not included in the consignments sent on from Philadelphia and Pittsburgh, Wilt purchased on four months' credit through Honey from Bates, who was at Herculaneum, a quantity of tow linen at 33 1/3 cents, bed cords at $4.50 a dozen, New England cottons at 36 to 38 cents, powder, glazed, at 62½ cents, and some dry

122 Wilt to Hertzog, September 18, 1813.
123 Wilt to Hertzog, October 23, 1813.

goods at 25 cents. "In purchasing at a percentage", he wrote to Honey, "the advance should be only on the cost, and the carriage added afterwards," and he continues, "if Colonel Hammond delivers a few hundred pounds of rice at a shilling, receive it on account and send it to me by the first opportunity."[124]

Douglas, paymaster of the troops, who brought $100,000 for the Missouri Rangers, had been detained at Louisville where he endeavored to negotiate his bills in order to have cash for the soldiers. He reached Saint Louis in February but Kerr, even after the new consignments had reached Saint Louis, refused to send goods either to Cape Girardeau or to Loutre Island. On account of this misunderstanding Wilt had little hope of gaining the profit that he had expected.

As spring approached in 1814 the expedition going up the river prepared to move. Wilt engaged Cameron to carry goods for him to the camp at Prairie du Chien. When he returned to Saint Louis, Cameron hoped to be honored with an appointment from the United States government as factor for the Sioux tribe. He was well-fitted for this work, since he was familiar with the manners and customs of the Indians, spoke their language fluently and had been for some time interpreter to the various tribes. Such an appointment would be of advantage to Wilt, for although Cameron, as factor, was forbidden to trade directly with the Indians, the law did not prevent his sending traders to the Saint Louis store, where their beaver would be taken in exchange for goods. This would be a "handsome exchange", for the beaver of the Sioux country was of an excellent quality. When spring opened Cameron, as sutler, went up the Mississippi with the troops, taking with him Wilt's invoice.

In connection with his sutling interests, Cameron promised to do some collecting for Wilt. There were notes due from Graham,[125] Bouthillier,[126] and Faribault,[127] the last amounting to $400. Brisbois, the previous summer, had purchased some

124 Wilt to J. Honey, October 7, 1813.

125 Duncan Graham, Indian trader at Prairie du Chien and Captain in the British Indian Department during the War. *The First Annual Report*

goods from Lucas, Wilt's agent, and in payment Wilt agreed to take lead. This lead Cameron would collect and ship. But because of the fact that the United States had lost the Prairie territory, which included the mines of the Sac and Fox Indians, Brisbois was disappointed in his attempts to procure lead, and in consequence Cameron could neither collect nor ship the lead to Wilt. In disposing of his wares Cameron was more successful. In June, he sent an order to Saint Louis which included carrot tobacco, and candles, but tobacco could not be purchased in Saint Louis, and the supply of candles was not sufficient to satisfy Wilt's local customers, because the candle business had suffered when Henderson, the candle-maker, went up with the expedition.[128] However, the results of these various business deals apparently did not affect the business too adversely, for in his letter to Hertzog dated December, 1814, Wilt wrote: "I calculate that by next June this concern will have cleared between 40 to 50 thousand, which in four years I do not consider bad business."[129]

In addition to his sutling enterprise, Wilt sent into the southwest a trading expedition which he entrusted to John C. Luttig, a German who had at one time been a prosperous Baltimore shipping merchant.[130] He appeared in Saint Louis in 1809, where he was employed as an assistant auctioneer by the Missouri Fur Company. After that company's 1812–1813 expedition, on which Luttig acted as clerk,[131] he entered the employ of Wilt. This was in early July, 1813. Wilt found him a very

and Collections of the State Historical Society of Missouri in the year 1854, II, 130.

126–127 Francis Bouthillier and Jean Baptiste Faribault, both Indian traders residing at Prairie du Chien. Report Historical Society of Missouri, II, 122.

128 Wilt to Cameron, June 26, 1814.

129 Wilt to Hertzog, December 3, 1814.

130 Wilt to Hertzog, July 3, 1813.

131 Drum, Stella, Introduction to Luttig's Journal of a Fur Trading Expedition on the Upper Missouri 1812–1813. (Kansas City, Missouri, 1921), p. 11.

capable clerk, but he hesitated to send him to represent the firm in New Orleans. He is an "excellent hand to sell goods, active as Mussina (their erstwhile Ohio agent) and withal a clever fellow" but, unfortunately, "he drinks, and while I could prevent it here in some measure, in New Orleans, he would be out of all bounds."[132] "Luttig stays with me no more," wrote Wilt in September, "General Clark could not do without him." Since Cameron was expected shortly, Wilt permitted Luttig to go, but in the following June, 1814, Luttig was back again and Wilt sent him on a three months' "trading voyage" to "the White River and in the Spanish country" where he had previously been and where prices "were encouraging". Luttig took an invoice of goods worth $2300 with him down the river and returned in the same boat early in September with deerskins and furs, the proceeds of which amounted to $1000. At his post on the White River he left 5000 pounds of tallow and his unsold goods amounting to $1800. Before the 10th of September, he went back on his second adventure with an additional cargo valued at $1700.[133] This included 10 barrels of whiskey, which was selling in Saint Louis for 80 cents a gallon. In early November Luttig dispatched a wagon load of peltries to Cape Girardeau in care of one Michael Steinbeck, with the message that he "had good prospects of doing well . . . and was selling his goods at high prices."[134] But in those pioneer days of ox-carts and unmade roads, travel was slow and difficult and this load of goods did not come into Cape Girardeau until late in February, and Steinbeck forwarded them from there to Saint Louis in a freight boat. On December 30, 1814, Luttig notified Wilt that he had hired John Duncan's boat and was sending 1000 pounds of shaved and unshaved deerskins, 1000 raccoons, buffalo robes, 3 barrels of tallow, buffalo tongues, beef, salted trout, turkey wings, hams, venison, and hides. He asked in return for plates

132 Wilt to Hertzog, July 3, 1813.

133 Wilt to Hertzog, September 10, 1814.

134 Wilt to Hertzog, December 16, 1814.

and other articles to complete his assortment.[135] Wilt sent Antoine Pourcelli, his clerk, down to White River on horseback with the cordelles and other articles Luttig needed, but plates which were selling in Saint Louis at $9 a dozen, he did not send lest they be broken in transit.[136]

Duncan's journey to the mouth of the Ohio took thirty-five days, but the bill of lading did not reach Saint Louis until the 27th of April. Duncan was instructed to leave the buffalo tongues and tallow at the mouth of the Ohio with Colonel Bird.[137] The latter was to send them on by Joseph Morin, who was bringing the "Captain Porter" to Saint Louis from Pittsburgh and would be passing the Point "within the next few days."

The other articles Duncan took on to Louisville where John Cromwell, on his way to Pittsburgh with Wilt's exports, was expected to meet him and pay the freight.[138] Duncan, however, reached Louisville about two weeks before Cromwell's arrival, and not finding anyone to take the load, offered it for sale at auction. Effecting no sales, he went up the Kentucky River to Lexington, where he stored the furs and the other articles he had on board his boat. Colonel Taylor, of Frankfort, Kentucky, to whom Cromwell had sent the original receipt which he had received from Wilt, prevented a sale but did not provide payment for the loading of the goods or for the payment of the freight. Duncan returned to Louisville, where he distributed handbills advertising his cargo for sale at public auction. On July 5, 1815, he sold 7 packs of raccoonskins, 4 packs of bearskins, 11 packs of deerskins, and 43 venison hams, which brought him enough to pay the freight and warehouse fees. The remaining articles Duncan placed in John T. Gray's warehouse, where according to a letter from David Howell of Louisville, the furs were in

135 Wilt to John Luttig, January 24, 1815; Wilt to John Cromwell, May 23, 1815.

136 Wilt to John Luttig, February 22, 1815.

137 Wilt to Bird, June 20, 1815.

138 Wilt to John Cromwell, May 23, 1815.

danger of being destroyed by worms.[139] Wilt notified Joseph Merrill, at that time acting agent for the Saint Louis firm, "to take proper steps to effect a settlement with Duncan and to sell the remaining furs." Wilt listed the raccoon at 25 to 30 cents, for according to the opinion of the Kentucky tanners, the raccoons from the Arkansas country did not compare with those of the Illinois, as one from Illinois was worth two from the South. They brought, when sold, 62½ cents a pound. The better deerskins were marked at 33 cents, and the bearskins at $2. The buffalohide might, in Wilt's opinion, be sold to the Kentucky tanners. If a sale could not be made, then Merrill was ordered, after examining and beating the furs, to ship them by the first opportunity to Messrs. Hepburn and Pleasants, merchants at New Orleans, who would send them to Joseph Hertzog of Philadelphia.[140] The buffalo meat, the tallow, and tar were sent on to Saint Louis. The tar brought in Saint Louis only 50 cents per gallon, by the barrel, which hardly paid the transportation. The small consignment of tallow, only 3 barrels, was a keen disappointment to the Saint Louis soap-maker, but Luttig had been unable to get more, because the Osages in the Arkansas country had put on their war paint and prevented the other Indian tribes and the white men from hunting the buffalo.

In February, 1815, according to his letter, Luttig was at Spring River where he disposed of a large quantity of dry goods "selling changeable silk at $4 a yard." He bought and sold horses, sending three, a black mare, a sorrel, and a roan, to Saint Louis where Wilt sold the former for $35, and the latter for $30, "which does not pay for their keeping, nor am I yet paid for them. I would therefore advise no more horse speculating."[141] Later Luttig exchanged salt at $2.50 a bushel and iron at 15 cents per pound for peltries to the amount of $1000, and at the same time purchased settlement rights on "Congress lands." To this Wilt objected, for later, cash would

139 Wilt to Andrew Wilt, July 31, 1815.
140 Wilt to Joseph Merrill, August 7, 1815.
141 Wilt to John Luttig, June 1, 1815.

be required to secure the lands and "I can do better with my funds by applying them to my business which is suffering for want of them."[142] Luttig, however, invested in other lands which he praised very highly. Some of this land he rented at a good rate of interest to the many new settlers who were coming into that section of the country, while he himself cultivated thirty-five acres which he estimated would yield at least 1200 bushels of corn and 2000 pounds of cotton. Wilt looked askance at the land speculation, but hoped Luttig's payments had been made in goods on which a good profit would be realized.

When Luttig discovered a lead mine on some of his land, he sent up a small parcel of the mineral which Macon, who leased the mines in the Missouri country, said would yield 80 per cent metal, and was quite superior to any he had seen.[143] Wilt sought advice relative to the purchase of the mine and Governor Clark warned that the government would not lease land for a lead mine until after a survey had been made. When James Kennerly,[144] who was not impressed with the prospects of the Southwest, discouraged Wilt in his investments in that section,[145] the latter warned Luttig "not to extend your business too much but endeavor to manage, so in case of necessity, you could close the business without leaving long-winded debts to collect."[146] This advice seemed dictated by a premonition, for on Saturday evening, July 20, 1815, James Moore, a young man from Arkansas, rode into Saint Louis with the word that Luttig died about twelve days before. Moore brought with him Luttig's account book and papers, with a letter from James Moore, young Moore's father, who offered to take care of the store, sell the remaining stock and make remittances. Wilt accepted, but ordered Antoine Pourcelli, who was still at White River to

142 Wilt to John Luttig, July 26, 1815.

143 Wilt to Hertzog, May 23, 1815.

144 James Kennerly came to Saint Louis in 1813. Later he became Chief clerk of Governor Clark in the United States Indian offices. Billon, *op. cit.*, p. 267.

145 Wilt to John Luttig, June 1, 1815.

146 Wilt to John Luttig, February 22, 1815.

remain until someone could be sent down to close the business.[147] "I fear I shall lose four or five thousand dollars," wrote Wilt to Andrew on July 31, as Luttig drank heavily, "ran into debt, scattered the business contrary to my instructions and made foolish speculations in settlement rights on Congress lands. This, with the loss on the shipments he made, makes it still worse."[148]

It was late in August before Wilt could send John Geiger to settle Luttig's affairs. Geiger, who had served during the war as lieutenant of the Mounted Riflemen under Captain James Rankin, seemed well-suited to undertake a long and perilous journey through the wilderness. Armed with power of attorney, Geiger went directly to White River where he met Moore, who had taken care of the business in the interim and who assisted him in selling or trading off the remaining goods. Wilt advised that while Geiger was in this section of the country he might collect a load of goods suitable for the New Orleans or the Saint Louis market, or for both. The New Orleans load ought to consist of deerskins purchased at not more than 12 to 18 cents, beaver at $2, otter $1 to $2 and a quantity of pork and beef. If Luttig's boat was in good repair Geiger was directed to send the boat down the river by a "confidential patroon well acquainted with the river," and consign the load to Messrs. Hepburn and Pleasants, who in turn would send the goods to Hertzog at Philadelphia. For Saint Louis, a load of tallow at 8 cents a pound should be provided. If neither was practicable, then Geiger could accept in payment from Luttig's debtors, hogs, cattle, and horses, which could be driven through the country to Saint Louis.[149] In conformity with the advice of Thomas Riddick, Geiger was not to sell the preëmption rights on the land because when the country was settled, as it was bound to be, these rights would be saleable at high prices.[150] Wilt was discouraged by this series of reverses and wrote to his brother:

147 Wilt to James Moore, (no date) 1815.
148 Wilt to Andrew Wilt, July 31, 1815.
149 Wilt to John Geiger, August 26, 1815.
150 Wilt to John W. Honey, August 7, 1815.

I shall try in the future to keep business more contracted and keep my goods, sooner than run too great risks. . . . This year is fraught with misfortune; the loss of the barging business; the loss in lead and merchandise by reason of the peace; I fear a loss by Henderson who is getting into his bad habits again and now, Luttig. It is time for bad fortune to change.[151]

News, as we know, traveled slowly in those early days, and weeks passed before word of the glorious victory at New Orleans reached Saint Louis. In writing Thomas Hill of Nashville, Wilt said:

The bankruptcy of the United States Treasury, disappointing our paymaster in funds for our troops (a part of which, the Rangers, are indebted to almost every class of people) causes a complete stagnation of business in the place. Gold and silver are not to be had here, bank paper would please me well enough if I could obtain it. The paymaster returned yesterday from Kentucky without money. He borrowed a good deal from merchants here and cannot pay them from his disappointment. If your militia prove themselves as good soldiers as your Jackson has proved himself a General, they will meet the sincere approbation of every citizen of these United States.[152]

But, "the darkest hour," so the proverb goes, "is the hour before the dawning," and in Wilt's case, this proved to be literally true. Fortune began to smile on his efforts. A month later, February 6, 1815, he was in better spirits, as he wrote to Hertzog:

We have been in considerable bustle here lately for the fate of New Orleans but which has now subsided. Many were of the opinion that if the British had taken the city they would send troops and Indians from Prairie du Chien and continue on to New Orleans, as nothing could stop them.[153]

151 Wilt to Andrew Wilt, July 31, 1815.
152 Wilt to Thomas Hill, January 7, 1815; Wilt to Hertzog, Dec. 31, 1814.
153 Wilt to Hertzog, February 6, 1815.

But New Orleans was saved and the defeat of the picked troops of Wellington by the raw frontier soldiers under Jackson, was a signal for general rejoicing throughout the whole western country. On the evening of February 18 the homes of the citizens of Saint Louis were illuminated, bonfires were built, and a federal salute was fired in honor of the brilliant success of the American Army and of Jackson, the idol of the Mississippi Valley.[154]

Word that peace had been signed reached Saint Louis during the early days of March. *The Favorite,* the British sloop of war, brought the news to Philadelphia, Sunday, February 13, and the *Missouri Gazette* of Saturday, March 13, published a copy of the Treaty in full. The people of the West did not believe that the peace could be a lasting one "as none of the differences for which they went to war had been adjusted." "It may be the policy of the United States," commented Wilt, "to blow a little about it, but the British have, no doubt, other views than the mere wish for peace."[155]

When peace had been established the government promised to send out two regiments of regular troops and establish a line of posts along the rivers. This would protect the frontier from the ravages of the red men, who were still restless, and would assure safety to the new settlers who were coming into the territories east of the Mississippi River.[156] A short time after the Treaty of Peace had been signed, business settled into normal channels again and the Saint Louis merchants looked forward to building up "bigger business" and opening new projects for financial gain to retrieve their fortunes which had been seriously affected.

154 *Missouri Gazette,* February 18, 1815.
155 Wilt to Hertzog, March 20, 1815.
156 Wilt to Hertzog, February 6, 1815.

CHAPTER VIII
POST-WAR READJUSTMENTS

THE ratification of the Treaty of Ghent, which marked the close of the War of 1812, brought to an end hostilities between Great Britain and the United States, but treaties between the American government and Britain's allies among the various Indian tribes had to be concluded before the red men along the frontier would leave the war path and return to their peaceful pursuits of hunting and fishing. In the late summer, September, 1815, representatives of the Sac Indians living near the Des Moines River met the United States Commissioners, William Clark, Ninian Edwards and Auguste Chouteau in the little Indian village of Portage des Sioux.[1] Here twelve chiefs and warriors signed a treaty promising to bury the tomahawk and to live in peace with their white brethren. The following day the same commissioners concluded a treaty with the Renard or Fox Indians who were represented by twenty-two braves and chieftains. Thus ended, for the time at least, the savage warfare that had devastated the frontier during hostilities with England. These treaties promised to the pioneers undisturbed peace in the pursuit of their various occupations and trades and insured safety for the home-builders in the wilderness, for the fur traders and trappers on the upper waters of the Mississippi and Missouri Rivers, and for the miners, manufacturers, and merchants of the Middle West.

After the establishment of peace the mode of living on the frontier underwent a gradual change. The demands of customers at the western stores revealed an increase in wealth and a desire for apparel that conformed a little more closely to the styles and fashions of the eastern cities. The merchandise that Wilt ordered from Philadelphia soon after the close of the war is interesting, because it includes many items not found in earlier memoranda. In writing to Hertzog, he said: "I now send you

1 Portage des Sioux, founded in 1799, was located on the bank of the Mississippi about six miles above the mouth of the Missouri.

a minute list of such articles as I think will be suitable and which will help my assortment."

```
 3 elegant silk shawls
30 prs. Russian and Grecian sandals, assorted
 4 pcs. fashionable gingham
     (fine 130 yds. Kermitch Hkf.
     6 yds. silk bandana & flag hkfs.)
 1 doz. parasols
 4 doz. men's fine socks $10
 2 doz. women's fine hose $18
 2 pcs. fine Irish Linen $1.75 and $2
 6 boxes raisins
 2 baskets best figs
 1 box best prunes
10 reams best writing paper
 6 pcs. fine cambric
 7 prs. brass hooks for shovel and tongs
 2 pr. window hinges (to project that the shutter lays against the wall.)
20 doz. fine knives and forks
 6 doz. fine dessert
 6 doz. fine scissors
 2 doz. fine Razors asstd.
10 lbs. sugar and lemon candy
 6 lbs. best ammatto
 6 doz. ½ pint bowls
 6 doz ½ pint glass bowls
 3 doz. ½ gal. glass bowls
30 sets enamelled cups and saucers
 4 sets blue printed cups and saucers
 4 sets china cups and saucers
 4 blue coffee pots
24 edged dishes assorted
```

Mrs. William Clark, who was always ready to give Wilt suggestions regarding things the housewives might need, asked him to include in the list "a dozen pineapple cheeses" for the use of her own table.[2] The entire invoice, which included many articles in addition to those enumerated, amounted to $10,000.

Wilt was also engaged at this time in the selection of furnishings for the home he was preparing for his prospective bride, Anna K. Wilson,[3] to whom he was married on January 10, 1815.

2 Wilt to Hertzog, March 27, 1815.

3 Born in Kentucky, January 20, 1798, Anne Wilson had come to Saint

He outfitted the second floor of his new brick store for house-keeping, and commissioned Luttig, who was still on an expedition in Arkansas, to purchase for him from a southern slave-holder two negro women to serve his household in Saint Louis. One of these, a strong young girl of about fifteen years of age, was to be the housemaid in the new home; the other, an older woman, was to act in the capacity of cook and do the general and heavy work of the house.[4] With them came a negro boy, one of whose chores was to bring water from the river, there being no other near-by source of supply. The river water was muddy, but, when the boy had filled the stone jars standing in the rear of the kitchen, the black cook stirred into it a handful of bran, or mustard seed, or white of egg[5] which cleared the water so that she could use it for her cooking and for all other domestic purposes.

For his dining room Wilt ordered "a set of dining tables" with leaves of solid mahogany around which "a dozen gilt chairs" were to be placed. The table, covered with white damask and lighted by large brass candlesticks placed at each end, and set with a pair of decanters, taper wine glasses, fluted tumblers, silver casters, sugar and cream pots, silver spoons, and a blue printed china dinner set, must have made an attractive board. Andrew Wilt sent the silver casters and the dozen silver table spoons as a wedding present, and Mrs. William Clark advised the purchase of the chinaware which she considered to be "much the cheaper crockery as more care is taken of this than of the common ones."[6]

Mrs. Wilt must have taken great pride in her new home; while it was a cozy place, it had at the same time, almost an air of

Louis with her father, Major George Wilson, whose early interest in the development of the Missouri Territory led him to make his home in the growing center of the western prairie in the valley of the Mississippi. Billon, *op. cit.*, p. 261 n.

4 Wilt to John Luttig, February 22, 1815. For the younger negro girl Luttig paid $300 and for the older woman $400.

5 Lionberger, *op. cit.*, p. 36.

6 Wilt to Hertzog, March 27, 1815.

elegance with its "armed gilt chairs, armed rocking chairs, gilt social settees, its bureau, bedstead, cornesto, and dressing glass, as well as two pairs of large plated candlesticks for mantle pieces, one dozen glass candle shades (barrel shaped and open at both ends), and one dozen common chairs."[7] All articles of furniture for the new house were made by McDonough's in Pittsburgh. The fact that Wilt asked Hertzog to send him some new piano music[8] suggests that a pianoforte might also have been part of the new furnishings.

Into this richly furnished "second-story residence," Wilt brought his young bride and there with the brightest prospects be began his married life. He planned to give a portion of his time in the future to recreation, and for that purpose he kept a "handsome gig," strong and well-made, with a good harness for his thoroughbred. Long accustomed to the use of horses in his business journeys through the state, he ordered from his brother Andrew in Pittsburgh a "complete saddle to cost about $25, something stylish, without stirrups unless they are good ones; and for a customer a neat gig and harness, the more dashing the better."[9]

The first business venture that Wilt undertook after he had settled in his new home was one in which he had been interested ever since coming to the West. Foreign wines and liquors were in great demand, as were home-manufactured whiskey, rum, peach brandy, and porter. With other merchants and manufacturers, he felt that the protection of home industry was of vital importance and he agreed with Joseph Charless, senior editor of the *Missouri Gazette,* when his paper proposed that an increased duty be put on some or even all of the foreign liquors "whether they be distilled or fermented or both." This, said the editor, would keep up the price of grain, fruits, and Louisiana sugars and molasses, for beer, ale, porter, cider, cherry, whiskey, apple brandy, peach brandy, and Louisiana rum "were manu-

7 Wilt to Andrew Wilt, May 15, 1815.
8 Wilt to Hertzog, March 27, 1815.
9 Wilt to Andrew Wilt, July 31, 1813.

factured from produce grown on the lands of the Missouri Territory. This consumption would of course beneft the sugar planters and the farmers throughout the country."[10]

Jacques Saint Vrain[11] had a log brewery at Belle Fontaine, only fourteen miles north of Saint Louis on the Missouri. Here the United States troops had been stationed after the withdrawal of the Spanish and French armies and the presence of the soldiers brought a great deal of specie into circulation, a fact that possibly influenced Saint Vrain in the selection of a site for his brewery. He employed Victor Habb to look after the brewing and they managed to turn out strong beer, table beer, and porter. Not less than sixty barrels of bottled porter were sold annually in Saint Louis, each barrel containing three dozen bottles. The contents of the barrels were sometimes sold by the bottle at 37½ to 50 cents; or the original package if sold entire, went for $18 which amounted to $6 a dozen.[12] What Saint Vrain asked for his porter is not recorded, but it is safe to conjecture that his price compared favorably with that of the foreign beverage. The price of his strong beer was ten dollars a barrel, if paid for in cash, or twelve dollars if paid for in produce; the table beer was sold for five dollars a barrel, cash, or six dollars in produce.[13] Buyers of small quantities of beer could be accommodated at either the brewery at Belle Fontaine, or at the home in Saint Louis of Edward Hempstead who kept a large supply of beer and porter in his cellar ready for sale.[14]

Saint Vrain's plant was destroyed by fire in 1813, and shortly afterward John Luttig and Victor Habb attempted to build a

10 *Missouri Gazette,* August 7, 1808.

11 Saint Vrain, was a brother of De Lassus, Lieutenant-Governor of Louisiana, 1799–1803 (Houck, *op. cit.,* II, p. 99 n.).

12 Wilt to Hertzog, December 26, 1813.

13 The produce, delivered at the brewery, was valued as follows:

    Wheat   @ 62½ cents per bushel
    Barley   @ 50 cents per bushel.
    Rye   @ 62½ cents per bushel
    Corn   @ 25 cents per bushel
    Green hops @ 10 cents per bushel
    Cattle and pork at market prices

14 *Louisiana Gazette,* July 12, 1810.

brewery "up town" in Saint Louis, but because their funds were limited their plans did not materialize.[15] According to Schoolcraft, Joseph Philipson owned the first brewery in the town of Saint Louis, a structure located on the west side of Main Street between Biddle and Carr Streets. The first finished product was turned out in the fall of 1817, evidently in limited vats, for Schoolcraft tells us that the beer was cooled in a pirogue.[16] Habb, who was the brewer, apparently did not remain long in the service of Philipson, as he began business on his own account in 1819. Through the columns of the *Missouri Gazette,* under date of March 1 of that year, he informed the public that he intended to commence running a cart through the streets of Saint Louis for the purpose of selling beer and vinegar, retail. By this arrangement, the citizens would be accommodated each day. Beer could also be had by the barrel at the brewery and at the store of Mr. Labadie. The price of vinegar was seventy-five cents per gallon and twenty-five cents per quart.[17]

There had been a brewery in this section even before 1809; it now seemed to Wilt and other enterprising citizens that the time had come for the establishment of a distillery; in fact, early in the year 1812 Joseph Philipson conferred with Wilt on the feasibility of building one in the Missouri Territory. Upon investigation they found that as many as five thousand barrels of whiskey were brought up the Ohio to Saint Louis each year where they were sold for seventy-five cents a gallon,[18] figures that made the proposed distillery seem a promising venture.

The garrison, which during the war was supplied through the sutlers, consumed considerable quantities of these beverages. For the manufacture of whiskey thousands of bushels of grain could be raised on the prairie near Saint Louis, and this quantity, the *Missouri Gazette* stated, "would be offered at a low price

15 Wilt to Hertzog, December 26, 1813.

16 Schoolcraft, *op. cit.,* p. 198.

17 *Missouri Gazette,* March 1, 1819.

18 *Missouri Gazette,* July 13, 1816.

to anyone who would establish a distillery."[19] Barley, the grain in demand for the manufacture of beer as well as whiskey, was not cultivated extensively in Missouri, but if assured of a ready market at harvest season, the farmers would gladly plant this grain. Saint Vrain had paid as high as a dollar a bushel for barley, when he conducted his brewery at Belle Fontaine, but hops grew wild in the woods and sufficient quantities could be had for the gathering. If, at a later date, the natural growth became exhausted, Wilt thought a sufficient amount for their needs might be grown on a single acre of ground.[20]

Wilt's first plan was to build a distillery in Missouri at New Hartford where the logs necessary for the construction could be easily obtained, and where, on an elevated tract, there was a pond that would supply the water needed for the manufacture of the various liquors.[21] However, on Wilt's tract in Illinois the Cahokia Creek flowed for some length through the stretches of his property. In this stream he found a waterfall which afforded a regular supply of cold water that would not only insure a superior quality of whiskey, but would also save the expense of pumping water into the vats and stills. And there Wilt erected a distillery in 1817. The liquor was easily ferried across the Mississippi for sale in the store in Saint Louis, since intoxicating liquors were sold, not in saloons, but in the retail stores. The quality of the liquor must have been good for it was a steady source of income, and found ready sale in the home market, in the Indian trade, in the cantonments of the United States troops along the frontier, and in several towns on the Mississippi, Missouri, and Ohio Rivers.

While business cares absorbed much of his time, Wilt was interested in all projects that might lead to the improvement of Saint Louis. We learn that in the summer of 1816 he and several other prominent citizens determined to bring about the erection

19 *Missouri Gazette,* July 13, 1816.
20 Wilt to Hertzog, December 26, 1813.
21 Wilt to Hertzog, March 19, 1814.

of a theater,[22] where the inhabitants might have an opportunity to spend their free hours in amusing and instructive entertainment. Among Wilt's fellow townsmen who furthered this project we find the names of James Kennerly, George H. Kennerly, John R. Guy, Thomas Hanley, Chas. S. Hempstead, William Turner, Henry S. Geyer, James Loper, Robert Wash, Stephen Rector, and others. The management of the enterprise was given into the hands of a committee composed of John Thompson, Christopher Price, and Thomas Hempstead, and they were authorized to purchase a tract of land in a suitable location and superintend the erection of the building. After some delay occasioned by disagreement in the selection of the site, they purchased a lot one hundred and twenty feet deep, with a frontage of fifty feet, on the south side of Chestnut Street. For this they paid the extravagant sum of $1500. Although they managed to begin the construction of a theater, they had proceeded only as far as the foundation when their funds were exhausted. The project therefore came to naught, as there was no possible source for collecting more money.[23]

The failure of this project was but one instance of the frustration and disappointment that Wilt had been called upon to endure, both in his business and in his efforts to develop the

22 In 1814 the old Baird blacksmith shop became the public hall of the town. Public meetings, exhibitions and religious exercises were held under its roof, and here, too, the young men's Thespian Society presented theatricals. The price of admission was one dollar, a rather high fee for that time and place, but the children's tickets cost only half that amount. The doors of the theater opened at half past five and the performance began at six-thirty. Among the dramas attempted by these amateurs one finds "Lovers' Vows", "The Poor Gentlemen," "Secrets Worth Knowing," "The Agreeable Surprise," and the tragedy "Douglas", in five acts. (Billon, *op. cit.,* pp. 74–75.)

23 For some years no change was made in the property but, finally, a new owner got possession and had a frame livery barn erected. From time to time, during the years that followed, the property changed hands. Among the successive owners we see such names as B. W. Alexander, Bob O'Blenis, etc. In the last turn of events the Arnots got possession and they had the present building, known as the post office of 1820, erected. This was on Chestnut Street, east of and adjoining the Republican building in which the former *Saint Louis Republican* was published. (Billon, *op. cit.,* p. 77).

social and cultural life of his adopted city. But these troubles and cares were overshadowed by the crushing sorrow that befell him during the Christmas season of 1816, when his young wife passed away after a brief illness. He now had to adjust himself to life without her encouragement and companionship, and to face the problem of rearing his infant son in that crude frontier town where a child's health, happiness, and well-being were peculiarly dependent on the guidance and tender care of its mother.

Two years after the death of Christian's wife, his brother Andrew, for some reason that has not been recorded, closed the store in Pittsburgh and came with his two sisters, Rachel and Juliana, to live in Saint Louis. Perhaps the growing business enterprises that Wilt was conducting in Saint Louis demanded greater and more detailed attention than he was able to give, and he invited Andrew to share his burdens, or possibly, the dark cloud of the coming panic (1819) had cast its shadow before and caused him to fear for the safety of some of his investments.

In Saint Louis, as throughout the entire country, the years from 1815 to 1819 had been a period of wild speculation in western lands, of excessive internal improvements, and of industrial expansion. The long cycle of wars, both in Europe and America, ending only in 1815, had encouraged the growth of an unstable and overdeveloped structure of credits and debits;[24] the system of banking seemed to produce abundant capital and this in turn induced speculation beyond all prudence.[25] When the storm broke in the spring of 1819 not only the settlement on the western frontier but the whole country was ruined. State bank issues were reduced from one hundred million dollars in 1817 to forty-five million in 1819; staple products fell to less than half their former price; merchants were bankrupt; laborers were out of work. Land values declined fifty to seventy-five per

24 Rezneck, Samuel, "The Depression of 1819–1822, a Social History", *American Historical Review*, XXXIX, p. 28.

25 Bezanson, *op. cit.*, p. 176.

cent,[26] bringing great hardship to the propertied class to which Wilt belonged. In the western states the Bank of the United States, whose holdings included property of every kind, suffered a loss of nearly two million dollars in bad debts; had it not been able to hold on until values were restored, it might have been even more seriously affected.[27] Distress prevailed throughout the country and business was completely paralyzed.

Whatever may have been Andrew Wilt's reason for moving to Saint Louis, he very soon formed a partnership with his brother and the firm of CHRISTIAN AND ANDREW WILT was established on February 10, 1819. This new firm, unfortunately, had only a brief existence, for Andrew had been in Saint Louis less than a year when he died on August 18, 1819, after an illness of only a few days. This must have been a great shock to Christian for he had been at all times greatly attached to this brother. We have no data to prove that this sudden bereavement had a bad effect on the health of the older brother, but the fact that he too passed away about six weeks later, when he was only thirty-one years of age, seems to confirm this conjecture. Four years later, in 1823, death claimed his son, a boy of seven years, his only descendant and the sole surviving member of his immediate family. We find no further reference to the family of Christian Wilt in the records of Saint Louis.[28]

26 Turner, *op. cit.*, p. 136.   27 Rezneck, *op. cit.*, p. 33.

28 Hertzog, Wilt's uncle, whose business in Philadelphia was affected by the panic of 1819 decided to remove with his family to the West. After six weeks spent in crossing the mountains they reached Pittsburgh where Hertzog fell ill of typhoid fever. This held him there for several months. Before he reached St. Louis both his nephews, Christian and Andrew, former business associates of their uncle, died. On arriving in St. Louis he found his affairs in a complicated and confused condition. Record of business transactions were incomplete; land titles were found unsound; debts were unpaid and much of the land mortgaged. All this proved too much for Hertzog at his advanced age and in his weakened condition. He carried on for a few years and then, worn with anxiety and care, discouraged by continued losses, crushed in spirit and broken in health, he succumbed to an attack of fever and died January 23, 1827, in his sixty-fourth year, at his home in Cahokia, Illinois.

Collins, *op. cit.*, p. 166; *Collections* of the Genealogical Society of Penn-

The *Missouri Gazette* of September 29, 1819, carried with the announcement of Wilt's death this brief appreciation of the young merchant:

Died: On Monday morning last, sincerely regretted by all who knew him, Mr. Christian Wilt, merchant of this place. He came to this town a youth about ten years ago, and has filled with high reputation those stations which entitled him to the respect and esteem of his friends and neighbors.[29]

Among Wilt's neighbors and friends were men distinguished in the early history of the West: General William Clark, United States Indian agent, Rufus Easton, first postmaster in Saint Louis, Edward Hempstead, the first territorial representative of Missouri in Congress, Alexander McNair, sheriff of Missouri and later its first governor, Benjamin O'Fallon, nephew of General Clark,[30] Joseph Miller[31] and Ramsey Crooks, members of John Jacob Astor's expeditionary party to the Pacific Ocean, James and George Kennerly, merchants, Thomas F. Riddick, patron of the public school system of St. Louis, Major Robert Wash, member of General Benjamin Howard's military staff, Pierre Chouteau, son of Auguste Chouteau, one of the founders of Saint Louis, Captain Gratiot, son of Charles Gratiot, noted early fur trader.

That Wilt, in the leisure time he allowed himself to take from his strenuous business affairs, played an active part in the social and civic life of the community in which he lived is evident from his interest in the Thespian Society which he helped to organize in 1814.[32] In the crude border settlement this was one of the few forms of amusement for those who sought to introduce some of the pastimes and pleasures that the young people of the East enjoyed. Wilt's interest in civic and national

sylvania, LXXIX, 239. Historical Society of Pennsylvania, Philadelphia, Pennsylvania.

29 *Missouri Gazette,* September 29, 1819.

30 Wilt to Hertzog, December 14, 1812.

31 Wilt to Andrew Wilt, May 15, 1813.

32 Billon, *op. cit.,* p. 77.

affairs was demonstrated during the war. He accepted willingly his share in picketing the town when it was feared the red men were about to attack the unguarded settlement,[33] and in 1813 he joined an expedition to the North against the Indians.[34] He was active with other citizens in providing a series of illuminations to celebrate the victories of the American troops. The first of these he described in a letter to Hertzog on October 12, 1813. "Hempstead arrived here the beginning of the week with the great news of Perry's capture of six sails of the English on Lake Erie. Our town illuminated in consequence thereof, and to heighten the sport we drew a canoe on fire through the streets. Let Chauncy do the same, and we shall perform the like ceremony."[35] On November 6, 1813, less than a month later, he was able to report, "Last night we illuminated for Chauncy."[36] A year prior to this, on October 11, 1812, he had written of the indignation of the Saint Louis colony over the treachery of General Hull: "Yesterday," to the accompaniment of howls and hisses, "we burnt, hung, and shot General Hull in effigy."[37] Of the last illumination referred to by Wilt, one held on February 18, 1815, to celebrate Jackson's victory at New Orleans, the *Missouri Gazette* says: "At least one candle burned in every window of the town in honor of the brilliant success of the American army at New Orleans."

Wilt's interests included banking and stabilization of the currency, and he was instrumental in organizing the Bank of Saint Louis. Speculation, especially in land, was extensive. Specie was scarce and bank notes were received in payment for the land. To provide currency, banks had been created on the east side of the river and their notes flooded the Saint Louis market.[38] To protect themselves, the merchants organized the Bank of Saint

33 Wilt to Hertzog, March 6, 1813.

34 Wilt to Andrew Wilt, August 7, 1813.

35 Wilt to Andrew Wilt, October 2, 1813.

36 Wilt to Hertzog, November 6, 1813.

37 Wilt to Hertzog, October 11, 1812.

38 Lionberger, *op. cit.,* p. 42.

Louis and later the Bank of Missouri. In the former Wilt invested heavily and acted as one of the commissioners in collecting its capital of $100,000; of the $250,000 capital of the Bank of Missouri, the second bank organized in Saint Louis, his share was $3000.

His widespread business activities included the establishment of a general store at Saint Louis and branch stores at Sainte Genevieve, Herculaneum, and New Hartford, Missouri; the operation of factories for the manufacture of red lead, white lead, candles and soap, all in Saint Louis; and the conduct of a shot factory at New Madrid. He operated a distillery on L'Abbe Creek in Cahokia, Illinois, engaged in land speculations both in the city of Saint Louis and in the surrounding country, and was actively interested in governmental affairs. He also kept on hand a supply of the best goods for the United States troops, and was ever ready to assist his fellow citizens by acting as agent in the collection and remittance of drafts when requested to do so.[39]

As Hertzog's partner in these various enterprises Wilt was to receive "one third without interest." Even after Mussina's withdrawal from the firm, his share of the profits remained the same. While Hertzog financed and outlined the general conduct of each new undertaking, he left Wilt free to work out the details of the business. He had implicit confidence in his partner's judgment, and rarely questioned the decisions which were made in St. Louis. Like every businessman, Wilt made some mistakes and experienced some disappointments, but his letters reveal a series of profitable undertakings. Sales were usually made on credit, and while collections were often slow, the firm seems to have lost little as the result of bad debts. Whenever possible Wilt sold for cash, but the bulk of his business was conducted on a barter basis. In selling lead, shot, or land Wilt accepted payment in specie, in long term drafts on eastern banks, or in notes of the Illinois or Kentucky banks. The proceeds from the various St. Louis enterprises were normally forwarded

39 Wilt to William Foster, June 11, 1814.

to Hertzog who occasionally complained of a protested draft or
a bad bank note. Wilt's working capital seems to have consisted
largely of the goods which Hertzog purchased in Philadelphia
and Pittsburgh and sent West. The St. Louis sales after the first
year made it possible for the firm to operate without investment
of additional funds. Wilt was successful in his business deals
and had not the panic of 1819 caused a complete stagnation of
all business, Hertzog would not have found his affairs in so
disordered a condition when he came to St. Louis in the year
of the disaster.

A glamor of romance and daring pioneering surrounds the
story of Christian Wilt. Through his letters, found in the old
leather-bound letterbook in the archives of the Missouri Historical Society of Saint Louis, runs the story of his failures
and his successes in the early commercial life of the present
metropolis of Missouri. In his early youth he left his family to
which he was affectionately attached, and went forth to seek a
home and fortune in the unexplored country of Upper Louisiana. He saw in the little western trading-post of more than a
century ago, the possibility of the great development that is
manifest in that city today. The significance of Wilt's story is
to be found not in the history of an individual merchant's business transactions but in the attempt to indicate, in a small way,
the value of the services of the pioneer mercantile class in
influencing trade and politics, in developing the natural resources
of the section and in transforming Saint Louis society from the
simplicity of its pioneer days to the complexity of modern times.

Strange as it may seem, the Saint Louis merchant was almost
wholly dependent for his immediate needs upon the movements
of world trade with all its ramifications; to him its uninter-
rupted continuance was of vast importance. The sturdy American clipper, the Spanish and Portuguese bottoms, and the swift-
sailing English vessels carried the furs of the Saint Louis
traders from the Eastern ports to the fur centers of Asia and
Europe—to Canton, Paris, Vienna, Amsterdam, Leipzig, London—where many of these furs were made into hats. While

fashions in the nineteenth century had changed somewhat, beaver from the trading posts on the Mississippi, used for hats alone, meant a fortune for both dealers and hatters as well as a living wage for felters and many other employees of these European cities.[40] On their return voyages the ships brought back steel from England and Germany; gin from Holland; indigo from Bengal; iron from England, Sweden, and Russia; wines from Lisbon, Sicily, and Marseilles; sheeting from Russia; sugar and coffee from Cuba, the West Indies and Santo Domingo; the tea, silk, and chinaware from China.[41] These, with some domestic goods, were floated in rudely built flat boats or keels sometimes of forty to sixty tons down to the mouth of the Ohio River and from there they were rowed, sailed, pulled or poled upstream to Saint Louis. If at times the current of the rivers was so swift that neither sails nor oars could make way against it, then long ropes called "cordelles" were used to tow the boat from the shore.[42] Sometimes the going up stream required long weeks of toil before the goods reached the merchants waiting in Saint Louis. When wars, blockades, embargoes, or British Orders in Council checked or prevented the importation of these goods the reaction upon the sales in the West was naturally very marked.

During the war with Great Britain, Saint Louis, which was in the immediate vicinity of hostile Indians, did little except engage in military operations. Business was in a large measure checked since communication with New Orleans, one of the avenues of trade with the East, was interrupted. The Indian tribes within the reach of British influence became hostile toward the American traders and the fur trade, the principal resource of its merchants was cut off. Money was at times so scarce that it could not be borrowed even on the best security and collection of debts was out of the question. Yet in no part of the country did the mass of able-bodied men—merchants, farmers, doctors, lawyers—show greater eagerness to take the

40 Skinner, *Beaver, Kings, and Cabins* (New York, 1933), p. 109.
41 Bezanson, *op. cit.,* pp. 14–16.   42 Lionberger, *op. cit.,* p. 33.

field, serving either in the enrolled militia or in the mounted rangers.[43]

The interests of the pioneer merchant were not confined to the disposal of goods on the shelves of his store but grew in ever widening circles as the resources of the country became known to him. As a class these merchants were men of intelligence and influence.[44] They invested in transportation companies, in industries of all sorts, and in lands and mines. In 1811 a cotton factory was opened in Saint Louis, but there is doubt as to its financial success. A "tobacco manufactory" was established in 1817, but even earlier Saint Louis boasted a lead factory, a soap and candle factory, a brewery, and two banks. In 1811 the assessed value of the town property was $134,516 with taxes at one and one-half per cent. Ten years later the value of the property of the city had reached the sum of $940,000. The United States opened the first Missouri land office in 1816 in Saint Louis, attracting numbers of speculators and adding to the competition for wealth and power.

The changes in Saint Louis' social life within a few years after Wilt came to open his store in 1810 were many. Sidewalks had been laid;[45] some streets had been paved in spite of the protests of the people who complained that the broken stones cut the wooden wheels of their wagons;[46] a theater, a Court House, and a Presbyterian Church had been erected, and, to the merchant, the most remarkable event, a steamboat[47] had docked at the levee.

To all of these improvements, social, industrial, financial, Wilt had given his time, his prestige and his wealth, and although premature death cut him off in his prime, just when his experience and his business acumen gave promise of success in all his undertakings, the records that relate in detail the material development of the city should include his name on the honor roll of "Laclede Village."

43 Chas. Gratiot's Letterbook, p. 166.
44 Lewis, *op. cit.*, p. 155.   45 In 1818.
46 Lionberger, *op. cit.*, pp. 40–41.   47 In 1817.

BIBLIOGRAPHY

PRIMARY SOURCES

MANUSCRIPTS

(Unless otherwise noted, these manuscripts are in the archives of the Missouri Historical Society in St. Louis.)

American Fur Company, Account Books (Invoices Outward) July 15, 1822, December 10, 1822.

Ashley, William H., Letters and Accounts, 1811–1836.

Bates, Frederick (Secretary of Missouri Territory and afterwards Governor of the State). Personal and official letters, appointments, and documents, 1807–1825.

Chouteau, Auguste, Collection of business and family papers, letters, notes, and accounts of the fur trade.

Chouteau, Pierre, Important collection of papers relating to the fur trade on the Upper Missouri, including several original journals and letter books.

Church Registers:

    Portage des Sioux, 1811–1836

    Saint Charles,   1792–1863

    Saint Ferdinand,   1796–1820

    Sainte Genevieve, 1850–1857. Book of Disbursements.

    First Reformed Church, Philadelphia, Pa., 1725.

Clark, William, Memorandum-book, September, 1820 to May, 1825; also letters and reports.

Crooks, Ramsey, Letters of Ramsey Crooks, John J. Astor, and American Fur Company, 1813–1846. Transcript made through the courtesy of Mr. C. M. Burton.

Darby, John F., Correspondence, personal and official of, 1826–1888.

Farrar, Dr. Bernard G., Account Books from 1807–1836, containing names of nearly all of the early residents of St. Louis.

Forsyth, Thomas, Collection of letters and reports while Indian Agent, 1811–1822.

Gratiot, Charles, Letter Book, March 6, 1798 to January 6, 1817.

Hempstead, Edward, Letters, 1805–1830, addressed to Stephen Hempstead.

Hertzog, Joseph (Merchant at Philadelphia). Letters to Christian Wilt and others, 1811–1815. (Hertzog-Wilt Manuscripts.)

Hunt, Theodore (Recorder of Land Titles). Hunt's minutes; the testimony relating to lands in the towns and villages of St. Louis, St. Charles, St. Ferdinand, Portage des Sioux, Carondelet, New Madrid, New Bourbon, Ste. Genevieve, Villa Robert (Missouri), and Village of Arkansas, February 13 to May 25, 1825. (Chouteau Collection.)

Kennerly, James, Memorandum book for 1824–1825 at Council Bluffs; same for 1839–1843 at St. Louis.

Lisa, Manuel, Collection of letters, contracts, deeds, accounts, and litigations, 1794–1820.

Missouri Fur Company, Book containing the Articles of Association, dated January 24, 1812, and minutes of the Board meetings from January 27, 1812 to January 17, 1814. The original of this is in the library of the Kansas State Historical Society, Topeka, Kansas.

Missouri Fur Company, Account Book, 1809–1812, signed by Manuel Lisa.

Major, George C. (Indian Agent), Letters, diaries, reports, personal and official, 1805–1850.

Philadelphia Archives, Original Deeds, 1683–1830. Register of Deeds' Office, City Hall, Philadelphia, Pa.

Philipson, Joseph (Merchant at St. Louis, 1807). Account Book, December 13, 1807 to July 31, 1809. Mercantile Library, St. Louis.

Sibley Letter Books, 1808–1849. Missouri Historical Society Archives, St. Louis, Mo.

Saint Cyr, Reverend (Pastor of Ste. Genevieve Parish). Account Book, 1850–1857. Ste. Genevieve, Mo.

Ste. Genevieve Archives, Marriage contracts, deeds, concessions, Circuit and Probate Court records, 1761–1854.

St. Louis Archives, Court records, 1764–1870; original land deeds, City Hall, St. Louis, Mo.

Proceedings of the Trustees of the Town of St. Louis, August 10, 1808, March 3, 1823. City Hall, St. Louis.

St. Louis Missouri Fur Company, Account books, containing also letters, articles of association and minutes of meetings, March, 1809–January, 1812.

Sublette Collection, Comprising the papers of William, Milton, and Andrew Sublette; business correspondence of Smith, Jackson and Sublette with Rocky Mountain Fur Co., 1826–1857.

Vallé, Captain Francois, Collection, 1796–1846.

Vallé, Jules F., Manuscript of Rules for the Valle Mines.

Vallé Mines, Account Book, Lead account, 1850.

Vallé Papers, Missouri Historical Society Archives in St. Louis.

Vallé and Ziegler, Account Books, Journal "A", Tobacco Manufacture, 1827–1830.

Walsh, Julius S., Collection, 1778–1922.

Wilt, Christian, Letters written at St. Louis to his uncle Joseph Hertzog of Philadelphia, John C. Luttig, and others, from July, 1812, to September, 1815. An important collection containing valuable material on the social and commercial life of St. Louis and on the War of 1812.

NEWSPAPERS

Missouri Gazette, 1808–1809; *Louisiana Gazette*, 1809–1812.

Missouri Gazette, 1812–1822.

Missouri Intelligencer (Franklin Missouri), 1822.

Missouri Republican, 1822.

Niles Weekly Register (Baltimore, 1811–1847), Vols. I. and II.

St. Louis Inquirer, 1819.

PUBLIC DOCUMENTS AND OTHER SOURCES

Acts of the Territory of Missouri, St. Louis, 1813–1818.

American State Papers, Documents, legislative and executive of the Congress of the United States. Public Lands, Vol. I–II. Navigation and Commerce, Vol. I. Finance, Vol. II. Washington, 1832–1861. 38 vols.

Annals of Congress, Debates and Proceedings in the Congress of the United States, 1789–1856. Washington, 1834–1856. 41 vols.

Ashe, Thomas, *Travels in America, 1806.* London, 1808.

Ashley-Smith Explorations and the Discovery of a Central Route to the Pacific, 1822–1829, with original Journals, H. C. Dale (ed.). Cleveland, 1918.

Audubon and His Journals, with Zoological and other notes, Audubon, Marie and Elliot Coues (ed.). London, 1898. 2 vols.

Austin, Moses, *Austin Papers, 1765–1836,* Eugene C. Barker (ed.). American Historical Association, *Report for 1919.* Washington, 1924.

Birkbeck, Morris, *Notes on a Journey from Virginia to Illinois.* London, 1818.

Boilvin, Nicholas, "Prairie du Chien in 1811". *Wisconsin State Historical Society Collections.* Reuben G. Thwaites (ed.). Vol. XI, Madison, 1888.

Bradbury, John, *Travels in the Interior of America in the Years 1809, 1810 and 1811.* London, 1819.

Brisbois, B. W., "Traditions and Recollections of Prairie du Chien". Notes by Lyman C. Draper, *Wisconsin State Historical Society Collections,* Vol. IX, Madison, 1882.

Brackenridge, H. M., *Views of Louisiana, together with a Journal of a Voyage up the Missouri in 1811.* Pittsburgh, 1814.

Chouteau, Auguste, "Journal". *Missouri Historical Society Collections,* Vol. III, 1911.

Clemens, James, Jr., *Travels on an Inland Voyage, 1807–1808.* New York, 1810. 2 vols.

Champion, Richard, *An American Correspondence of a Bristol Merchant, 1766–1776.* Berkeley, 1934.

Edwards, Ninian W. (ed.), *Life and Times of Ninian Edwards,* Springfield, 1870.

Geyer, H. S., *Digest of the Laws of Missouri.* St. Louis, 1818.

Gregg, Josiah, *Commerce of the Prairies.* New York, 1844. 2 vols.

Laws of the Missouri District, Louisiana. St. Louis, 1804–1808–1810.

Leonard, Zenas, *Adventures of Zenas Leonard, Fur Trader and Trapper, 1831–1836.* Cleveland, 1904.

Lewis, Meriwether and William Clark, *Journal of the Lewis and Clark Expedition.* Gass, Patrick (ed.). Philadelphia, 1810.

Luttig, John, *Journal of a Fur-trading Expedition on the Upper Missouri, 1812–1813.* Drumm, Stella (ed.). St. Louis, 1920.

New York Price Current, 1805–1810, 1812–1814. New York, 1814. 6 vols.

Philadelphia Directory, 1811. Philadelphia, Pa.

Pennsylvania Archives, 3rd and 6th Series, Vols. 14, 15, 25. 1730–1898, Philadelphia.

Schoolcraft, Henry Rowe, *A View of the Lead Mines of Missouri.* New York, 1819.

——, *Journal of a Tour into the Interior of Missouri and Arkansas.* London, 1821.

——, *Scenes and Adventures in the Semi-Alphine Region of the Ozark Mountains of Missouri and Arkansas.* Philadelphia, 1853.

Stoddard, Major Amos, *Sketches, Historical and Descriptive of Louisiana.* Philadelphia, 1812.

SECONDARY SOURCES

Adams, Henry, *History of the United States of America.* New York, 1891–98. 9 vols.

—— (ed.), *Writings of Albert Gallatin.* Philadelphia, 1879. 3 vols.

Alvord, C. W., and Carter, C. E., "The New Regime, 1765–1767". *Illinois Historical Collections,* Vol. XI. Springfield, 1916.

Alvord, Clarence Walworth, *The Mississippi Valley in British Politics.* Cleveland, 1917. 2 vols.

——, *The Critical Period.* Springfield, 1915.

Babcock, Rufus (ed.), *Forty Years of Pioneer Life: Memoir of John Mason Peck,* edited from his journals and correspondence. Philadelphia, 1864.

Bakewell, B. G., *The Family Book of Bakewell, Page and Campbell.* Pittsburgh, 1896.

Beers, Henry P. *The Western Military Frontier, 1815–1846.* Philadelphia, 1935.

Beidelman, William, *The Story of the Pennsylvania Germans.* Easton, Pa., 1898.

Bell, Charles N., *The Earliest Fur Traders on the Upper Red River, and Red Lake Minnesota, 1783–1810.* Winnipeg, 1928.

Bezanson, Anne, *Wholesale Prices in Philadelphia, 1784–1861.* Philadelphia, 1936.

Billon, F. L., *Annals of St. Louis in Its Early Days under the French and Spanish Dominations.* St. Louis, 1886.

——, *Annals of St. Louis in Its Territorial Days, 1804–1821.* St. Louis, 1888.

Biographical Encyclopedia of Pennsylvania of the Nineteenth Century. Philadelphia, 1874.

Bolles, Albert S., *Pennsylvania, Province and State.* Philadelphia, 1899.

Bowen, Daniel, *A History of Philadelphia.* Philadelphia, 1839.

Boyd, Julian P., *The Susquehanna Company.* Yale Press, 1935.

Brackenridge, H. M., *Recollections of Persons and Places in the West.* Philadelphia, 1834.

Brown, Henry Collins (ed.), *Valentine's Manual of Old New York.* New York, 1921.

Bryan, W. S., and Rose, Robert, *History of the Pioneer Families of Missouri.* St. Louis, 1876.

Burpee, Lawrence J., *A Chapter in the Literature of the Fur Trade.* Bibliographical Society of America Papers, Chicago, 1910. 5 vols.

Cable, John R., *The Bank of the State of Missouri.* New York, 1923.

Campbell, R. A., *Gazette of Missouri*. St. Louis, 1875.

Carpenter, W. H., *History of Pennsylvania from Its Earliest Settlement to the Present Time*. Philadelphia, 1882.

Carr, Lucian, *Missouri, A Bone of Contention*. Boston, 1888.

Charlevoix, Rev. P. F. X., S.J., *A Voyage to North America undertaken by the Command of the present King of France*. Dublin, 1866. 2 vols.

——, *History and General Description of New France*. New York, 1866. 6 vols.

Chittenden, Hiram Martin, *American Fur Trade of the Far West*. New York, 1902. 3 vols.

——, *History of Early Steamboat Navigation on the Missouri River*. New York, 1903.

Collet, O. W., *General Index to the Archives in the Office of the Recorder of Deeds for the County of St. Louis*. St. Louis, 1876. 6 vols.

Collins, William H., *Genealogical Records of the Descendants of John Collins, Sr., 1640–1760*. Quincy, Ill., 1897.

Coman, Katherine, *Economic Beginnings of the Far West*. New York, 1912. 2 vols.

Cox, James, *The Old and New in St. Louis*. St. Louis, 1894.

Cramer, Vadox, *Navigator*. Pittsburgh, 1821.

Dale, H. C., *Ashley-Smith Explorations and the Discovery of a Central Route to the Pacific, 1822–1829*. Cleveland, 1918.

Edwards, Richard, *The Great West and Her Metropolis*. St. Louis, 1860.

Essex, James Cartwright, *An Autobiography*. Missouri Historical Society Pamphlet. St. Louis, 1934.

Flint, Timothy, *Recollections of the Last Ten Years in Occasional Journeying in the Valley of the Mississippi*. Boston, 1826.

Gayerré, Charles, *History of Louisiana, the French Domination*. New York, 1867.

Genealogical Society of Pennsylvania Collections, Vol. 79, Philadelphia, 1903.

Goebel, Dorothy B., *William Henry Harrison, A Political Biography*. Indianapolis, 1926.

Gouge, William M., *A Short History of Paper Money and Banking in the United States*. Philadelphia, 1833.

Hall, James, *The West, Its Commerce and Navigation*. Cincinnati, 1848.

Harrington, Virginia, *The New York Merchants on the Eve of the Revolution*. New York, 1935.

Hazard, E., *Register of Pennsylvania*. Philadelphia, 1828–35.

Herrick, Francis Hobart, *Audubon the Naturalist, A History of His Life and Times*. New York, 1917. 2 vols.

Holdsworth, J. T., *Report of the Economic Survey of Pittsburgh*. Pittsburgh, 1912.

Houck, Louis, *History of Missouri*. Chicago, 1908. 3 vols.

——, *The Spanish Regime in Missouri*. Chicago, 1909. 2 vols.

Hunt, Freeman, *Lives of American Merchants*. New York, 1856. 2 vols.

Hyde, William, and Conrad, H. L., *Encyclopedia of the History of St. Louis.* St. Louis, 1899. 2 vols.

Irving, Washington, *Astoria.* Philadelphia, 1841. 2 vols.

——, *Rocky Mountain Sketches.* Philadelphia, 1832. 2 vols.

James, Thomas, *Three Years Among the Indians and Mexicans.* Waterloo, 1846. Reprinted and edited by Walter B. Douglas. St. Louis, 1917.

Jenkins, Howard M. (ed.), *Pennsylvania, Colonial and Federal, 1608–1903.* Pennsylvania, 1903. 3 vols.

Johnson, Ida Amanda, *The Michigan Fur Trade.* Michigan Historical Publications, Vol. 5, 1919.

Jordan, John W., *Colonial and Revolutionary Families of Pennsylvania.* New York,1911. 3 vols.

Kellogg, Louisa P., *The British Regime in Wisconsin.* Madison, 1935.

Knox, J. J., *The History of Banking in the United States.* New York, 1903.

Laut, Agnes C., *The Fur Trade of America.* New York, 1921.

Lewis, John F., *The History of an Old Philadelphia Land Title.* Philadelphia, 1904.

Lightfoot, Mrs. Joseph Vallé, *A Tale of Sainte Genevieve.* St. Louis, 1934.

Lionberger, Isaac H., *The Annals of St. Louis, 1764–1928.* St. Louis, 1929.

Lippincott, Horace M., *Early Philadelphia; its People, Life and Progress.* Philadelphia, 1917.

Lucas, C. P., *The Canadian War of 1812.* Oxford, 1906.

Marshall, Thomas M., *Life and Letters of Frederick Bates.* St. Louis, 1926. 2 vols.

Martin, Francois Xavier, *The History of Louisiana From the Earliest Period.* New Orleans, 1882.

Mereness, Newton D., *Travels in the American Colonies.* New York, 1916.

Missouri Geological Survey Reports, "Dr. Litton's Report", *Annual Report of the Geological Survey of Missouri,* 1853–1854, Jefferson City, 1856.

Missouri Historical Society *Collections.* St. Louis, 1875–1927.

Muschamp, Edward A., *Audacious Audubon.* New York, 1929.

Nevins, Allan, *Fremont, The West's Greatest Adventurer.* New York and London, 1928. 2 vols.

Parkman, Francis, *Oregon Trail.* Boston, 1882.

Pittman, Philip, *The Present State of the European Settlements on the Mississippi.* (Original Edition, London, 1770). Cleveland, 1906.

Pittsburgh in 1816. Compiled by the Carnegie Library of Pittsburgh, on the One Hundredth Anniversary of the Granting of the City Charter, 1916.

Poore, Benjamin P., *The Political Register and Congressional Directory, 1778–1878.* Boston, 1878.

Porter, Kenneth Wiggins, *John Jacob Astor, Business Man.* Cambridge, Mass., 1931. 2 vols.

Pratt, Julius, *Expansionists of 1812.* New York, 1925.

Reavis, L. U., *St. Louis, the Future Great City of the World.* St. Louis, 1875.

Reynolds, John, *The Pioneer History of Illinois, 1673–1818.* Chicago, 1887.

Rich, Wesley E., *History of United States Post Office to the Year 1829.* Cambridge, Mass., 1924.

Rickard, T. A., *A History of American Mining.* New York and London, 1932.

Ritter, Abraham, *Philadelphia and Her Merchants.* Philadelphia, 1860.

Rothensteiner, Rt. Rev. John, *A History of the Archdiocese of St. Louis.* St. Louis, 1928.

Rozier, Firmin A., *A History of the Early Settlement of the Mississippi Valley.* St. Louis, 1880.

Ruxton, George F., *Life in the Far West.* New York, 1894.

Scharf, J. Thomas, *History of St. Louis City and County.* Philadelphia, 1883. 2 vols.

Scoville, Joseph A., *The Old Merchants of New York.* New York, 1863.

Shepherd, Elihu H., *The Early History of St. Louis and Missouri.* St. Louis, 1870.

Shortfield, Luke., *The Western Merchant, Hints for Those who Design Emigrating to the West.* Philadelphia, 1849.

Skinner, Constance Linsay. *Beaver, Kings and Cabins.* New York, 1933.

——, *Adventurers of Oregon.* New Haven, 1920.

Stevens, Walter B., *St. Louis One Hundred Years in a Week.* (Celebration of Centennial of Incorporation, October third to ninth). St. Louis, 1909.

——, *St. Louis Centennial Association.* St. Louis, 1909.

——, *St. Louis, the Fourth City, 1764–1909.* St. Louis, 1909. 3 vols.

——, *Missourians One Hundred Years Ago.* St. Louis, 1908.

Stevens, Wayne E., *The Northwest Fur Trade 1763–1800.* Urbana, Ill., 1926.

Stewart, Sir William D., *Edward Warren.* London, 1854.

Sturgis, William, *The Northwest Fur Trade and the Indians of the Oregon Country.* Old South Leaflet. General Series, V. 9, No. 219.

Thomas, W. L., *History of St. Louis County, Missouri.* St. Louis, 1911. 2 vols.

Thwaites, Reuben G., *Daniel Boone.* New York, 1924.

——, *The History of Wisconsin.* Boston, 1891.

Tohill, Louis A., *Robert Dickson, British Fur Trade on the Upper Mississippi.* Ann Arbor, 1927.

Turner, Frederick Jackson, *The Frontier in American History.* New York, 1920.

——, *The Rise of the New West, 1819–1829.* New York, 1906.

——, *The Character and Influence of the Fur Trade in Wisconsin.* Baltimore, 1891.

Utley, Henry, and Cutcheon, Bryon M., *Michigan as a Province, Territory and State.* New York, 1906. 4 vols.

Veech, John, *The Monongahela of Old, Historical Sketches of South-Western Pennsylvania to the Year 1800.* Pittsburgh, 1858.

Violette, Eugene M., *A Hisory of Missouri.* Chicago, 1918.

Weiser, C. Z., *Life of John C. Weiser, German Patriot.* Reading, Pa., 1876.

Williams, Walter, *The State of Missouri.* Columbia, Mo., 1904.

——, *Missouri, Mother of the West.* Chicago, 1930. 5 vols.

PERIODICALS

Atherton, Lewis E., "The Western Merchants." *Mississippi Valley Historical Review,* Vol. XXIV, No. 2, 1937.

Cruckshand, Ernest A., "Robert Dickson, the Indian Trader," *Wisconsin State Historical Society Collections,* Vol. XII, Madison, 1892.

Douglas, W. B., "Manuel Lisa." *Missouri Historical Society Collections,* Vol. III, St. Louis, 1911.

Drumm, Stella M., "More About Astorians." *Oregon Historical Society Quarterly,* December, 1923.

Missouri Geological Survey Reports, "Dr. Litton's Report." *Annual Reports of the Geological Survey of Missouri, 1853–1854,* Jefferson City, 1856.

Papin, Edward Villeré, "The Village Under the Hill. A Sketch of Early St. Louis, Mo." *Missouri Historical Society Coll.,* Vol. V, October, 1927.

Rezneck, Samuel, "The Depression of 1819–1822: A Social History." *American Historical Review,* XXIX, No. 1, Oct. 1933.

Rothensteiner, Rt. Rev. John, "Earliest History of Mine La Motte." *Missouri Historical Review,* January, 1926.

Thwaites, Reuben G., "Notes on Early Lead Mining in the Fever (Galena) River Region." *Wisconsin Historical Society Collections* Vol. XIII, 1895.

Wesley, Edgar B., "James Callaway in the War of 1812." *Missouri Historical Society Collections,* October, 1927.

White, John Barber, "A Missouri Merchant One Hundred Years Ago." *Missouri Historical Review,* Vol. 13, St. Louis, 1919.

INDEX